THE R

MALTA

AND GOZO

Forthcoming titles include

The Algarve • The Bahamas • Cambodia
Caribbean Islands • Costa Brava
New York Restaurants • South America • Zanzibar

Forthcoming reference guides include

Children's Books • Online Travel • Videogaming
Weather

Rough Guides online

www.roughguides.com

Rough Guide Credits

Text editor: Polly Thomas
Series editor: Mark Ellingham
Production: Michelle Draycott and Andy Turner
Cartography: Ed Wright

Publishing Information

This first edition published November 2001
by Rough Guides Ltd,
62–70 Shorts Gardens, London WC2H 9AH

Distributed by the Penguin Group:

Penguin Books Ltd, 80 Strand, London WC2R 0RL
Penguin Putnam, Inc., 345 Hudson Street, New York 10014, USA
Penguin Books Australia Ltd, 487 Maroondah Highway,
PO Box 257, Ringwood, Victoria 3134, Australia
Penguin Books Canada Ltd, 10 Alcorn Avenue,
Toronto, Ontario, Canada M4V 1E4
Penguin Books (NZ) Ltd,
182–190 Wairau Road, Auckland 10, New Zealand

Typeset in Bembo and Helvetica to an original design by Henry Iles.
Printed in Spain by Graphy Cems.

© Victor Paul Borg, 2001
432pp, includes index
A catalogue record for this book is available from the British Library.

ISBN 1-85828-680-8

THE ROUGH GUIDE TO

MALTA
AND GOZO

by Victor Paul Borg

ROUGH
GUIDES

We set out to do something different when the first Rough Guide was published in 1982. Mark Ellingham, just out of university, was travelling in Greece. He brought along the popular guides of the day, but found they were all lacking in some way. They were either strong on ruins and museums but went on for pages without mentioning a beach or taverna. Or they were so conscious of the need to save money that they lost sight of Greece's cultural and historical significance. Also, none of the books told him anything about Greece's contemporary life – its politics, its culture, its people, and how they lived.

So with no job in prospect, Mark decided to write his own guidebook, one which aimed to provide practical information that was second to none, detailing the best beaches and the hottest clubs and restaurants, while also giving hard-hitting accounts of every sight, both famous and obscure, and providing up-to-the-minute information on contemporary culture. It was a guide that encouraged independent travellers to find the best of Greece, and was a great success, getting shortlisted for the Thomas Cook travel guide award, and encouraging Mark, along with three friends, to expand the series.

The Rough Guide list grew rapidly and the letters flooded in, indicating a much broader readership than had been anticipated, but one which uniformly appreciated the Rough Guide mix of practical detail and humour, irreverence and enthusiasm. Things haven't changed. The same four friends who began the series are still the caretakers of the Rough Guide mission today: to provide the most reliable, up-to-date and entertaining information to independent-minded travellers of all ages, on all budgets.

We now publish more than 150 titles and have offices in London and New York. The travel guides are written and researched by a dedicated team of more than 100 authors, based in Britain, Europe, the USA and Australia. We have also created a unique series of phrasebooks to accompany the travel series, along with an acclaimed series of music guides, and a best-selling pocket guide to the Internet and World Wide Web. We also publish comprehensive travel information on our Web site: **www.roughguides.com**

Help us update

We've gone to a lot of trouble to ensure that this Rough Guide is as up-to-date and accurate as possible. However, things do change. All suggestions, comments and corrections are much appreciated, and we'll send a copy of the next edition (or any other Rough Guide if you prefer) for the best letters.

Please mark letters "**Rough Guide Malta and Gozo Update**" and send to:

Rough Guides, 62–70 Shorts Gardens, London WC2H 9AH, or Rough Guides, 4th Floor, 345 Hudson St, New York, NY 10014.

Or send email to: mail@roughguides.co.uk
Online updates about this book can be found on
Rough Guides' Web site (see opposite)

The author

After growing up roaming the beaches of Gozo and playing hide-and-seek among the Ġgantija Temples, the author first tasted foreigners' perceptions of his country by hanging out with the children of British expatriates in his teens. He now works as a freelance writer, and has published over 400 pieces in Maltese, British and American publications, as well as producing a weekly column for a Maltese newspaper. He currently lives in London.

Acknowledgements

Thanks above all to Mark Vassallo and Kevin Pesci for putting me up, and my parents for their endless support. I was lucky to have an extended group of friends in Malta who provided good times and insiders' tips: Franco and Laura Vassallo, Julian Manduca, Carmelo Vassallo, Alex and Estrella Cali, Carol Agius, Mario Sant, Michelle Camilleri and Victor and Rose Grima. Special thanks go to Chris Camilleri for taking me out and sharing his knowledge of cuisine and the restaurant scene, Julian Sammut of *Rubino* for showing me what can be done with Maltese cuisine, Michael Axiak of *Pulena* for his excellent culinary insights, and Noel Agius for some fact-checking, drinks and inspiration. I am indebted to the Malta Tourism Authority for smoothing out the research, particularly Victor Bonnett in London and Carlo Micallef in Malta. At Rough Guides, I'm grateful to Paul Gray for his genteel direction and the larger picture; Polly Thomas for her sharp editing and for putting up with my rebelliousness; Matthew Teller for editing portions of this book, Andy Turner for typesetting, Ed Wright for cartography, Russell Walton for proofreading and Sharon Martins for picture research.

ACKNOWLEGMENTS

CONTENTS

MAP LIST

MAP SYMBOLS

═══	Road	✖	Swimming area
═ ═ ═	Unpaved road	🤿	Scuba-diving area
- - -	Path	⊠	Gate
──	Coast/waterway	🅿	Parking
⋯⋯	Seasonal river	ⓘ	Information office
──	Wall	⊠	Post office
✈	Airport	@	Internet café
🗼	Lighthouse	◉	Hotel
⚊	Campsite	▣	Restaurant
♖	Castle/fort	▬	Building
▮	Tower	✚	Church (town maps)
Ⓗ	Heliport	✝	Church (regional maps)
⌂	Cave	⊙	Statue/monument
∴	Archeological site	▱	Salt pan
🏛	Palace/stately home	▦	Beach
ⵛ	Public gardens	▦	Gardens/park
	(regional maps)		(town maps)
♦	Point of interest		

Introduction

Mention Malta and the images that spring to mind – the Knights of St John, the Maltese Falcon, the George Cross – evoke dignity and glory, chivalry and endurance. **Malta**, **Gozo** and **Comino** together comprise 316 square kilometres of land, barely half the size of London, and this cluster of tiny islands, strategically located in the central Mediterranean some 96km south of Sicily, 353km north of Libya, and equidistant from Gibraltar and Alexandria, have taken on an importance completely out of proportion to their size. They have stood up to the might of the Ottoman Empire during the Great Siege of 1565, cradled the core of Europe's aristocracy for 268 years under the Knights of St John, and endured more bombing than any other country during World War II. From the Phoenicians to the British, all the great powers have fought over these dusty, windswept rocks, and courted the proud and defiant citizens, as laid-back and irreverent a people as they are industrious and adaptable.

Since attaining independence from Britain less than forty years ago (the only time the islands have not been ruled by an outside power), Malta has developed into a wealthy, modern democracy with a burgeoning **tourism** industry, now the mainstay of the economy both in the mainland and on Gozo and Comino. Over one million visitors

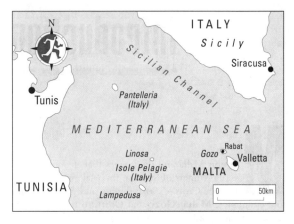

descend each year, most drawn by the two-week sun-and-sea packages for which the islands have come to be known. The north coasts of Malta and Gozo are peppered with fully fledged **resorts**, which hold all categories of accommodation as well as a wealth of restaurants and cafés serving up Maltese, Italian and French delicacies, hordes of lively bars and the odd nightclub. In terms of **beaches**, you can choose between some gorgeous sandy swaths – some with unusual orange sand – or the rocky stretches of coastline, equipped with ladders for easy access to the water, which are equally popular spots from which to dive into the sparkling Med. Most of the popular beaches hold **watersports** outlets during the summer, and the calm seas that surround the island are ideal for anything from jet-skis and banana boats to snorkelling and scuba; Maltese waters are said to offer the best **diving** in the Mediterranean. However, if you're after some seclusion by the sea, there are dozens of undeveloped, less easily accessible coves and rocky shorelines which you'll often have all to yourself.

There's far more to Malta than beachlife, though, and you'd be missing out if you didn't take time to explore the islands' extensive **historical sights**, most of which are located in the fortified capital of Valletta, now designated a World Heritage City. The magnificent **Neolithic temples** scattered over Malta and Gozo – the oldest human-built structures in the world – are second to none: there are more major complexes here than in the whole of the rest of Europe, and they're an absolute must-see. The Catholic church remains hugely influential in the Maltese islands: 99 percent of the populace are affiliated to the faith, as attested by the 350-plus **churches** that pierce the skyline (more than one for every square kilometre). Ranging from tiny rural chapels thronged by pilgrims to grandiose parish churches and ornate cathedrals, these shrines showcase some invaluable works of art as well as superlative Baroque architecture.

Where to go

The Maltese islands are essentially the peaks of submerged mountains that were shifted during movements of tectonic plates many thousands of years ago. A huge earthquake sometime in the last 6000 years tilted the islands, and as a result, northern shorelines slope gently down to sea (and hold the best beaches and busiest resorts), while southern coastlines are mostly characterized by dramatic girdles of meandering cliffs, and make more peaceful bases, ideal for hikers or birdwatchers.

Malta is one of the most densely populated countries in the world, a jumble of towns that mesh together seamlessly and lend it the epithet "city-state". The bulk of the inhabitants live on the north coast, and it's likely that you'll spend much of your time here, too. Jutting finger-like into the appropriately named Grand Harbour, **Valletta** is suffused with historical atmosphere, home to the islands'

Malta is a truly **bilingual** country. Both **Maltese** and **English** enjoy equal weight; official documents, for example, must be in both languages to be legally binding. This is reflected by the fact that you'll see some place and street names in Maltese, and others in English; a few sights even stick with the Italian title as bestowed by the Knights of Malta. We've followed suit throughout this guide, using whatever you'll see on the ground.

largest concentration of Baroque buildings and military architecture as well as the major museums, the cathedral and an absorbing gallery. However, it's short on facilities and as it pretty much shuts down after dark, it's not a place to base yourself if you like things lively. On the opposite side of the harbour, the "Three Cities" of **Vittoriosa**, **Senglea** and **Cospicua** are also ringed by fortifications and hold some important sights, particularly the Inquisitor's Palace and Fort St Angelo, the current home of the Knights of Malta, though again, these are primarily residential zones with little in the way of tourist infrastructure. A better option is on the other side of Valletta, across the waters of Marsamxett Harbour, where **Sliema** or **St Julian's** hold a wealth of tourist accommodation and restaurants, as well as most of the island's clubs and bars within the buzzing **Paceville** district. Moving northwest along the coast, **Buġibba** is Malta's major resort, a string of high-rise hotels and apartment blocks set around the glittering St Paul's Bay, a pacific body of water that gives its name to the neighbouring settlement of **St Paul's Bay**, a smaller, less package-dominated former fishing village that retains a feel of the past. Both towns are within easy distance of some excellent sandy **beaches**.

An aged and delicately preserved Baroque city that still retains the town plan and some of the palazzos of its medieval origins, **Mdina** is central Malta's major draw. The southeast, though mostly characterized by crowded residential towns and heavy industry, has a few scattered sights worth checking out, top of which is the **Hypogeum**, an underground Neolithic burial shrine. Ħaġar Qim and Mnajdra **Neolithic temples** are equally significant relics, their ambience reinforced by their dramatic setting atop a rocky plateau above the majestic seacliff and gorge scenery of **Wied Iz-Żurrieq**. The region has little tourist infrastructure, and the only attractive beach, cut majestically into white, chalky cliffs, is at **Xrobb L-Għaġin** beyond **Marsaxlokk**, a fishing town that, together with its neighbour Marsascala, hold some of the islands' best **fish restaurants**.

Regular ferries connect the Maltese islands. As you make the short journey to Gozo, the ferry glides past **Comino**'s southern cliffs, topped by the stout St Mary's Tower. Virtually uninhabited and somewhat barren, Comino has just one hotel, as well as the inviting turquoise water of the **Blue Lagoon**, and the islands' largest tract of **garigue**, an unspoiled rocky habitat harbouring hundreds of flowering plants, including some endemic species and rare orchids. If you're looking for a nature retreat by the sea, Comino is as good as any place in the Med – lovely beaches, no motor vehicles, sharp light, fabulous sunsets and good snorkelling and scuba diving as well as watersports. As the ferry docks in **Gozo**'s single port, you get a succinct picture of what's to come: terraced fields, church domes and spires punctuating the skyline, and a rural gentility complemented by the whiff of drying hay and freshly turned soil. Although it has its own walled town within the capital, **Rabat**, as well as the **Ġgantija temples**, the oldest of any built in the Maltese islands during the Neolithic era, Gozo has fewer historical sights than its larger neighbour. It's an island of lore and legend, populated by 30,000 down-to-earth, deeply conservative citizens, and what it lacks in nightlife and facilities, it makes up for in rural tranquillity, pristine beaches and fabulous, walkable coastline. Gozo never really gets congested, even at the height of summer, but it's more seasonal than Malta, with many restaurants and a few hotels shutting down from December or January to March.

When to Go

Most people visit during the May and October **high season**, with the busiest months being July and August; at this time, Malta gets pretty hectic. It's searingly hot, beaches get impossibly crowded and everyone seems to be on holiday – including the Maltese. Summers also offer the majority of *festas*, with their dazzling fireworks displays, as well as pumping nightlife. Rain is a rare occurrence between May and September, though, and the countryside is parched dry, so it's not the best time to visit if you plan on doing a lot of walking. Things get quieter during **winter**: many hotels and guesthouses slash their prices and you don't have to jostle with shuffling throngs of other tourists at the country's main sights. Winter weather is usually mild, rainfall is occasional, and the countryside wears an attractive green cloak, while the sun shines strong enough for you to pick up a tan. Nightlife picks up on weekends, the historical sights open longer hours, and restaurants will give you more attention.

The **best time to visit** is during the spring or autumn shoulder seasons, when accommodation is less expensive than in summer, and it's hot enough to swim. In spring, the clear blue skies complement the blaze of wild flowers, and the countryside blooms into variegated reds, purples and yellows. Spring and autumn see hundreds of thousands of birds migrating through the islands, and birders can expect to see some spectacular birds of prey. However, bear

MALTA'S CLIMATE

	AVERAGE DAYTIME TEMP °C	AVERAGE DAYTIME TEMP °F	AVERAGE SEA TEMP °C	AVERAGE SEA TEMP °F	AVERAGE DAILY RAINFALL MM
Jan	12.3	54	14.5	58	90.1
Feb	12.3	54	14.5	58	60.8
March	13.4	56	14.5	58	44.7
April	15.4	59.5	16.1	61	24
May	19.1	66	18.4	65	8.9
June	23	73	21.1	70	3.8
July	25.7	78	24.5	76	0.9
Aug	26.2	79	25.6	78	8.8
Sept	24.1	75.5	25	77	40.4
Oct	20.5	69	22.2	72	123.6
Nov	17	62.5	19.5	67	76.8
Dec	13.9	57	16.7	62	100.2

in mind that autumn is characterized by brief but fierce rainstorms, and that high winds can be a bit maddening during spring.

BASICS

Getting there

Malta is well-served by direct flights from European hubs, plus some Mediterranean and Middle Eastern airports. There are also high-speed ferry services from Sicily several times a week, as well as car-ferry services (sometimes on cargo ships that also take a limited number of passengers) from some Italian ports.

Airfares always depend on the **season**, with the highest being around June to September; fares drop during the "shoulder" seasons – October to December and March to May (excluding Christmas and New Year, and Easter, when prices are hiked up and seats are at a premium) – and you'll get the best prices during the low season, January to March. Note also that flying on weekends is often marginally more expensive than midweek; price ranges quoted below assume midweek travel.

You can often cut costs by going through a specialist **flight agent** – either a consolidator, who buys up blocks of tickets from the airlines and sells them at a discount, or a discount agent, who, in addition to dealing with discounted flights, may also offer special student and youth rates and a range of other travel-related services such as insurance, car rentals, tours and the like. Because Malta is a popular holiday destination for short breaks, many agents offer **charter**

flights that may be cheaper than anything available on a scheduled flight, but again departure dates are fixed and withdrawal penalties are high. Since Malta is a major package holiday destination, buying a **package holiday** that includes accommodation often works out cheaper than a scheduled or charter flight and accommodation organized independently. You can sometimes stumble on good deals in the classified travel pages of national Sunday newspapers, or, in the UK and Ireland, on Teletext or Ceefax.

BOOKING FLIGHTS ONLINE

Many airlines and discount travel websites offer you the opportunity to buy your tickets **online**, and this is often the cheapest option: good deals can be found through discount or auction sites, as well as the airlines' own websites.

Online booking agents and general travel sites

ⓦ **www.etn.nl/discount.htm**
A hub of consolidator and discount agent Web links, maintained by the non-profit European Travel Network.

ⓦ **www.princeton.edu/Main /air800.html**
An extensive list of airline toll-free numbers and websites.

ⓦ **www.flyaow.com**
Online air travel info and reservations site.

ⓦ **www.smilinjack.com/airline s.htm**
Lists an up-to-date compilation of airline website addresses.

ⓦ **http://travel.yahoo.com**
Incorporates a lot of Rough Guide material in its coverage of destination countries and cities across the world, with information about places to eat, sleep, etc.

ⓦ **www.cheaptickets.com**
Discount flight specialists.

ⓦ **www.cheapflights.com**
Flight deals, travel agents, plus links to other travel sites.

ⓦ **www.lastminute.com**
Offers good last-minute holiday package and flight-only deals.

Ⓦ **www.expedia.com**
Discount airfares, all–airline search engine and daily deals.

Ⓦ **www.travelocity.com**
Destination guides, hot Web fares and best deals for car hire, accommodation and lodging as well as fares. Provides access to the travel agent system SABRE, the most comprehensive central reservations system in the US.

Ⓦ **www.hotwire.com**
Bookings from the US only. Last-minute savings of up to forty percent on regular published fares. Travellers must be at least 18 and there are no refunds, transfers or changes allowed. Log-in required.

Ⓦ **www.priceline.com** and
Ⓦ **www.priceline.co.uk**
Name-your-own-price US- and UK-based websites that have deals at around forty percent off standard fares. You cannot specify flight times (although you do specify dates) and the tickets are nonrefundable, nontransferable and nonchangeable.

Ⓦ **www.skyauction.com**
Bookings from the US only. Auctions tickets and travel packages using a "second bid" scheme. The best strategy is to bid the maximum you're willing to pay, since if you win you'll pay just enough to beat the runner-up regardless of your maximum bid.

Ⓦ **www.travelshop.com.au**
Australian website offering discounted flights, packages, insurance and online bookings.

Ⓦ **www.uniquetravel.com.au**
Australian site with a good range of packages and good-value flights.

FLIGHTS FROM THE UK AND IRELAND

Air Malta and British Airways run several **scheduled direct flights** (3hr) daily from Gatwick and Heathrow, plus direct flights approximately every other day from Manchester, Birmingham and Glasgow. Return fares on these scheduled services range from £100 in winter to

£300 during peak season, which includes Easter. You can also pick up occasional competitive deals with European airlines such as Swissair, Lufthansa and Alitalia, though these flights entail changing planes in their respective national hubs.

Since Malta is primarily a package holiday destination, the cheapest way to get there is is to hop on one of the **charter flights** that operate every day from the main airports in London, Birmingham, Manchester, Glasgow and Dublin throughout the year.

Airlines

Air Malta ☎ 0845/607 3710; in Republic of Ireland ☎ 01/872 1175; ⓦ www.airmalta.com.

Alitalia ☎ 0870/544 8259; in Republic of Ireland ☎ 01/677 5171 ⓦ www.alitalia.it.

Britannia Airways ☎ 01582/424155; ⓦ www.britanniaairways.com.

British Airways ☎ 0845/773 337; in Republic of Ireland ☎ 0141/222 2345; ⓦ www.britishairways.com.

Lufthansa ☎ 0845/773 7747; in Republic of Ireland ☎ 01/844 5544; ⓦ www.lufthansa.com.

Swissair ☎ 0845/601 0956; in Republic of Ireland ☎ 01/677 8173; ⓦ www.swissair.com.

Flight and travel agents

CIE Tours International, Dublin ☎ 01/703 1888; ⓦ www.cietours.ie. General flight and tour agent for Malta packages.

London Flight Centre ☎ 020/7244 6411; ⓦ www.topdecktravel.co.uk. Reliable discount flight agent.

Neenan Travel, Dublin ☎ 01/676 5181; ⓦ www.neenantrav.ie. Efficient and fast for packages and flights, including connections with European airlines.

North South Travel ☎ & ⓕ 01245/608291; ⓦ www.northsouthtravel.co.uk.

Friendly, competitive travel agency, offering general fares – profits are used to support projects in the developing world.

usit CAMPUS
ⓣ 0870/240 1010;
ⓦ www.usitcampus.co.uk.
General flight agent specializing in students and youth travel.

PACKAGE TOURS

Since Malta is a major **package** destination, choosing a deal that includes flight and accommodation can often work out cheaper than booking both independently, although this of course limits your choice of accommodation and locale. There are dozens of companies offering package tours to Malta at very competitive rates; low-season packages start at around £150 for seven nights including flight and accommodation. The Bargain Holidays website (ⓦ www.bargainholidays.com) sells package tours by several tour operators.

Tour operators

Airtours ⓣ 0870/241 2567;
ⓦ www.airtours.co.uk. Well-established operator offering a range of options in Malta's busier resorts.

Aquatours ⓣ 020/8255 8050;
ⓦ www.aquatours.com. Specialists in scuba diving holidays in Gozo.

Chevron ⓣ 01753/851267;
ⓦ www.chevron.co.uk. Sun-and-sea geared packages to mid-range hotels, as well as self-catering accommodation.

Edirectholidays
ⓣ 0800/015 2797;
ⓦ www.edirectholidays.co.uk. Lack of overheads for this internet-based operator ensures some of the cheapest deals based on sun-and-sea attractions.

First Choice
ⓣ 0870/750 0499;
ⓦ www.firstchoice.co.uk. Resort-type holidays in a range of hotels and self-catering apartments.

Thomas Cook
ⓣ 0870/566 6222;
ⓦ www.thomascook.co.uk.
Large tour operator (with offices in Malta) offering the full range of packages, as well as car rental and wire money transfers.

FLIGHTS FROM THE US AND CANADA

There are **no direct flights** to Malta from the US and Canada, so you'll have to change planes at a European hub. Flexible and fast connections can be had with the mainstream European carriers, changing flights in their respective national hubs – particularly in London, Frankfurt and Rome – with tickets costing around US$1000 return.

Airlines

Alitalia ⓣ 1-800/223-5730; in Canada ⓣ 1-800/361-8336; ⓦ www.alitalia.com.

British Airways ⓣ 1-800/247-9297; ⓦ www.british-airways.com.

EgyptAir ⓣ 1-800/334-6787; in Canada ⓣ 1-800/263-2899; ⓦ www.egyptair.com.eg.

Lufthansa ⓣ 1-800/645-3880; in Canada ⓣ 1-800/563-5954; ⓦ www.lufthansa.com.

Swissair ⓣ 1-800/221-4750; ⓦ www.swissair.com.

Discount agents and consolidators

Air Brokers International ⓣ 1-800/883-3273 or ⓣ 415/397-1383; ⓦ www.airbrokers.com. General flight agent, specializing in tailored RTW tickets.

Council Travel ⓣ 1-800/226-8624 or ⓣ 617/528-2091; ⓦ www.counciltravel.com. Discount student and youth flight agent, offering occasional Mediterranean tours that include Malta.

STA Travel ⓣ 1-800/777-0112 or ⓣ 1-800/781-4040; ⓦ www.sta-travel.com. Long-established agent offering a wide range of options, including tailor-made deals for groups.

Travel Cuts in Canada ⊤ 1-800/667-2887; in US ⊤ 416/979-2406; ⓦ www.travelcuts.com. Excellent for discount flights, and can also arrange hostel bookings.

Worldtek Travel ⊤ 1-800/243-1723; ⓦ www.worldtek.com. General flight agent that sometimes features Mediterranean cruises that include Malta.

PACKAGE TOURS

Malta is only a fringe **package destination** for the US and Canadian markets, and as such, choices are pretty slim. Although it can work out cheaper taking a tour than booking flight and accommodation independently – it's not unheard of to come across a deal which includes flight, accommodation and taxes for around US$500 – general, resort-type package tours are seldom on offer. Most other packages are **specialized all-inclusive tours** that cost around US$2000 (lodging in mid-range accommodation), and are geared around sites of religious importance or history, as well as trips for older people and the "New Age goddess" pilgrimages detailed on p.181.

Tour operators

Academic Tours ⊤ 1-800/875-9171; ⓦ www.academictours.com. Among the cheapest one-week tours from the US, including mid-range accommodation and wide programme of excursions to the main sights.

Elderhostel ⊤ 1-877/426-8056; ⓦ www.elderhostel.org. All-inclusive programmes focused on learning, including workshops and lectures, for people over 55.

Golden Escapes ⊤ 1-800/668-9215; ⓦ www.goldenescapes.com. Canada-based operator

PACKAGE TOURS FROM THE US AND CANADA

offering rather expensive tours combining Malta and Sicily, focused on history and geared toward mature travellers.

Heavenly Tours
ⓣ 1-800/322-8622; ⓦ www.heavenlytours.com. Three tours to Malta, all whirlwind trots around the main sights.

Legacy Tours ⓣ 1-877/874-4445; ⓦ www.legacy-tours .com. Roman Catholic Church pilgrimages and workshops.

Mediterranean Destinations ⓣ 610/789-1108; ⓦ www.ibrcusa.com. Accommodation and flights as well as various Mediterranean cruises that include Malta.

FLIGHTS FROM AUSTRALIA AND NEW ZEALAND

The cheapest means of flying to Malta from Australia is to take connecting flight with one of the less reputable airlines: Aeroflot, with a stop in Moscow, or EgyptAir, changing in Cairo – both offer return tickets for around A$1500. Return fares with mainstream European carriers such as British Airways, Lufthansa, SwissAir and Alitalia usually start at around A$2000. Given the distance between Australia and New Zealand and Malta, you might want to opt for a RTW ticket, which will enable you to visit more destinations for only a little more than the cost of a return ticket; at the time of writing, tailor-made RTW tickets from Australia, including a stop in Malta, cost about A$2500.

If you're flying from New Zealand, the mainstream carriers detailed above are the most straightforward option. You can also fly with Air New Zealand to London and then get a connecting service to Malta. Since prices hover at around NZ$3000, you may prefer to fork out an extra NZ$700 for a **RTW ticket**.

Airlines

Aeroflot Australia ☎ 02/9262 2233; ⊛ www.aeroflot.com.

Air New Zealand Australia ☎ 13 2476; New Zealand ☎ 0800/737 000 or ☎ 09/357 3000; www.airnz.com.

Alitalia Australia ☎ 02/9244 2400; New Zealand ☎ 09/302 1452; ⊛ www.alitalia.com.

British Airways Australia ☎ 02/8904 8800; New Zealand ☎ 09/356 8690; ⊛ www.british-airways.com.

EgyptAir Australia ☎ 02/9267 6979; ⊛ www.egyptair.com.eg.

Emirates Australia ☎ 02/9290 9700 or ☎ 1300/303 777; New Zealand ☎ 09/377 6004; ⊛ www.emirates.com.

Lufthansa Australia ☎ 1300/655 727 or ☎ 02/9367 3887; New Zealand ☎ 09/303 1529 or ☎ 008/945 220; ⊛ www.lufthansa.com.

Qantas Australia ☎ 13/13 13; New Zealand ☎ 09/357 8900 or ☎ 0800/808 767; ⊛ www.qantas.com.au.

Swissair Australia ☎ 02/9232 1744 or ☎ 1800/221 339; New Zealand ☎ 09/358 3216; ⊛ www.swissair.com.

Travel agents

Flight Centre Australia ☎ 02/9235 3522 or for nearest branch ☎ 13 1600; New Zealand ☎ 09/358 4310; ⊛ www.flightcentre.com.au. Somewhat expensive flights from both Australia and New Zealand with mainstream airlines.

STA Travel Australia ☎ 13 1776 or ☎ 1300/360 960; New Zealand ☎ 09/309 0458 or ☎ 09/366 6673; ⊛ www.statravel.com.au. Flights to Malta from both Australia and New Zealand.

Thomas Cook Australia ☎ 13 1771 or ☎ 1-800/801 002; New Zealand ☎ 09/379 3920; ⊛ www.thomascook.com.au. Efficient service, and tickets with all the mainstream carriers.

FLIGHTS FROM AUSTRALIA AND NEW ZEALAND

PACKAGE TOURS

Since most Australians who visit Malta do so because of familial connections, package tours from Australia – and even more so from New Zealand – are virtually unheard of. Choices are very limited, and tours are only likely to be marginally cheaper than travelling independently.

Kompas Holidays Australia ⓣ 07/3222 3333 or ⓣ 1800/269 968; ⓦ www.kompasholidays.com .au. Limited number of historical tours to Malta.

FLIGHTS AND FERRIES FROM ITALY AND NORTH AFRICA

Malta is well connected to Italy and parts of North Africa – you can **fly** to the island or take a **ferry** from Italy or Tunisia. Air Malta also flies direct from Istanbul and Cairo.

Air Malta (Malta ⓣ 00356/234397; Rome ⓣ 06/488 3106; Milan ⓣ 08/646 3650; Catania ⓣ 313308; ⓦ www .airmalta.com) flies daily to Malta from Rome, from Catania in Sicily, and weekly from Milan; midweek fares in high season are around L373,957/€193 from Catania, about L582,855/€301 from Rome, and L665,365/€343 from Milan. **Alitalia** (in Rome ⓣ 665621; ⓦ www.alitalia.it) also operates daily flights to Malta from Rome and Milan for similar prices.

By sea from Italy, the fastest and most efficient option is to take a high-speed ferry from the Sicilian towns of Catania, Pozzallo or Licata with Virtu Ferries Ltd (Malta ⓣ 00356/318854, ⓕ 345221; ⓦ www.virtuferries.com); there are several trips per week depending on season, and return tickets start at L194,271/€100 one-way, and L247,687/€127 return; journey time is two hours. Note that fares dip by five percent in the low season. **Sea Malta,**

based around Malta's Grand Harbour at Flagstone Wharf, Marsa (℡00356/232230, ℱ225776), operate a weekly merchant vessel, which also takes a limited number of passengers, from Genoa in north Italy; one-way tickets throughout the year cost L349,649/€180, or L422,489/€218 with a motor vehicle; journey time is eighteen hours.

Air Malta operate several flights per week from **North Africa**; high-season return fares are about TD222 from Tunis in Tunisia (℡01/703229), LD155 from Tripoli in Libya (℡21/3350578) and £E940 from Cairo in Egypt (℡02/5782692). **Tunis Air** (Tunisia ℡701717; ⓦwww.tunisair.com.tn) operates direct flights from Tunis that cost TD288 in the high season. **Sea Malta** offer a weekly service from Tunis; year-round one-way fares are TD228, and TD275 with motor vehicle. Keep in mind that the trip from Tunis to Malta sometimes detours via Genoa and Marseilles and takes six days. The trip from Malta to Tunis is direct (16hr).

FLIGHTS AND FERRIES FROM ITALY AND NORTH AFRICA

Red tape and visas

Nationals of EU and Commonwealth countries, as well as the US, Canada, Australia and New Zealand, do not need visas for stays of up to ninety days; you merely present your (valid) passport when you enter Malta. Nationals of Austria, Belgium, France, Germany, Greece, Italy, Luxembourg, the Netherlands, Portugal, Spain and Switzerland can produce a valid national ID card rather than a passport.

If you want to **extend your stay**, you need to apply at the Immigration Office in the Police Headquarters on Pjazza San Kalċidonju in Floriana (☎224001); take four passport photos and proof that you have enough money to support yourself, and a ninety-day extension will be granted immediately.

Embassies and consulates in Malta

Australian Embassy, Villa Fiorentina, Ta' Xbiex Terrace, Ta' Xbiex ☎338201.

Canadian Consulate, 103 Triq L-Arċisqof, Valletta ☎233121 or ☎233126.

UK High Commission, 7 Triq Sant' Anna, Floriana ☎233134 or ☎233135.

US Embassy, 3rd Floor, Development House, Triq Sant' Anna, Floriana ☎235960 or ☎235961.

Maltese embassies abroad

Australia and New Zealand 38 Culgoa Circuit, O'Malley, ACT 2606 ☎ 02/6290 1724.

North America 2017 Connecticut Ave NW, Washington, DC 20008 ☎ 202/462-3611.

UK Malta House, 36–38 Piccadilly, London W1V 0PQ ☎ 020/7292 4800.

Information, websites and maps

G iven Malta's economic dependence upon tourism, there's a huge amount of information available. Offices of the Malta Tourism Authority on the island and abroad will send out leaflets on sights, activities, tour operators, car rental agencies, accommodation and airlines, as well as an annual calendar of events.

Staff at offices in Malta are generally friendly and helpful, and can usually help with specific queries. There are five

tourist offices, with the headquarters at 280 Triq Ir-Repubblika in Valletta (☏ 224444). The office in Malta International Airport (see p.47) is open 24 hours a day, and the others – in Valletta (see p.47) and two in Gozo (see p.186) – are detailed in the relevant guide sections.

The most comprehensive **listings** of cultural, historical and political events are published every Sunday in the lifestyle section of the local Sunday newspaper *Malta Today*.

There's not a huge amount of Malta-related information on the **internet**, and few websites have independent and in-depth content. However, the sites listed below provide a good starting point for researching the islands, as well as the opportunity to buy Maltese books and goods online.

Maltese tourist offices abroad

Australia World Aviation Systems, 403 George St, Sydney, NSW 2000
☏ 02/9321 9514,
☏ 9290 3641.

Republic of Ireland J. Walter Thomson Communications, 1 Christchurch Hall, High St, Dublin 8
☏ 01/405 8200, ☏ 473 2962;
ⓔ office.ie@visitmalta.com.

UK Malta House, 36–38 Piccadilly, London W1V 0PP
☏ 020/7292 4900,
ⓕ 7734 1880
ⓔ office.uk@visitmalta.com.

USA 300 Lanidex Plaza, Parsippany, NJ 07054
☏ 973/884-0899,
ⓕ 425/795-3425;
ⓔ office.us@visitmalta.com.

Useful websites

Gozo.com
ⓦ www.gozo.com
The best online source of info on Gozo, from sights to directories of boat trips, town feasts and bus schedules, as well as listings of self-catering apartments and villas for rent.

Malta Tourism Authority
ⓦ www.visitmalta.com
The best starting point for online information, from sights

and activities to a hotel directory, calendar of events, news and features on contemporary events.

Search Malta

Ⓦ www.searchmalta.com/index .shtml

Extensive site, with daily news, weather forecasts, features, accommodation listings (some with online booking) and directories of links, ranging from the economy to the environment.

Government of Malta

Ⓦ www.magnet.mt

Pretty mundane design, but with contacts for all the government departments, as well as further official info on state institutions.

Megalithic Temples of Malta

Ⓦ http://web.genie.it/utenti/m/ malta_mega_temples/index .html

Background on, and photographs of, each of Malta's Neolithic temples, plus special features that use virtual animation to illustrate the calibration of the equinoxes in some temples, and how their interior looked when intact.

MAPS

You can buy foldable visitor **maps**, published by various companies, from travel outlets at home as well as newsagents, souvenir shops and bookshops in Malta. They're all much of a muchness, with a general road map of Malta, Gozo and Comino as well as city maps of Valletta, the Three Cities, Sliema and St Julian's, Mdina and Rabat, Buġibba and St Paul's Bay. If you're not wandering off the beaten track, these maps will suffice, but if you want to feel confident about more adventurous forays – particularly if you're driving – it pays to invest in *The Maze* by Frans Attard; it costs Lm4.95 and is relatively bulky, but clearly shows every named street in Malta and Gozo. Most local stationers and bookshops have it in stock.

MAPS

Insurance

Although Malta has reciprocal agreements with the UK and Australia to provide free healthcare for citizens of those countries, you'd do well to take out an insurance policy before travelling to cover against theft, loss and illness or injury.

Before paying for a new policy, however, it's worth checking whether you are already covered: some all-risks home insurance policies may cover your possessions against loss or theft when overseas, and many private medical schemes include cover when abroad, including baggage loss, cancellation or curtailment and cash replacement as well as sickness or accident. In Canada, provincial health plans usually provide partial cover for medical mishaps overseas, while holders of official student/teacher/youth cards in Canada and the US are entitled to meagre accident coverage and hospital inpatient benefits. Students will often find that their student health coverage extends during the vacations and for one term beyond the date of last enrolment. Some bank and credit cards include certain levels of medical or other insurance and you may automatically get travel insurance if you use a major credit card to pay for your trip. Lastly, travellers from the UK should bear in mind that though travel agents and tour operators are likely

ROUGH GUIDE TRAVEL INSURANCE

Rough Guides offers its own travel insurance, customized for our readers by a leading UK broker and backed by a Lloyds underwriter. It's available for anyone, of any nationality, travelling anywhere in the world.

There are two main Rough Guide insurance plans: Essential, for basic, no-frills cover; and Premier – with more generous and extensive benefits. Alternatively, you can take out annual multi-trip insurance, which covers you for any number of trips throughout the year (with a maximum of sixty days for any one trip). Unlike many policies, the Rough Guides schemes are calculated by the day, so if you're travelling for 27 days rather than a month, that's all you pay for. If you intend to be away for the whole year, the Adventurer policy will cover you for 365 days. Each plan can be supplemented with a "Hazardous Activities Premium" if you plan to indulge in sports considered dangerous, such as skiing, scuba-diving or trekking. Rough Guides also does good deals for older travellers, and will insure you up to any age, at prices comparable to SAGAs.

For a policy quote, call the Rough Guide Insurance Line on UK freefone ☎ 0800/015 0906; US toll-free ☎ 1-866/220-5588, or, if you're calling from elsewhere ☎ +44 1243/621046. Alternatively, get an online quote and buy your cover at ⓦ www.roughguides.com/insurance

to require some kind of insurance when you book a package holiday, UK law prevents them from making you buy their own policy (other than a £1 premium for "schedule airline failure").

After exhausting the possibilities above, you might want to contact a specialist travel insurance company, or consider the travel insurance deal we offer (see box, above). A typical travel insurance policy usually provides cover for the loss of baggage, tickets and – up to a certain limit –

cash or cheques, as well as cancellation or curtailment of your journey. Most of them exclude so-called dangerous sports unless an extra premium is paid: in Malta this can mean scubadiving and windsurfing. Many policies can be tweaked to exclude coverage you don't need – for example, sickness and accident benefits can often be excluded or included at will. If you do take medical coverage, ascertain whether benefits will be paid as treatment proceeds or only after return home, and whether there is a 24-hour medical emergency number. When securing baggage cover, make sure that the per-article limit – typically under £500 – will cover your most valuable possession. If you need to make a claim, you should keep receipts for medicines and medical treatment, and in the event you have anything stolen, you must obtain an official police report.

Costs, money and banks

Malta can't be described as cheap, and rapid economic development is pushing up prices each year. Accommodation will account for a major part of your daily expenditure. Supermarket prices are roughly the same as those in the UK, and more expensive than North America, Australia and New Zealand. In restaurants, expect to pay an average of Lm10 for a three-course meal excluding drinks, while spirits and pints of local or imported beer are under Lm1. Public transport and attraction and museum entry are cheap, and although accommodation is likely to account for a major part of your daily expenditure, it's still possible to enjoy yourself on a budget.

The cheapest **accommodation** option is a hostel bunk, at around Lm2 per night; guesthouses charge about Lm6 per night, and Lm12 or so will get you a comfortable hotel room with airconditioning, en-suite bathroom, telephone, TV and kitchenette. If you're looking to cut costs, it's well worth visiting during the low season, when many hotels and guesthouses slash their rates by up to fifty percent. Getting around by public **transport** is pretty inexpensive, with average fares at Lm0.15 – you can also buy a weekly travel pass for Lm5.50, which covers unlimited travel on all buses. If you want to drive yourself, expect to pay around Lm10 per day to rent a car, and Lm4 per day for a scooter. **Eating out** can also hit your pocket hard, with a full meal at a fancy restaurant costing around Lm10; however, there are plenty of cheaper places where you can eat for Lm7, and if you restrict yourself to takeaways, you'll spend under Lm2 per day. Alcohol is relatively cheap – about Lm3 for a bottle of mid-range Maltese wine from a supermarket and under Lm1 for a pint of beer or spirit shot in a bar. If you're on a tight budget, you can get by on under Lm10 per day. If you opt for more decent accommodation, a rented car, meals in mid-range restaurants and nights out, you're looking at a **daily budget** of about Lm40.

CURRENCY

Malta's currency is the **lira** (Lm), plural Liri; when speaking English, Maltese people call the lira the Pound. A lira is divided into 100 cents. **Notes** come in Lm2, Lm5, Lm10 and Lm20 denominations and there are 1¢, 2¢, 5¢, 10¢, 25¢, 50¢ and Lm1 **coins**. At the time of writing the **exchange rate** was Lm0.65 to the pound sterling, Lm0.45 to the US dollar, and Lm0.24 to the Australian dollar. For up-to-date currency conversion rates, visit ⓦ www.xe.net/ucc/full.shtml.

BANKS AND EXCHANGING MONEY

There are four **banks** in Malta – HSBC, Bank of Valletta, APS and Lombard; all open between Monday and Saturday from 8.30am to 4pm, and branches are numerous; in built-up areas, you'll never be more than a ten-minute walk away from the nearest bank. All the branches have **ATMs** (or cashpoints) from which you can withdraw Maltese currency with a credit card. Some ATMs – HSBC's particularly – take debit cards issued by major non-Maltese banks, but it's wise to check with your issuing bank before you travel. It is possible to **exchange** foreign currency notes – particularly British sterling, US dollars and German deutschmarks – in banks, exchange bureaux, most hotels and 24-hour exchange machines in Valletta, Sliema, Buġibba and Victoria in Gozo. All these places will also cash **travellers' cheques**, though you'll need to present your passport. Banks generally offer the best rates for all currency transactions.

The major **credit cards** – Visa, MasterCard, American Express, Diners – are widely accepted to pay for meals, accommodation, goods purchased and car rental. American Express (14 Zachary St, Valletta ☎232141), and Thomas Cook issue their own travellers' cheques; the latter has five strategically located and conspicuous branches in Valletta (☎233629), Sliema (☎334759), Buġibba (☎570178), Paceville (☎378881) and Rabat, Gozo (☎559961).

You can have money **wired** to you in Malta via Western Union: call ☎0800/773773 to locate the nearest branch.

Getting around

Given the size of the Maltese islands, getting around is a pretty simple business. The cheapest way to travel, and virtually the only mode of public transport available, are the buses, though they're somewhat slow and inefficient. Renting a car is of course the most convenient option, particularly if you want to go out late at night, although keep in mind that signage is fairly inadequate, the roads in a poor state, the driving chaotic and congestion common in the built-up centres. Busy roads with no cycle lanes, combined with the intense summer heat and hilly topography mean that bicycles are fairly uncommon.

BUSES

Malta is well covered by an inexpensive – if inefficient – **bus network**, mostly comprised of creaky postwar vehicles which can be slow and uncomfortable. Virtually all services originate from and return to the main Valletta bus terminus, and there are two other small bus stations in Sliema and Buġibba that offer more tourist-tailored direct services to places such as the Three Cities, Mdina and Rabat, Marsaxlokk, Ċirkewwa (for the Gozo Ferry), and the beaches of Għajn Tuffieħa and Golden Bay.

Services from the Valletta terminus start operating at 5.30am and stop between 9pm and 11pm, depending on the route; on weekends there is an extended service between Paceville and Valletta until 2am. Buses from the terminuses at Sliema and Buġibba are less frequent and their schedule changes seasonally, with more services in the summer; you can pick up the latest schedule from information booths at the terminuses. Fares come in three prices: Lm0.15 for all routes operating from Valletta, Lm0.40 for all specialized direct routes from Sliema and Buġibba, and Lm0.50 for the route to Paceville. Fares are paid on board, but you should carry small change as drivers cannot change large notes. The Public Transport Association (☎250007) issue **bus passes**, covering unlimited travel, valid for one, three, five or seven days and costing Lm1.50, Lm4, Lm4.50 and Lm5.50 respectively; these can be bought from the bus terminuses.

Although buses are numbered, destinations along the route are not listed, so ascertaining if a **route** serves the place you want to go to can be difficult. However, drivers are normally happy to tell you where to get off. You can pick up a free list of all bus routes at the bus terminuses, but for a better illustrated map of the routes, invest in the bus route map available from stationers and bookshops for Lm0.35.

CAR AND MOTORBIKE RENTAL

For daytime excursions, buses will pretty much suffice, but if you want to go out regularly at night to different parts of the islands, your choice is limited to **renting a car** or paying hefty taxi prices. This is especially true if you're staying in the northwest or outside the centres of Valletta, Sliema, St Julian's and their satellites.

CAR AND MOTORBIKE RENTAL

To rent a car or a motorbike, you need an **international driving licence**, which you obtain in your country of origin. Rental agencies will ask to see this as well as your passport or identity card, and some ask for a deposit of Lm50 to cover any traffic fines incurred. You have the option of paying an extra Lm2 a day to be **comprehensively insured**, and this is recommended given Malta's high accident rates; otherwise, in the event of an accident or damage, you may be liable for the insurance excess of Lm150. Bear in mind that though the legal driving age is eighteen, virtually all Maltese rental companies will turn you away if you're under 25.

Average rental rates for a two-door, four-seater car are about Lm10 a day – less in the low season – and are usually discounted if you rent for longer than five days. Before you commit yourself to a car from a particular agency, check with the airline that flew you to Malta and the place where you're staying to see if they offer discounts on cars from certain companies. Listed opposite are the most reputable Maltese rental companies, from which you're guaranteed good service and competitive prices. All of them can arrange for cars to be picked up and left at Malta International Airport.

Given the short distances and amiable weather, **motorbikes** are a lot more suitable for the Maltese islands, and cheaper than a car: prices start at around Lm6 for a day, and are discounted for rentals of more than five days. The downside of a motorbike is the poor state of the roads and dangerous driving by Maltese motorists: you have to keep one eye out for potholes and another on those who drive as if other road users don't exist. Road surfaces can also be very slippery, so be cautious when navigating corners and bends.

Car rental companies

Avis, 50 Msida Sea Front, Msida ☎ 225986, ⓕ 241308, airport office ☎ 232422.

Budget, Mexico Buildings, Zimelli St, Marsa ☎ 241517, ⓕ 244626, airport office ☎ 244023.

Europecar, Alpine House, Naxxar Rd, San Ġwann ☎ 388516, ⓕ 373673, airport office ☎ 803140.

Gozo United, 31 Republic St, Rabat, Gozo ☎ 556291.

Hertz, United House, 66 Gzira Rd, Gzira ☎ 314636, ⓕ 333153, airport office ☎ 232811.

Mayjo, 34 Republic St, Rabat, Gozo ☎ 556678, ⓕ 553744.

Motorbike rental companies

Albert's, 200 Upper Saint Albert St, Gzira ☎ 340149.

Islander Tourist Services, Triq It-Turisti, Buġibba ☎ 576039.

Lillywhites, St George's Rd, St Julian's ☎ 335921.

Victor Sultana, Main Gate St, Rabat, Gozo ☎ 556414.

DRIVING IN MALTA

A combination of excessive congestion (there are some 160,000 vehicles), slippery, potholed, badly constructed roads and blistering summer heat can make **driving** in the islands a hair-raising experience, and after a few hours behind the wheel, it's not difficult to understand why Malta has the highest per capita accident rate in the world. Local drivers will frequently cut you up, pull out after an absent-minded glance over their shoulder, butt in at roundabouts and corners, overtake in spectacular zigzag patterns and in tunnels, but will rarely use indicators. At the other end of the extreme are the over-cautious, who crawl along in the outer lane or habitually put on their hazard lights in tunnels.

DRIVING IN MALTA

Trucks, buses and taxis are largely driven by bullies with a bully mentality: the biggest reigns. Don't try to argue or expect others to obey the rules, and don't respond with rude gestures at those whose driving is less than perfect, as road-rage tussles are fairly common.

However, away from the towns and throughout Gozo, the roads are fairly quiet. Employing defensive driving techniques and keeping a sharp eye on the road should minimize the possibility of potential problems. The crucial thing to bear in mind is that it's personal interaction rather than rules which govern the roads, and you'll soon get the knack of making eye contact with other motorists to find out their intentions. At all times, err on the side of caution, and don't take things for granted based on past experience; while flashing high-headlight beams signals the intention to give way in most parts of the world, it can signify the exact opposite here.

TAXIS

Official **taxis** are white and have their registration number painted on the side of the car. There are plenty of strategically located taxi stands in the central areas, airports and ports, and along the nightlife and tourist circuits. Though some taxis have meters, these are rarely used, and **fares** are fairly arbitrary, often dependent on how the day's business has gone, how naive you appear to be or the time of day (fares go up after dark). Make sure you agree to a price before starting out, and bear in mind that haggling is an acceptable custom. In general, though, taxis are not cheap, and after the buses have stopped running after 11pm, prices generally go up by about a third, but once again, this is arbitrary. Expect to pay at least Lm5 from Valletta to Sliema during the day, and anything up to double that at night. The fare from the airport to the Gozo Ferry in Ċirkewwa, one of the longest journeys you're likely to take, is around Lm15.

If you're taking a taxi from the nightlife area of Paceville, the cheapest option is to go to Wembley's Taxis (☎374141 or ☎374242) on St George's Road, from where you can share a taxi or minibus with passengers heading to the same destination and split the fare. Even if you have to take a taxi alone, Wembley's are guaranteed to offer a more professional service, more luxurious cars and lower rates than the official white taxis, and they're available 24-hours a day.

CYCLING

At face value, given the short distances, Malta may seem ideal to explore on a **bicycle**, but there are various disadvantages. The landscape – especially in Gozo – is hilly, and cycling in the intense summer heat can easily lead to dehydration or sunstroke. Few Maltese cycle, and there are no bicycle lanes, so you'll also have to contend with congested roads and haphazard Maltese driving habits. Having said that, bicycles can be a pleasant means of exploring Malta's rural areas. You can **rent bikes** for about Lm2 per day from the motorbike rental agencies listed on p.27.

Communications and the media

Keeping in touch while in the Maltese islands is relatively easy. Telephone connections, both local and international, are generally reliable and efficient, and although mail services are not on a par with parts of Western Europe, the service is improving swiftly.

TELEPHONES

As hotels usually impose substantial surcharges on calls, it's best to use **phone booths** for both local and international calls. Maintained by the state-owned telephone company, Maltacom plc, these are numerous, and all take phonecards only; these come in denominations of Lm2, Lm3 or Lm5, and are available from stationers and souvenir shops. If you want to make a **reverse-charge** international call, dial the overseas operator on ☏194. Local calls cost 5¢ per five minutes during peak times (6am–6pm), and a flat rate of 5¢ between 6pm and 6am.

The country **code** for incoming international calls to Malta is 356.

TELEPHONE NUMBER CHANGES

Since this book went to print, economic liberalisation within Malta's telecommunications industry has resulted in changes to the configuration of local phone numbers. To get through to all the six- and eight-figure terrestrial numbers listed in this guide, you need to add the new area code, **21**, to the start of the original number. Hence what's listed in the book as ☎232141 should be dialled as ☎2123241. **Mobile phone** numbers which started with 0 have also been adjusted; you must now replace the initial 0 with a 9. Hence numbers in this book configured as ☎09470377 should be dialled as ☎99470377. Bear in mind that changes are ongoing; check with tourist offices for recent updates.

MAIL

There are **post offices** in virtually every town in Malta and Gozo; most open Monday to Saturday from 8am to noon, but the two main offices – in Valletta and Rabat, Gozo – stay open until 4pm. **Mail** takes about three days to reach a UK destination, about a week to North America, and two weeks for Australia and New Zealand. Postboxes, the same red type in use in the UK, are numerous and situated strategically in the centres of towns.

NEWSPAPERS

Malta has four national daily **newspapers** and five Sunday titles. Two of the dailies are written in Maltese and serve mostly as propaganda mouthpieces for the MLP and PN political parties. The remaining two are in English, and are rather archaic in tone and content: *The Times* is stiffly conservative, and many of its stories are simply parroted from politicians' speeches, while the *Malta Independent* makes a lame show at breaking the conservative, establishment mould of its rival. The liberal English-language Sunday title *Malta Today* is the boldest of all independent newspapers, willing to uncover shady dealings by politicians where others have balked; it also champions green issues and prints some of the most analytical political comment. All the English-language newspapers feature **listings** of upcoming events.

Many **international newspapers**, particularly British national dailies and Sunday newspapers, and the American titles *USA Today* and the *International Herald Tribune*, are available in Malta. Weekly news-magazines such as *Newsweek*, *Time* and *The Economist* are also easy to get hold of, as are British and American glossy magazines. All are sold in newsagents.

RADIO AND TELEVISION

There are several **radio stations** in Malta. Most are amateurish community-driven attempts, or the unashamedly biased mouthpieces of political parties, but some offer a good range of music. Island Radio (101.8 FM), Bay Radio (89.7 FM) and Radio Calypso (103.3 FM) are worth checking out, though their chat shows and phone-ins are usually conducted in Maltese.

Of the three national **TV stations**, two are unashamed propaganda machines owned by the PN and MLP. The state-owned Television Malta (TVM) broadcasts mainly in Maltese, as well as showing a few popular British and US imports. **Cable TV** is widely available, with stations from the UK and Italy. Satellite dishes are also ubiquitous, and virtually all hotels have TV sets in their lobby or lounge showing broadcasts from international stations such as CNN, Euronews and the BBC World Service.

Health

The level of local healthcare, mostly provided by the state, is on par with the standards you expect in Western Europe, and all doctors speak English. You don't need any vaccinations or inoculations, and tap water is safe to drink, but mosquitoes and jellyfish can give you annoying stings. The major health hazards are sunstroke and dehydration in the heat of the summer; take precautions during possible lengthy exposure to direct sunlight and drink plenty of water. The emergency services are normally well organized and deployed rapidly.

The state operates two general **hospitals**. St Luke's, in Msida on the outskirts of Valletta (☎241251 or ☎247860), is the largest and best equipped, while Gozo has the smaller Gozo General (☎556851) in Rabat. There are also eight health centres, which generally deal with non-emergencies and minor examinations or treatments. These are situated in Cospicua (☎675492), Floriana (☎243314), Gzira (☎337244), Mosta (☎433256), Paola (☎691314), Qormi (☎484450), Rabat in Malta (☎459082), and Rabat in Gozo (☎561541). There are also two **private hospitals**: St Philip's (☎442211), situated a couple of kilometres west of Valletta in Santa Venera, and Capua Palace (☎335235) in the centre of Sliema; these are more modern, efficient and less crowded than the state hospitals, but they cannot take emergencies, and their prices reflect the extra comforts and luxuries.

There are plenty of **pharmacies** situated strategically in the town squares or centres of towns. Most are open during regular shopping hours (Mon–Sat 9am–1pm & 4–7pm), and a select number are open, on rotation basis, every day until 10pm, including public holidays; these are listed in the daily and Sunday newspapers. If you need a **prescription**, it will work out a lot cheaper to get one at the state health centre than through seeing a doctor recommended by a pharmacy, whose special visit will invariably result in a hefty fee.

For an ambulance, call ☏ 196; for
helicopter rescue call ☏ 244371.

MOSQUITOES AND JELLYFISH

In the summers, **mosquitoes** come out in droves at twilight, particularly where there is greenery and uncovered fresh water. Although they don't transmit diseases, the itch from mosquito bites can be annoying and unsightly, and it helps to carry some kind of repellent. Fortunately, most buildings have netting covering the doors and windows. The Mediterranean is plagued by sporadic blooms of **jellyfish**; none are deadly poisonous, but their sting is painful and produces a rash that takes weeks to disappear. Before wading or jumping into the water, it pays to scan the shoreline for floating specimens.

Police, trouble and drugs

Malta is one of the safest countries in the Mediterranean. Muggings, rape and other instances of violent crime are rare, and burglaries are uncommon, although theft from cars is not so infrequent. Generally speaking, the police are professional and helpful, and deal with violent crime seriously.

The best way to ensure a safe stay is to employ your **common sense**. Don't leave valuables visible in cars, and don't flash jewellery, cash or expensive cameras around. Always lock your car, and don't leave your belongings unattended while swimming. If you're inebriated and staggering home at night alone, you're an easy target for trouble. Though the Maltese are known for their short tempers, you can usually settle any problems that arise peacefully with a ready smile and an apology. If problems do occur, you'll find **police stations** in virtually every town centre. The Police Headquarters is at Pjazza San Kalċidonju in Floriana (☎224001), while the main police station in Gozo is on Triq Ir-Repubblika, Rabat (☎556011). If you do get something stolen, make sure you obtain a police report in order to claim on your insurance.

In rural areas, farms and houses generally have savage guard dogs that can surprise you as you approach; the general rule is to be cautious and look out for any signs of dogs. Also in the countryside, bird hunters and trappers are generally uncomfortable about inquisitive passers-by, and stories of hunters instigating their dogs to attack strollers or even shooting at ramblers are common. Besides, hunters are very trigger happy, and every year there are incidents of people in the countryside being injured or blinded in shooting accidents. Hence if you do cross paths with a hunter or trapper, it's best to be on your way pretty quickly.

EMERGENCY NUMBERS

Police ☏ 191	Fire service ☏ 199
Helicopter rescue ☏ 244371	Coastguard ☏ 238797

DRUGS

Illegal drugs are dealt with heavily by the Maltese police and courts. **Possession**, even of small amounts for personal use, will lead to deportation, while small-scale trafficking will almost always mean a prison term. Importing drugs is punishable by a minimum sentence of six months imprisonment. There have been a couple of cases where foreigners caught with a few grams of marijuana were given the mandatory six-month prison term, and despite harsh criticism by some sections of the media, the government shows no intention of relaxing the law. Random **roadblocks** are set up to search vehicles for drugs, while at rave parties, you are searched at the door by police, and inside, plain-clothes officers keep an eye out for drugs.

DRUGS

WOMEN TRAVELLERS

Malta is generally safe for solo **women travellers** and, thankfully, there are only several instances of rape every year. More common are **flashers**, particularly at night and on the beaches. If you choose to sunbathe or swim nude, try to do so when with a group, as stories of Peeping Toms and flashers abound. Maltese males tend to have a macho, Latin-type attitude, and solo women will need to get used to dealing with a constant barrage of male attention, almost always harmless. For local contacts, get in touch with the Commission for the Advancement of Women, Ministry for Social Policy, 2 Cavalier St, Valletta ☎25905296 or ☎25905345; ⓦ www.msp.magnet.mt.

THE GUIDE

THE GUIDE

Valletta and Floriana

C lustered attractively in a tight grid of narrow streets behind grand fortifications, Baroque **Valletta** – capital of Malta – is surrounded on three sides by sea. This early-to-bed town sits at the seaward tip of the hilly Sciberras Peninsula, a wedge of land defining the northern flank of the **Grand Harbour**, which penetrates deep inland midway along Malta's northeast coast. Ever since 1530, when the Knights of Malta shifted the island's power-base from Mdina to Vittoriosa, the Grand Harbour – later with Valletta at its core – has been the island's commercial and political centre. Facing Valletta to the south across the Grand Harbour are two tongues of land jutting out into the water, occupied by the so-called Three Cities of Vittoriosa and Senglea, both out on a limb separated by the Dockyard Creek, and Cospicua further east at the head of the creek; all three have their own chapter, beginning on p.90.

The history and present-day look of Valletta are intimately connected with the history of the **Knights of Malta**: they planned and built the town, filled it with a range of highly decorated churches and splendidly grand *auberges* (inns), and sealed it off from attack on all four sides with stout fortifications that still stand today. After suffering extensive bomb damage in World War II, Valletta has seen some shabby rebuilding work, but for the most part the city's sixteenth-century ambience remains, acknowledged by UNESCO, who granted Valletta the status of a **World Heritage City**. It's a calm and attractive place for a couple of days' meanderings, taking in the mighty **cathedral**, a clutch of museums and the impressive fortifications which extend to **Floriana**, an eighteenth-century suburb sprawling west of the centre. Nightlife is not Valletta's strong point: this may be the capital, but after the shops and tourist sights have shut, the city winds down. Stay to sample the historic atmosphere and to draw breath away from some of the island's more over-touristed spots, but don't expect a bustling metropolis.

Valletta

Built on the peninsula that divides Grand Harbour to the south from Marsamxett Harbour to the north, **VALLETTA** is a small city of some nine thousand inhabitants. It's less than 2km in length from end to end and easily walkable.

The main thoroughfare is **Triq Ir-Repubblika** (Republic St), which runs from the **City Gate** in the southwest (location of the main bus terminus) to **Fort St Elmo** in the northeast and divides the city into two halves. It defines one of Malta's main shopping and business districts, and along its length are the city's most important sights – principally the vast and elaborate **St John's Co-Cathedral** with its blaze of Baroque art, the equally monumental **Grand Master's Palace**, and the newly revamped **National Museum of Archeology** with displays covering Malta's sophisticated and protracted Neolithic era.

Other highlights, found in the web of streets and alleys to either side of Triq Ir-Repubblika, are the **Auberge de Castille**, one of the Knights' inns of residence and the most impressive secular Baroque building in Malta, and – in a quite different vein – the **Lascaris War Rooms**, nerve-centre for the Allied Mediterranean fleet in World War II. The **Upper Barakka Gardens** and **Hastings Gardens** are two of Valletta's loveliest open spaces, both perched high on the city's fortifications and offering panoramic views over the city and its harbours.

Some history

Over four hundred years after it was built, Valletta still bears the legacy of the Knights' crowning achievement. Yet it came into being as a military necessity: the Knights, bottled up in Vittoriosa, saw the bulk of Mount Sciberras across the Grand Harbour as a threat, a no-man's-land where an enemy would have the advantage of altitude. Their worst predictions came true in the **Great Siege** of 1565, when the Turks, occupying the heights, were able to bombard the garrison holed up in Fort St Elmo into submission (although they were eventually themselves defeated in a bloody battle later in the same year). After the conflict, with pledges of funding from Europe, **Grand Master Jean Parisot de la Vallette** revived the plans for a fortress atop Mount Sciberras. The Knight's overlord, Pope Pius V despatched **Francesco Laparelli**, a renowned military engineer, to Malta in 1566 to draw up plans for the new city.

For more on the Great Siege of 1565, see p.336.

Laparelli's designs were highly innovative. A curtain wall of **fortifications** was to be built around Mount Sciberras, effectively sealing the new city off from attack from either land or sea. The streets within this enclosure were to be laid out on a grid plan to facilitate natural ventilation, and infrastructure was installed for sewage and rubbish collection. Every building had to have a rainwater cistern and sewer, and every corner house exterior decoration. The exhaustively detailed planning brief stipulated how much would be spent on each building, and which sections of the city would be allocated for palazzi. Laparelli even envisaged slicing off the humpback of Mount Sciberras in order to make level ground for the new city; these plans were hurriedly abandoned when intelligence – subsequently proved to be false – suggested a new Turkish invasion was imminent. La Vallette himself laid the first stone of the new city in March 1566, and an army of eight thousand construction workers, mostly slaves, moved in to start erecting the fortifications.

In 1568, La Vallette died before the city that would bear his name took shape, and Laparelli – having set the wheels in motion – returned to Italy, leaving his assistant, the Maltese architect **Ġirolmu Cassar**, in charge. Many of Valletta's grandest surviving buildings were the work of Cassar; in just over a decade, he designed and built St John's Co-Cathedral, the Grand Master's Palace, the seven lavish Knightly *auberges* and a host of smaller churches and private dwellings. The Knights moved to Valletta in 1571 when it was still mostly a shell, but within thirty years it was a bustling community of about four thousand people. They pumped money into the defence of the city and the Grand Harbour, attracting goods and services to the area, and Valletta soon became the island's most populous and prosperous urban centre. In the early eighteenth century, as the Knights came to dominate the central Mediterranean, they embarked on a makeover project for their city, redesigning many of Valletta's buildings in the florid **Baroque** style.

With Malta occupying such a key strategic location, and the Grand Harbour offering protected docks, the city was an obvious choice for Britain (the controlling power after 1800) to use as the headquarters of its Mediterranean fleet. Later, it was an equally obvious choice to serve as the Allies' regional headquarters in **World War II**, a status which invited intense bombing from Axis aircraft. Although the Grand Master's Palace, the Co-Cathedral and some other major sights emerged unscathed, most of the city has been reconstructed, parts of it with little regard for aesthetic sensibility.

After 1945, the population of the Grand Harbour region, especially the younger generation, migrated to the suburbs of the new towns being built to the south and north, where they enjoyed larger houses, wider roads and more modern infrastructure. Today, the Grand Harbour region is the most socially and economically depressed region in Malta. Valletta's gentle commercial life continues with little regard for the healthy numbers of tourists wandering the streets, and after the shops and offices shut in the late afternoon, the city rapidly empties. Few Maltese now choose to live in Valletta, and the handful of young locals who have recently trickled back into the converted townhouses, charmed by the city's bohemian beauty, have failed to stir up any challenge to Paceville's monopoly on nightlife in the area (see p.117). However, Valletta can now boast some of Malta's best **restaurants**, a handful of which have opened or relocated here.

For details of Valletta's restaurants, see p.266.

VALLETTA

Arrival and information

Malta's international **airport** is situated in Luqa, 5km south of Valletta. The arrivals hall has money-exchange bureaux, banks and a small tourist information office (daily 24hr). From outside the terminal building, beyond the car park, bus #8 runs to Valletta (every 30min; Lm0.15; 15min), or you could plump for a taxi: the set fare into Valletta or Sliema is Lm8.

Valletta's **bus terminus** occupies a circular open-air plaza just south of City Gate. Buses arrive here from all over the island, including from the airport, and on the plaza there's a Public Transport Authority booth (daily 5.30am–11pm) that can provide details of bus routes and fares. From the plaza, a bridge heads northeast across the dry moat into Valletta itself, while Floriana extends to the southwest. Given Valletta's narrow streets, buses do not enter the town, but it's an easy walk of about 1km into the centre from the bus terminus.

Arriving **by sea** from Italian ports (see p.12 for more), you'll come into the ferry terminal on Pinto Wharf, below the southeastern walls of Floriana overlooking the Grand Harbour. There are no money-exchange facilities here, and no public transport; you must either shell out for a taxi or take the steep, signposted 1km walk up to Valletta's bus terminus.

From Sliema, north of Valletta (see p.110), **ferries** run on a scenic 5min route across Marsamxett Harbour (daily 9am–7pm, every 30min; Lm0.30), dropping off at the Mandareggio district on the north flank of Valletta, near the water-polo pitch, from where it's a ten-minute uphill trek to Triq Ir-Repubblika in the city centre.

All cars need a **permit** to drive in Valletta (motorbikes are exempt). If you must drive in the town, check with your rental agency in advance that your car has the permit (most rented cars do). Once you have the permit, it can still be hell trying to drive in Valletta's one-way systems and car-choked streets, and yet more hellish finding **parking**; you'd do well to leave your vehicle in the multistorey car park (Map 2, F8) just south of the bus terminus towards Floriana (Lm0.30/hr).

Information

Valletta's lacklustre **tourist office** (Mon–Fri: mid-June to Sept 8.45am–1.30pm; rest of year 8.45am–5pm; ☎237747) is in Freedom Square (Misraħ Il-Ħelsien; Map 2, G7), just through the City Gate from the bus terminus, with another office in the airport arrivals hall (daily 24hr). Both stock plenty of useful brochures for sights in Valletta and around the island, including street-plans and lists of forthcoming events (which include a number of pageants celebrating the city's Knightly past). They can also supply lists of self-catering accommodation and hotels, as well as details of bus routes and the ferries to Gozo.

CITY GATE AND FREEDOM SQUARE

Map 2, G7.

Across from the bus terminus and over the concrete bridge spanning the dry moat of the fortifications, the rebuilt **City Gate** exemplifies the kind of bland architecture applied insensitively after World War II. In Laparelli's original design, this was the smaller Baroque Gate of St George, complete with drawbridge; it was later renamed Porta Reale, then King's Gate during British rule, and the present uninspiring structure was erected in 1964. It opens into the frenetic **Freedom Square**, rebuilt after the bombing of World War II, a paved-over plaza of makeshift car parks, fringed by flat arcades and humdrum shops. Amidst the streams of pedestrians stand stalls flogging trinkets alongside creaky-voiced buskers.

Across the square from the City Gate, another impromptu car park occupies the ruined foundations of the former **Royal Opera House**, pending extensive renovation work. The original was designed in the 1860s by Edward Middleton Barry (who also designed the Royal Opera House in Covent Garden, London), but it fell victim to German bombs in 1942. After the war, only the rubble was cleared; the surviving foundations were left in place for eventual rebuilding, an idea that itself fell victim to fifty years of official procrastination. Plans for a new opera house are now finally in train (see below). Facing the remains of the Opera House is **Palazzo Ferraria**, built in the nineteenth century as the residence of a wealthy wheat importer but now converted into offices. Its facade, essentially Baroque, has been adorned with folds of panelling around the door and flower-shaped cutouts doubling as ventilators in an attempt to counterbalance the heavy Neoclassicism of the Opera House, but now that its opposite number has gone, the palazzo simply looks overdone.

At last, however, plans are in the offing to rebuild the whole area of the bus terminus, City Gate, Freedom Square and the Royal Opera House, under a project called the **Valletta Master Plan**. The designs, by the Genoese architect **Renzo Piano** (who recently worked on Berlin's rejuvenated Potsdamer Platz) and Malta's most famous architect **Richard England**, are partly derived from Laparelli's original designs, sensitive to the Baroque architectural character of Valletta while also introducing innovative modern styles. Expected to cost Lm42 million, and funded mostly by the government, the Master Plan is due to start in 2002 and take five years to complete. There is an exhibition of the scheme's designs and sketches at the St James Cavalier Centre for Creativity (see p.52).

AUBERGE DE CASTILLE

Map 2, H7. Pjazza Kastilja.

Just south of the Royal Opera House ruin, the road opens into Pjazza Kastilja (Castille Square), a square dominated by the facade of the **Auberge de Castille**, the largest and most impressive of Valletta's four surviving *auberges*, or inns of residence (three of the original seven have been destroyed). This was the *auberge* of the Spanish and Portuguese *Langue*, originally entitled the "Auberge de Castille, Léon et Portugal". It is Malta's most monumental secular building, bombastically occupying an entire city block, its two storeys punctuated by a series of louvred windows with elaborate shell ornamentation. Originally designed by Ġirolmu Cassar in the 1570s in the austere style preferred by the Knights, the *auberge* was commissioned to be rebuilt in the eighteenth century by Grand Master Pinto de Fonseca, as part of the drive to give Valletta a Baroque makeover. The building was completed in 1744 in a style of grand Baroque, with an imposing facade dominated by a column-framed doorway. Above is a bust of Grand Master de Fonseca and his coat of arms alongside that of the *Langue* of Castille, Léon and Portugal, flanked with motifs of flags, swords, drums and shells, all of them symbols of power and prestige. The *auberge* now houses the Office of the Prime Minister, and there's no public access.

There are two monuments to public figures in Pjazza Kastilja. The first, across the road northwest of the *auberge*, is dedicated to **Sir Paul Boffa**, the first post-World War II Prime Minister, who oversaw the reinstatement of the Maltese constitution. On the roundabout in Pjazza Kastilja is a monument to **Manwel Dimech**, a socialist activist who was exiled by the colonial authorities to Egypt, where he died in 1921, for attempting to set up a trade union; the plinth describes him as "the first Maltese socialist teacher and martyr".

UPPER BARAKKA GARDENS

Map 2, I8. Daily 7.30am until dusk; free.

South of Auberge de Castille, a short street leads to the gate of the beautiful little **Upper Barakka Gardens**, created in 1661 by the Italian knight Flaminio Balbiani as a retreat for the Knights. Back then, the arcaded courtyard at the southern part of the garden was covered, but when Grand Master Francisco Ximenes de Texada learned in 1775 that dissident knights plotting against him were holding rendezvous here, he symbolically stripped the roof. Today, the garden, lush with ficus trees, palms, Aleppo pines and a fountain at its centre, is a breezy place of refuge from the bustle and heat of the city, full of locals and visitors lounging on its wooden benches and feeding the flocks of feral pigeons.

However, the garden's star attraction lies past the courtyard – its lofty terrace with a stunning panoramic **view** over the Grand Harbour, the Three Cities and the Malta Drydocks. From here, you can also get an idea of how impenetrable Valletta was in its heyday by peering down over the fortifications, perched above a sheer 100m drop into the dry moat.

THE LASCARIS WAR ROOMS

Map 2, H8. Lascaris Bastion. Mon–Fri 9.30am–4pm, Sat & Sun 9.30am–12.30pm; Lm1.75.

Southwest of Pjazza Kastilja, some 20m down Triq Ġirolmu Cassar, a signposted passageway on the right directs you through winding tunnels cut through the rock to the **Lascaris War Rooms**, located in the heart of the bastion. This was originally where the Knights kept their slaves under lock and key, until Napoleon granted a general amnesty when he ejected the Knights from Malta in 1798.

In World War II the British forces converted the dank and mouldy dungeons into the centre of operations for Malta and also the headquarters of the Royal Navy's Mediterranean Fleet. Working conditions were claustrophobic – a thousand people worked here, 240 at a time in six-hour shifts – but it was from Lascaris that the Allies changed the course of the war in the Mediterranean by severely disrupting Axis supply-lines to North Africa, launching the invasion of Sicily, and eventually engineering Italy's unconditional surrender. The network of rooms has now been opened as an interesting **museum**, with the wartime atmosphere re-created by means of wax dummies and all the original maps, props and equipment. Audioguides (in English) are available from the ticket desk.

Highlights include the **Navy Plotting Room**, which reconstructs the attack on Taranto Harbour in 1941, when the Italian fleet was destroyed in port. Note the ominous J-type contact mine that floated just beneath the water's surface; the Italians planted 200,000 of these mines around Malta's seas. The **Anti-Aircraft Guns Operations Room** illustrates the umbrella of fire around Malta that enemy planes had to penetrate – what the Italians called "the gates of hell". The **Coast Defence Operation Room** provided the quietest jobs, if only because Hitler's planned invasion of Malta never came to fruition. Finally, the largest room at the back of the complex is devoted to **Operation Husky**, the title given to the 1943 Allied invasion of Sicily, directed by General Eisenhower. A map of the island, lined and scribbled, charts the complex troop, air and sea campaign.

THE LASCARIS WAR ROOMS

ST JAMES CAVALIER CENTRE FOR CREATIVITY

Map 2, G7. Triq Papa Piju V. Daily 10am–5pm; free.

From the west end of Pjazza Kastilja, Triq Papa Piju V heads north across the top of the City Gate. A short way along on the right is the **St James Cavalier Centre for Creativity**, an engaging centre for postmodern Maltese art, cinema, literary events, drama and classical music.

The building is one of the two Cavaliers in Valletta (the other is St John's Cavalier, located further north along Triq Papa Piju V on the other side of City Gate; see p.53). Originally built in the 1570s, the Cavaliers are pentagonal towers topped by heavy gun emplacements, designed to act as rearguard defence positions looming over the city's land front. The walls are several metres thick, packed with an infill of rubble, and the interior is filled by a ramp that spirals to the roof in order to deploy cannon and a series of half-barrel chambers to store ammunition. The British altered the building in 1868 to incorporate two water reservoirs, and in the early twentieth century – taking advantage of the thick walls – parts of the Cavalier were converted into shelters against chemical warfare.

In 1995, after the Cavalier had suffered several years of disuse, the government commissioned the celebrated Maltese architect **Richard England**, one of the co-designers of the Valletta Master Plan, to restore it as an arts centre (designs and sketches for the Master Plan are displayed in one of the Cavalier's exhibition halls). Circular architecture is Richard England's trademark, and here it is the dominant motif of what is a sensitive restoration: the half-barrel chambers have been left intact, while a theatre-in-the-round and an atrium with a glass-domed roof have been incorporated in the former water cisterns.

The building's eleven halls now house an array of attractions, not least of which is a small permanent exhibition of

postmodern Maltese art. Most works, particularly the paintings, are derivative of the mainstream trends in Western European postmodern art; standout pieces include **Gabriel Caruana's** psychedelic splash-paintings on recycled wood that has been fashioned into different shapes, and the most original installation is *Gossip*, poignantly illustrating the banality of speech with voices blathering away from inside empty cans of tomatoes built into an intricate structure. Alongside the permanent collection are changing exhibitions; local artists to keep an eye out for include Norbert Attard, Vince Briffa, Austin Camilleri and Pierre Portelli.

Also tucked away in the complex is a small **cinema** that screens European art-house films, and a circular **theatre** staging anything from plays to ballet to concerts of classical music.

The Valletta tourist office stocks leaflets giving full details of artistic and cultural events in and around the city.

HASTINGS GARDENS

Map 2, F6. Daily 7.30am until dusk; free.

At the northern end of Triq Papa Piju V, past **St John's Cavalier** (which is now home to the embassy of the Knights of Malta; see p.340), is the entrance to **Hastings Gardens**. This fine garden of Mediterranean oaks and flowers is dedicated to Lord Hastings, the British governor from 1824 to 1826, who died at sea in 1827 and was buried in the Neoclassical shrine which now stands at the centre of the garden. These days a popular haunt of young lovers smooching in the sun, the garden sprawls just behind the ramparts of the walls, from where you can get the most impressive views of the curving and twisting Valletta fortifications, which are about 100m high here; beyond, views stretch to Marsamxett Harbour winding into the yacht marina of Msida Creek, and, to the north, the outline of Fort Manoel and the urban sprawl of Sliema and St Julian's (see p.108).

NATIONAL MUSEUM OF FINE ARTS

Map 2, G6. Triq Nofs In-Nhar. Mid-June to Sept daily 8.30am–1.30pm; rest of year Mon–Sat 8.30am–4.30pm, Sun 8.30am–3.30pm; Lm1.

Less than 100m east of Hastings Gardens is the rather disappointing **National Museum of Fine Arts**, on Triq Nofs In-Nhar. The building, originally the home of a French knight, is a large Baroque townhouse, designed round a courtyard on two floors; it has a sumptuous staircase but its large rooms have been much tinkered with over the centuries. Under the British, it was the residence of the naval chief commander, and was retitled Admiralty House. Despite some fine works, the art collections are only of passing interest, and many paintings (and the building itself) are crying out for restoration. To make matters worse, the descriptions are sketchy and the canvases lit so badly that some are hard to discern through the reflective shimmer. A visit can be a frustrating experience.

The 24 rooms exhibit paintings dating from the fourteenth century to the present, originating from Malta, Italy, Venice and the Netherlands. A tour begins on the upper floor. **Room 1** showcases fourteenth-century religious icons, most of them sculpted or painted on wood, while the highlight of the religious art in **room 2** is the striking *Nativity* by Maestro Alberto. **Room 3**'s sixteenth-century Italian works include Filippo Paladini's stirring *Martyrdom of St Lawrence*, and the finest Venetian-school work in **room 4** is Andrea Vincentino's haunting *Raising of Lazarus*. Next door in **room 5** is the excellent but misogynistic *Portrait of a Lady* by Jan van Scorel, showing the subject's hands clenched in frustration and her stare cold and suspicious. A few large canvases, mostly unremarkable, populate **rooms 8–11**, including the tortured rendition of the *Martyrdom of St Agatha* by Giovanni Baglione, and a stately portrait of Grand Master Alof de Wignacourt. **Rooms 12** and **13** hold pieces by the Italian artist Mattia Preti, famous for his work in St John's Co-Cathedral – most notably *The Drunkenness of Noah* and *The Incredulity of St Thomas*.

On the ground floor, in **room 14**, the eighteenth-century French artist Antoine de Favray aims to capture the chivalry and pomp of the Knights, but his best piece is the *Maltese Lady Visiting Her Lady Friend*, a study of the contrast in garb and demeanour between the humble Maltese lady and her wealthy foreign counterpart. **Rooms 18–19** display some realist renditions of Maltese cityscapes, including, in **room 19**, the excellent 1867 *Death of Dragut* by the Maltese Giuseppe Cali. **Rooms 20–23** are full of nineteenth-century Malta-scapes by local artists, mostly realistic, if glorified, canvases of Valletta streets and magnificent ships anchored in the Grand Harbour. The **basement** holds Knightly paraphernalia, including silverware from the Sacra Infermeria and a collection of Maltese Crosses.

NATIONAL MUSEUM OF ARCHEOLOGY

Map 2, H6. Triq Ir-Repubblika. Mid-June to Sept daily 7.45am–2pm; rest of year Mon–Sat 8.15am–4.30pm, Sun 8.15am–4pm; Lm1.

From the National Museum of Fine Arts, it's a short walk southeast to the main Triq Ir-Repubblika. At the corner with Triq Melita sits the grand **National Museum of Archeology**. This stately building, its facade decorated with engaged columns and ornate Baroque windows, was built by Girolmu Cassar as the Auberge de Provence in 1575 to house the French knights. During the British era, it was converted into the British Union Club, pompous meeting-place for British expatriates and colonial rulers.

At the time of writing, the only visitable part of the museum was the ground floor, which showcases Malta's Neolithic Age discoveries, from the beginnings of Għar Dalam to the end of the period of the temple-builders (5000–2500 BC). Although the collection is small, the pottery, figurines and motifs found in the Neolithic temples are impressive works of art, acclaimed as the world's most sophisticated Neolithic pieces so far discovered. Labelling is good, and each room has detailed notes giving contextual background to the works on display.

At the time of writing, the museum's upper floor was being renovated to house exhibits from the Bronze Age, Phoenician and Roman periods, but the opening date for these sections had not been fixed. Contact the Valletta tourist office for up-to-date information.

The remains of the Għar Dalam and Skorba phases in the **Pre-Temple** room are understandably crude, mostly incised pottery ware and pendants of rodents' teeth similar to those found in Sicily that date from the same period. The next room, the **Tarxien Hall**, houses two important discoveries. First is a specially fashioned stone slab with spiral motifs that was wedged across the passageway in Tarxien's Middle Temple to mark the inner shrine, so holy that only special shamans could enter. Also here is the altar, with similar spiral reliefs and a stone headdress framing a square, hollow niche. The altar itself is hollow, lidded by the wedge of stone near its bottom; inside, Sir Temi Zammit, the father of Maltese archeology, discovered animal-bone remains and flint knives, sole but definitive proof of animal sacrifices in the temples. In the **Prehistoric Architecture** room, note the architectural details of the stone model of a temple – the larger corner megaliths for structural support, the stepped, slightly domed roof of megaliths, and the concave facade. Here, also, is the illustration of a theory put forward by British archeologist John Evans that the outline of the temples evolved from the lobed, egg-shaped chambers of the Żebbug Phase tombs.

Interest picks up in the next room, which is dedicated to the **Human Figure**. Here are stone phallic symbols and chunky female figures, dubbed **"fat ladies"** by archeologists, which were found in the Neolithic temples (3600–2500 BC). There are various human sculptures, some with pleated skirts and headdresses, but most of them are headless, so that different heads – perhaps even animal heads – could be added to the loop at their neck for different ceremonies. The most famous is the well-endowed nude figurine dubbed the *Venus of Malta*, found in Hagar Qim, one of the temples. The left hands of the "fat ladies" almost always rest on their bellies, symbolizing fertility; indeed, one theory to explain the outline of the temples suggests that they were modelled on the outline of the seated figurines, which are thought to personify fertility (see p.329). Highlight of this section is the **Sleeping Lady**, a small, hand-sized figurine found in the Hypogeum that shows a large woman reclining on a couch. It's a delicate piece of art, carved in minute detail and infused with metaphor: some archeologists have proposed that this figurine represents the pregnant women who would crouch in the grave chambers of the Hypogeum (see p.178) so that the spirit of the dead would enter their unborn child.

NATIONAL MUSEUM OF ARCHEOLOGY

ST JOHN'S CO-CATHEDRAL

Map 2, I6. Misraħ San Ġwann. Mon–Fri 9.30am–12.30pm &
1.30–4.30pm, Sat 9.30am–12.30pm; closed public holidays;
cathedral free; museum and oratory Lm1.

Dominating a relaxed, pleasant square just off Triq Ir-
Repubblika in the heart of Valletta is the magnificent **St
John's Co-Cathedral**, Malta's finest church by far, which
is effortlessly awe-inspiring for its architecture, for the opu-
lence of its vast, frescoed interior, and for the quality
of painting and sculpture within (including one of
Caravaggio's finest works).

The building was designed by Ġirolmu Cassar, and constructed between 1573 and 1578 to serve as the conventual
church of the Knights following their arrival in the new
city of Valletta. The austere, panelled facade reflects the
Knights' early sensibility, but in the latter half of the seventeenth century, with the advent of Baroque in Roman
Catholic countries, they set about transforming its plain
interior in the most ambitiously artistic project the order
ever undertook. They commissioned the Italian artist
Mattia Preti (1613–99) to supervise the scheme and also
to produce many of the cathedral's paintings; in some years
more money was spent on the Co-Cathedral than on military defence.

The result is an interior that is artistically overwhelming,
the flamboyance and frothiness of Baroque filling every surface within the impressively huge space. Knightly vanity is
evident in the self-aggrandizing memorials to various
Grand Masters that dominate the side-chapels: each chapel
is dedicated to a particular *Langue*, which oversaw its design
and installed monuments celebrating each Grand Master
elected from that *Langue*. In 1816, in an acknowledgement
of the magnificence of the church, the Maltese ecclesiastical
authorities promoted the conventual church of St John to a

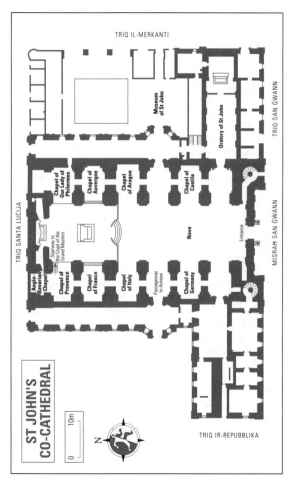

TRIQ IL-MERKANTI

TRIQ SANTA LUĊIJA

TRIQ SAN ĠWANN

MISRAĦ SAN ĠWANN

TRIQ IR-REPUBBLIKA

Museum of St John

Oratory of St John

Chapel of Our Lady of Philermos

Chapel of Auvergne

Chapel of Aragon

Chapel of Castile

Anglo-Bavarian Chapel

Stairway to the Crypt of the Grand Masters

Chapel of Provence

Chapel of France

Chapel of Italy

Passageway to Annexe

Chapel of Germany

Nave

Entrance

ST JOHN'S CO-CATHEDRAL

0   10m

N

ST JOHN'S CO-CATHEDRAL

position of equality with St Paul's, located across the island in Mdina (see p.126), thus giving rise to the odd name of "Co-Cathedral". To absorb it all could take three hours or more.

The nave

As you step into the vast **nave**, it takes a while for your eyes to adjust to the dimness of the interior. The side walls rise solidly, fashioned into thick, arched pillars that provide access to the side chapels and are stamped with folds of Baroque ornamentation interspersed with Maltese Crosses. Working directly on the porous limestone, it took Preti five years to paint the vault; the eighteen vignettes, showing episodes from the life of St John, mark the apex of Preti's artistic career and exemplify what has been dubbed the High Baroque style. He was one of the first painters to work on a concave surface without distorting true perspective, a trick he managed by using directional shadows to give the vignettes a perspective of their own. Between the vignettes are the coats of arms of the two **Cotoner Grand Masters**, the brothers Rafael and Nicolas who presided over the transformation of the church during their period as Grand Masters from 1660 to 1680.

The floor of the nave is a chequerboard of 364 unique inlaid **marble tombs**. Each tomb has a Latin scroll extolling the virtues of the knight buried beneath, followed by an epitaph, both of them framed by symbols of prestige and immortality, glory and evil – eagles, angels, skulls, flags, lions, crowns and ghoulish skeletons brandishing sickles. In tribute to his artistry in the Co-Cathedral and other Maltese churches, the Knights awarded Preti the title of "Knight of Grace". He lies beneath one of the cathedral's simplest tombstones, on the passageway to the sacristy to the left of the entrance.

This account of the cathedral's lavish internal **chapels** begins to the left of the main entrance, and follows a clockwise direction around the cathedral interior, starting on the north wall. Alongside the main cathedral building to the south is a small **museum**.

The Chapel of Germany

Inside the main doors on the left is the passageway to the sacristy, with a doorway off it to the right opening into the **Chapel of Germany**, dedicated to the Epiphany of Christ. Since the only German Grand Master was Ferdinand von Hompesch, who was impeached and stripped of his title for capitulating to Napoleon, this is the only chapel without a Grand Master's monument. Nonetheless, the chapel interior is still fluidly Baroque, and the gilt-stone altar, typical of Preti's influence, is the only one in the church that has not been subsequently altered.

Beneath the threshold of the bare **Passageway to the Annexe** alongside the chapel is buried Anselme de Cays, a French knight who clearly felt victimized by real or imaginary power struggles, and who took his grudges to the grave: he lies beneath a tombstone which bears the curse, "You who tread on me will be trodden on."

The Chapel of Italy

The next bay is the **Chapel of Italy**, dedicated to St Catherine. Preti painted the altarpiece's *Mystic Marriage of St Catherine*, an emotional portrait capturing the saint's visage lurid with inspirational sanctity. The monument to Grand Master Gregario Carafa is humble, his head turned sideways to face the altar and Preti's painting.

ST JOHN'S CO-CATHEDRAL

The Chapel of France

In the 1830s Giuseppe Hyzler, curator of the Co-Cathedral, started stealthily tinkering with the **Chapel of France**, alongside the Chapel of Italy. He considered the excesses of Baroque to be a corruption of Catholicism, so he set about cleansing the chapel of its Baroque influence. He replaced the altar, hacked the trimmings from Grand Master Emmanuel de Rohan Polduc's monument, and whittled the decor on the walls down to their present blue background broken by motifs of the Maltese Cross, crown and leaf. By the time Hyzler had started on the monument of Grand Master Adrien de Wignacourt he'd provoked a storm of protest – and was fired shortly after.

The Chapel of Provence

The last chapel on the north aisle is the **Chapel of Provence**, dedicated to St Michael, which holds the monuments of Grand Masters Jean Paul de Lascaris Castellar and Antoine de Paule. To give the monuments a symmetrical and compositional unity, Preti topped both with a single painting, depicting a knight raising a sword while angels trumpet glory. The bust of Grand Master Castellar fully conveys his fierce and authoritarian character, with a heavy-set jaw and goatee beard, wide brow, and bulging nose and forehead.

The Anglo-Bavarian Chapel

To the right of the Chapel of Provence is the **Anglo-Bavarian Chapel**, enclosed by a bronze gate and dedicated to St Charles Borromeo. It's the smallest and simplest of the chapels, reflecting the obscurity of the Anglo-Bavarian *Langue* that was set up in 1784 as a way of reviving the Anglican *Langue* in exile; at that time, there were so few

British knights that they had to be annexed to their Bavarian counterparts. No Grand Master was ever elected from these regions. To the right of the altar, the wood-carved figure of St John served as figurehead for the *Gran Caracca*, one of the galleys which bore the Knights from Rhodes to Malta in 1530. In 1798, Napoleon stripped the chapel of its silver caskets to finance his military adventures.

The Crypt of the Grand Masters

To the right as you face the Anglo-Bavarian Chapel is a staircase leading down to the **Crypt of the Grand Masters**. This is the only part of the Co-Cathedral that retains the original, restrained architectural tastes. This simple crypt is the resting-place of two of the most influential Grand Masters – Jean Parisot de la Vallette and Philippe Villiers de L'Isle Adam, the sarcophagi of both of whom are raised up on legs and feature sculptures of their subjects reclining, with their hands steepled in prayer. A tablet commemorates the knight Oliver Starkey, secretary to La Vallette, granted the unusual honour of burial in the Co-Cathedral. Note the altar, typical of simple vernacular altars in medieval Malta. The crucifixion group is a rare example of local sixteenth-century wood-carved sculpture.

The Chapel of Our Lady of Philermos

Crossing the nave from the crypt stairs leads you to the **Chapel of Our Lady of Philermos**. Legend has it that the silver balustrades which divide the chapel were painted black so that Napoleon wouldn't be tempted to rip them out to sell. Now restored to their pristine state, they glint in the light of the chandelier. At the head of the chapel is a small, gilded icon of the Madonna, partly embedded in its frame, which has been dubbed Our Lady of Carafa. This

ST JOHN'S CO-CATHEDRAL

THE KNIGHTS' HERALDIC SYMBOLS

Throughout Malta, and particularly in Valletta, it's impossible to avoid the distinctively symmetrical **Maltese Cross**, four identical arrowheads meeting at their points, which served as the Knights of Malta's badge of identity from their foundation in Jerusalem in 1113 onwards: they flaunted it everywhere, in their buildings, clothes and armaments. Its four equal arms represent the virtues of Temperance, Prudence, Justice and Fortitude, and are coloured white to symbolize the purity of the Knights' mission as hospitallers, caring for pilgrims. The cross's red background is a graphic symbol of the blood spilt on the battlefield in the name of the Christian faith. The base of each arrowhead is divided into two points, which together represent the eight Beatitudes proclaimed by Christ in the Sermon on the Mount (Matthew 5).

The Knights' history imbued the Maltese Cross with associations of chivalry, prestige and care for the sick, prompting many organizations around the world to adopt it as their own, not least the Knight Templars, a thirteenth-century offshoot of the Knights of Malta, who reversed its colours, using a red cross on a white background. The Maltese Cross is also bandied about by many modern humanitarian organizations, including the St John's Ambulance Brigade (sometimes called St John's Rescue Corps and represented in virtually all the

replaced the original icon of Our Lady of Philermos, which the Knights took with them when they left Malta two centuries ago.

The Chapel of Auvergne

Following a route back through the chapels on the south wall towards the main cathedral entrance, the next is the **Chapel of Auvergne**, dedicated to St Sebastian, which

Commonwealth countries), which was formed in Britain in 1831 by the English *Langue* without formal approval by the Knights themselves. In addition, there are dozens of bogus Knights' organizations around the world, particularly in the USA, who display the cross and who will sell you a knighthood, irrespective of your background. The Maltese Cross also appears as a motif in some medieval rock-cut churches in the Turkish region of Cappadocia.

The Knights also liberally stamped their **coats of arms** over Valletta. Every building erected by them bears its owner's escutcheon mounted prominently on the facade as an assertion of individuality and historical familial connections: the Cotoner brothers, for instance, who came from a family of cotton growers and who both served as Grand Masters in the seventeenth century, have cotton plants adorning their coats of arms. Sometimes buildings have more than one escutcheon, perhaps as a reflection of the transfer of ownership between different individuals, or possibly to indicate different layers of use or ownership, since each *Langue* also had its own coat of arms.

Today, even those Maltese without aristocratic or noble titles have taken to the tradition of upholding their coats of arms with pride: many families flaunt their escutcheon to this day, if not mounted on the facade then framed and taking pride of place in the living room.

boasts elaborately twisted columns framing an altarpiece painting depicting the martyrdom of the saint. Grand Master Annett de Clermont de Chattes Gessan is buried in the crypt beneath his bust.

The Chapel of Aragon

Alongside the Chapel of Auvergne is the superb **Chapel of Aragon**, dedicated to St George, which showcases three paintings by Preti including the grand altarpiece of an invincible, mounted St George. But it's the monuments of the four Spanish Grand Masters that dominate: the two nearest the altar, of Martin de Redin and Rafael Cotoner, are restrained busts enclosed in modest niches, but those to Nicolas Cotoner and Ramon Perellos y Roccaful are as big as wardrobes, the busts presiding over angels and triumphant motifs of flags, guns and swords.

The Chapel of Castille

Beyond a passageway leading to the museum (see p.67) is the **Chapel of Castille**, dedicated to St James the Less. It holds another Preti mural entitled *St James Assisting the Spaniards in Defeating the Moors*, with beautiful muted colours – autumn-orange and russet. Two monuments commemorate Grand Masters Antonio Manoel de Vilhena and Manoel Pinto de Fonseca. The former is huge, the most sumptuous in the church: de Vilhena, flanked by angels, sports locks of shoulder-length hair that resemble the manes of the lions which support the whole monument.

The Oratory of St John

The final bay, dubbed the Passageway to the Oratory, leads south to the **Oratory of St John**. Originally a place of worship for novice Knights, the oratory is home to Malta's most important artwork, **Caravaggio's** magnificent *Beheading of St John the Baptist*. Painted in 1608, it's widely considered to be the finest painting of the seventeenth century, and has all the qualities of a masterpiece – most notably the perfectly balanced composition and the virtuoso use of light and shade, the application of halftones and subtle illumination bringing the subjects to life. Caravaggio was the first artist to use directional light effectively to add depth and texture to his paintings, and here he graphically conveys the tortured tribulations of the protagonists: they are furtive, their brows furrowed, and you can't help surmising that this is one execution they will deny even to themselves. An old woman is clutching her hands to her head in grief, the prison guard is evasively turning his attention away from the beheading, and the executioner, his body clenched stiff, is stealthily unsheathing his knife to cut clean through John's neck, which has already been sliced with a sword.

Also hanging here is another painting by Caravaggio, a small *St Jerome* that was recently moved here from its original place in the Chapel of Italy for security reasons. It frames the saint's upper torso as he writes on a parchment, the artist giving him a wise demeanour and compassionate eyes. Once again, Caravaggio's use of directional light and halftones breathes life into the work.

The Museum of St John

A corridor from the oratory leads past the largely bare, roofless **cemetery**, resting-place of many knights, including some of those killed during the Great Siege of 1565. There is no public access to the cemetery itself, which you can only glimpse through the museum windows. The corridor leads on to the **Museum of St John**, whose prize exhibits are some majestic Flemish tapestries dating from 1702 that were formerly hung in the church's nave. Grand Master Roccaful commissioned the three sets of tapestries from the Belgian artist Jodicos de Vos for a price equivalent almost to the Knights' annual defence budget. The first set has fourteen panels depicting episodes in the life of Christ from the Annunciation to the Resurrection; the second depicts Christian fables such as *The Triumph of Charity* and *The*

ST JOHN'S CO-CATHEDRAL

Destruction of Idolatry; and the third portrays Christ, the disciples, the Madonna and the gracious donor.

THE NATIONAL LIBRARY

Map 2, J6. Misraħ Ir-Repubblika. Mid-June to Sept Mon–Sat 8.15am–1.15pm; rest of year Mon–Fri 8.15am–5.45pm, Sat 8.15am–1.15pm; free.

The main Triq Ir-Repubblika heads northeast past the Co-Cathedral and the Neoclassical colonnaded **Law Courts** (built on the ruins of the Auberge de Auvergne, which was bombed in World War II) before opening out into Misraħ Ir-Repubblika (Republic Square), filled with the coo of pigeons bobbing and pecking. A small, faded statue of Queen Victoria in the square is lost amid the rows of café tables.

Misraħ Ir-Repubblika is lined with cafés and is an atmospheric place to stop for a snack or a drink.

At the south end of the square is the **National Library**. This was the Knights' last building, erected in the 1790s, the more usual Baroque architecture here giving way to Neoclassical columns and a pediment. The grand building is a depository for both Malta's official records and for the archives of the Knights, from the order's foundation in 1113 to 1798, including the documents that attest to each knight's sixteen lines of nobility, necessary in order to join the order. Since 1612, all books and private papers belonging to deceased knights have been lodged here.

Upstairs is the long **main hall** and reading room; the handful of researchers, sitting at tan wooden desks, are outnumbered by the streams of visitors shuffling through the hall. The 400,000 books stacked floor-to-ceiling along the hall are covered with a film of dust, many of the brown spines cracked and peeling. Changing displays showcase notable documents and books, not least of which is the deed signed by **Charles V** of Spain in 1530, which granted Malta to the knights: "The Emperor Charles V and his mother Joanna the Mad grant and bountifully bestow on the Grand Master the islands of Malta and Gozo and the castle in Tripoli, to be held in feudal tenure by sole acknowledgement of a falcon, each All Saints' Day to be delivered to the Viceroy of Sicily."

THE GRAND MASTER'S PALACE

Map 2, J5. Misraħ San Ġorġ. Mon–Sat 9am–4.30pm; closed when parliament is in morning session and during official state visits; free.

Opening off Triq Ir-Repubblika, diagonally opposite Misraħ Ir-Repubblika, is Misraħ San Ġorġ (also known as Pjazza Palazz) – these days prosaically used as a car park. In the square is a monument depicting peasants clinging to the Maltese flag, which commemorates the Sette Giugno Riots of June 7, 1919, when nervous British troops shot four people dead.

The **Grand Master's Palace**, another of Ġirolmu Cassar's designs from 1571, dominates the south side of the square. Its two entrances, framed by columns, punctuate the high exterior wall that is ringed by an enclosed balcony. The building has served as Malta's seat of government since its construction in the 1570s as the residence originally of the Grand Master, then of British governors; today it houses the President's office and the parliament. From the balcony above the southwest entrance a succession of leaders have addressed crowds thronging Misraħ San Ġorġ, from Queen Elizabeth II to President Roosevelt, Pope John Paul II, and various newly-elected Maltese Prime Ministers.

PRINCELY EXCESS

When he visited Malta from Sicily in the 1770s Lord Patrick Brydon wrote: "We found ourselves in a new world. The streets were crowded with well-dressed people… Assassinations and robberies are very uncommon. Knights have much the appearance of gentlemen and men of the world." At the time, there were several hundred Knights in Malta, presiding over the best hospital and most famous naval academy in Europe.

But by the eighteenth century, the Knights – supreme in the Mediterranean – had abandoned their vows of chastity and celibacy to lapse into princely excess. Private servants groomed and dressed them, served them dinner on silver dishes, and carried them through Valletta on wooden sedan chairs. The Grand Master could choose between four magisterial palaces, in Valletta, Mdina, Buskett Gardens and San Anton Gardens. Garbed in velvet, he lunched with Knights, Chaplains and Sergeants as an orchestra played, typically eating partridge or quail and drinking wine from a cellar of the finest French wines. A staff of forty, headed by the Master of the Horse, fussed over his 52 horses; the Master Falconer, with a staff of sixteen, trained the Maltese peregrine falcons that the Grand Master gifted to friends and sovereigns. Two pages accompanied the Grand Master – to carry his stick and hat, fan him in the summer, light his way at night, groom him and dress him. At St John's Co-Cathedral, the Grand Master sat on his throne by the altar while his pages fanned him with gold-handled peacock-feathered fans.

The Knights' over-complacency was their downfall. The bubble burst towards the end of the eighteenth century, as overindulgence ate into Malta's coffers. The economic austerity measures that resulted, including a hike in the price of bread, led to widespread discontent, and the loss of French financial support following the 1798 French Revolution bankrupted the Knights. When they left Malta, the country had to shoulder their debts.

THE GRAND MASTER'S PALACE

Much as with the Co-Cathedral, the dourly grand facade of the palace ill prepares you for an interior awash with excessive quantities of **art**. In portraits gracing the corridors and coats of arms adorning the marble floors, each Grand Master etched his legacy on the building, with British governors later adding portraits of their own monarchs. Maltese presidents have contributed little save for a few plaques, preferring instead merely to install themselves in the Grand Master's state apartment, converting the grand bedchamber into an office.

Behind the facade at street-level are a pair of beautiful internal **courtyards**, tranquil retreats from the bustle outside. From here, stairs lead up to the building's **upper floor**, where the halls and grand state rooms, adorned with frescoes, damask, magnificent portraits, *objets d'art* and furniture, open off a U-shaped corridor.

The Courtyards and the Armoury

The northeast entrance on Misraħ San Ġorġ gives into **Neptune's Courtyard**, a garden of ficus and palm trees with a marble monument bearing the coat of arms of Grand Master Ramon Perellos y Roccaful. The bronze statue of Neptune at the centre of the courtyard is a thinly veiled portrait of Grand Master Alof de Wignacourt (1601–22).

On the western flank of the courtyard, a doorway leads through into **Prince Alfred's Courtyard**, named after Queen Victoria's second son, who planted an auricaria tree here in 1858 (it's now four storeys high). Mounted high on a wall at one end of the courtyard is Pinto's Clock, named after Grand Master Manoel Pinto de Fonseca, who had it installed here in 1745. It's a grandiose object, with four concave dials – one to record the time in hours and minutes, another the date, another the month, and the fourth the phases of the moon. Three bells top the dials, and statues of Moorish slaves wield the hammer that strikes the bells every quarter-hour. Their sharp peal can be heard throughout Valletta.

The Armoury

Same hours as Grand Master's Palace; Lm1.

The corridor running along the southwest flank of Neptune's Courtyard leads to the palace **Armoury**, an impressive exhibit of militaria spread over two barrel-vaulted halls that were formerly used as the palace stables. The displays were moved here in 1976, when Malta's parliament took over the original armoury, located on the upper floor of the palace.

With the weaponry of deceased Knights passing automatically into the Armoury, by 1785 the Knights had amassed forty thousand muskets and enough military hardware to equip an army of 18,000 men. However, most of this has since been looted, and only a fraction remains – some five thousand pieces, dating from the sixteenth to the eighteenth centuries that were produced in Malta and the European mainland.

The whole range of armaments is on display – crossbows, helmets, lances, shields, swords, guns, pistols, muskets, cannon, and the tableau of twelve jigsaw pieces of body armour that encased each knight in battle. Highlights include the full damascened suit of armour that belonged to Grand Master Alof de Wignacourt, and the breast- and back-plate worn by Grand Master La Vallette in the Great Siege, although the most inventive item is a German-made piece dating from 1550, a sword that intriguingly doubled up as a pistol.

The upper floor

From the northwest corner of Neptune's Courtyard, a staircase leads up to the **Entrance Corridor**, lined with framed portraits of Grand Masters and, above them, lunettes depicting the Knights' naval battles. Manoel Pinto de Fonseca, perhaps the most vain and artistic of all Grand Masters, is shown flaunting his red velvet cape, shoving the Ottoman flag to one side with decisive finality. The ceiling

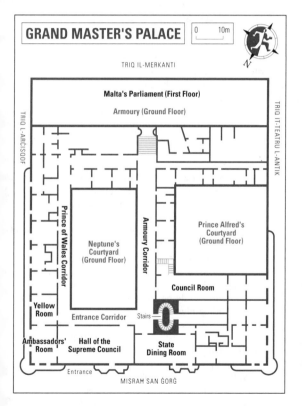

GRAND MASTER'S PALACE

0   10m

TRIQ IL-MERKANTI

Malta's Parliament (First Floor)

Armoury (Ground Floor)

TRIQ L-ARĊISQOF

TRIQ IT-TEATRU L-ANTIK

Prince of Wales Corridor

Neptune's Courtyard (Ground Floor)

Armoury Corridor

Prince Alfred's Courtyard (Ground Floor)

Yellow Room

Council Room

Entrance Corridor

Stairs

Ambassadors' Room

Hall of the Supreme Council

State Dining Room

Entrance

MISRAĦ SAN ĠORĠ

THE GRAND MASTER'S PALACE

is covered in frescoes of geometric designs, which have the unfortunate look of old, tattered wallpaper.

From the top of the staircase, turn left into the **State Dining Room**, decorated with two crystal-glass chandeliers and portraits of British royalty from George III to Elizabeth II. Their portraits are uncannily similar in size and hue to the Grand Masters' portraits that hang in these rooms, but fail to surpass them.

The next room off the Entrance Corridor was the setting for official state functions. Dubbed the **Hall of the Supreme Council**, it has a coffered and panelled timber ceiling, with the lower half of its walls covered in dull yellow brocade. Twelve remarkable frescoes, executed in 1576 by the Italian painter Matteo Perez D'Aleccio, line the upper part of the walls, depicting the major episodes of the Great Siege. The gilded balcony that dominates the head of the room was originally part of the stern of a galley; its six panelled paintings show details from the first chapter of Genesis.

Continuing clockwise, the **Ambassadors' Room** was where foreign envoys presented their credentials to the Grand Master, amidst suitably impressive decor – red damask covering the lower half of the walls, a red carpet, and chairs upholstered in red velvet. Gilded pendants stud the panelled timber ceiling, and D'Aleccio's frescoes recount key events of the Knights' history. There is a full-length study of Louis XVI (1774–93), flanked by more portraits of Grand Masters. Antoine de Favray's painting showing Grand Master Philippe Villiers de L'Isle Adam receiving the keys to Mdina illustrates a certain capacity for spin: the painting shows well-dressed nobility and dignified guards kneeling in front of L'Isle Adam, but in truth the nobles resented the Knights and met them at the gates of Mdina accompanied by a gang of men-at-arms.

The **Yellow Room**, so called because of the gold pendants adorning its coffered ceiling, is next door. This was originally named the *Paggeria*, or Pages' Room, and served as the withdrawing room for the Grand Master's sixteen pages. D'Aleccio's frescoes here show scenes from the Knights' life in Jerusalem in the thirteenth century; note the two groupings of knights depicted, the Knights of Malta (then called the Order of St John of Jerusalem) and the Knights Templar, the latter recognizable by their red-on-white Maltese Cross. The room's decor clashes rather oddly, the white and blue damask covering the walls below the frescoes contrasting with the green carpet.

From the Yellow Room, you emerge into the **Prince of Wales Corridor**, its marble floor inlaid with the coats of arms of Grand Masters. Along the walls are more beautiful lunettes of the Knights' glorious naval battles.

Back at the top of the stairs, the long **Armoury Corridor** heads off to the left, so called because it leads to what was formerly the Armoury and what since 1976 has been used as the Maltese **parliament** (no public access). More portraits of Grand Masters line the corridor, with lunettes depicting idealized Maltese landscapes and cityscapes.

The Knights' executive body, the Council, met in the **Council Room**, which opens off the Armoury Corridor near the top of the stairs. Between 1921 and 1976, this was also the chamber for the Maltese parliament, but these days has been emptied to show off the magnificent **Gobelin Tapestries** which line its walls. The tapestries depict lush jungle scenes of Brazil and the Caribbean, and have the romantic exoticism of early Europeans travelling in the New World, to such an extent that the hunters and animals look equally angelic. They are based on paintings by Francois Post and Albert Eckhout, who accompanied the German Prince Johan Mauritz of Nassau on expeditions between 1636 and 1644. In 1679, Prince Johan donated the paintings to Louis XIV of France, who commissioned his personal painter Charles Le Brun to make copies of them,

THE GRAND MASTER'S PALACE

which were then in turn used by Etienne Le Blondel, one of the king's weavers, as the basis for the tapestries. The knight Ramon Perellos y Roccaful bought the tapestries on completion, and then donated them to the palace on his election to Grand Master in 1697. The tapestries almost never made it: mid-voyage, the galley carrying them to Malta was waylaid by pirates, who managed to extract an on-the-spot full-price ransom for the artworks from the luckless captain.

ST PAUL'S SHIPWRECK CHURCH

Map 2, J6. Triq San Pawl. Daily 9.30am–noon & 1–5pm; free.
Triq It-Teatru L-Antik (Old Theatre St), cluttered by a squalid flea market, runs south from Misraħ San Ġorġ.

THE MALTESE FALCON

In his lifelong passion for falconry, Frederick II – who ruled Malta as King of Sicily in the first half of the thirteenth century – was always looking for the best **falcons**. In Malta, his nineteen falconers weaned and trained the peregrine falcons that bred naturally on the islands, and at some point Frederick seems to have decided that Maltese peregrines possessed the sharpest finesse: since his word carried the weight of authority, Malta's birds quickly became so famous – by this time dubbed the **Maltese Falcons** – that when Emperor Charles V of Spain granted the islands to the Knights in 1530, all he asked for in return was a single Maltese falcon each year.

The Knights also took an interest in falconry, and the Grand Masters practised the sport in Buskett Gardens, among other places (in 1568, Grand Master la Vallette died from a stroke partly caused by the strain after one such hunt). They reinforced the reputation of the Maltese Falcons by gifting falcons

Two blocks south is Triq San Pawl, with **St Paul's Shipwreck Church** on the right. (If the main door is shut, use the smaller side-door round the corner to the left.) This is one of Valletta's earliest churches – another Ġirolmu Cassar creation in the 1570s – and so it's fitting that it is dedicated to the legendary shipwreck of St Paul on Malta in 60 AD (see p.158). The church is sandwiched between buildings, its facade unremarkable. The **interior**, with the plan of a Latin cross, is typical of Maltese parish churches in many ways: lit with silver chandeliers, it has side-chapels adorned with altars, paintings and frescoed ceilings, most surfaces caked in marble and decorated with Baroque plumes. This church was used as a resting-place for knights and ecclesiastical officials who couldn't be buried within St John's Co-Cathedral due to lack of space,

trained by their master falconer and his staff to kings and allies all over Europe.

Over the centuries, Maltese falcons took on such a powerful symbolism of speed, pride, sharpness and invincibility that **Dashiell Hammett** seized on the image to weave a hard-boiled 1930s detective thriller around the theft of a golden, jewel-encrusted statuette of a falcon, imaginary gift of the Knights to Charles V in 1530; the subsequent movie of his *Maltese Falcon*, starring Humphrey Bogart, projected the image into the public consciousness, and perhaps indirectly led to the birds' extinction: Maltese trappers used to risk life and limb climbing down Ta Ċenċ Cliffs in Gozo, the falcons' breeding stronghold, in order to steal the peregrines' eggs and hatchlings for onward sale on the black market. Eventually, and despite being declared legally protected in 1980, the last pair of the Maltese subspecies of peregrine falcons were shot by hunters in 1982 off the Ta Ċenċ Cliffs.

ST PAUL'S SHIPWRECK CHURCH

and its floor is set with a chessboard of marble tombstones. The dull Baroque vault paintings re-create St Paul's life, including his imagined shipwreck on Malta. In the chapel nearest the main altar on the nave's east flank sits a minor altar carved in intricate Baroque style in 1629 by the famous Maltese artist and architect **Lorenzo Gafà**, and the west aisle holds an elegant wooden gilded statue of St Paul sculpted by Lorenzo's brother Melchiorre Gafà. Sadly, the church's most cherished relics – the silver throne of the Knights, a bone from St Paul's arm and a fragment of the column on which Paul was beheaded – are locked away for safekeeping.

THE JESUIT CHURCH

Map 2, K6. Triq L-Arċisqof. Daily 6am–12.30pm, Sat also 4.30–8pm; free.

Five minutes' walk north along Triq San Pawl from the Shipwreck Church is the cross-street Triq L-Arċisqof, the junction marked by the **Jesuit Church**. This was Malta's first Baroque building, designed in the 1640s by the father of Maltese Baroque and the Knights' resident engineer Francesco Bounamici on the model of Rome's Jesuit Church; it even takes the Italian name *Chiesa di Gesu*. The church is in the centre of the former Jesuit complex that occupies a whole block; entrance is from a side door and corridor that cut through the outer wall of the complex. Unlike other Baroque churches, the interior is simple, with the walls painted beige and marble conspicuously absent. Above the altar, twisted columns support a podium for a sculpture of a naked adolescent Jesus flanked by angels, with his handsome pose and curly locks looking more classically pagan than divine.

SACRA INFERMERIA

Map 2, M5. Mediterranean Conference Centre. Mon–Sat 9.30am–4pm; Lm1.40.

Almost at the northeastern end of Triq Ir-Repubblika, just over 100m beyond the fine Valletta palazzo known as Casa Rocca Piccola (more enticing on the advertising posters than in reality), **Triq L-Isptar Il-Qadim** heads right (southeast). This shaded alley retains part of the city's original housing fabric, its four-hundred-year-old facades filmed in soot and redolent with the smell of mould on stone. Turn left into Triq Il-Merkanti and then the first right brings you to the **Sacra Infermeria**, the hospital of the knights.

This was one of the first buildings in Valletta, erected in the 1570s to honour the Knights' founding pledge of ministering to pilgrims and Crusaders on their way to the Holy Land. All Knights, including Grand Masters, attended to patients on a roster basis, and the sick (except criminals) were served food of the highest quality, presented on silver plates and cups. By 1787 the hospital had 536 beds, and benefited from the expertise of Mikielang Grima, Europe's leading surgeon, who – in the days before anaesthesia – could perform an operation to remove bladder stones in a record two-and-a-half minutes. When the French were blockaded in Valletta (1798–1800; see p.344), the constant bombardment of cannon shells forced them to move all the patients into tunnels hewn beneath the hospital; in two years underground, 555 French and 2468 Maltese died from epidemics triggered by malnutrition. World War II bombs flattened the hospital, and after the war it was stylishly rebuilt in its original rustic style and rechristened the **Mediterranean Conference Centre**.

Today, there is a small permanent **exhibition** about the workings of the Sacra Infermeria in the arched cellars that

AUDIOVISUAL HISTORICAL SHOWS

Several **audiovisual shows** repackaging Malta's key historical events have sprung up in recent years – and, giving their ubiquitous advertising, it's hard to ignore them. In Valletta, there are several to choose from, some good, some mediocre. Following is a selection of the best.

The Great Siege of Malta and the Knights of St John
Map 2, J6; *Café Premier* complex, Misraħ Ir-Repubblika
ⓣ 247300; ⓦ www.cities.com.mt/great-siege. Daily 9am–4pm; Lm3.50.
Walk-through show using virtual reality, video clips and theatrical reconstructions to re-create the Knights' story from their inception to their downfall in Malta. Children will love the drama of the place, but the presentation skimps on historical detail, so can be unsatisfying.

Wartime Experience
Map 2, J5; 113 Triq L-Arċisqof ⓣ 247891. On the hour: Mon–Fri 10am–4pm, Sat 10am–1pm; Lm2.
Housed in the same building as the amateurish Valletta Experience, this is a gripping film documentary on Malta's experiences in World War II. The narrative is accurate and detailed, yet tight and urgent, and the black-and-white period footage has been edited well. Reading about these events is no substitute for being able to see the drama unfolding on the screen. Highly recommended.

The Malta Experience
Map 2, M5; St Elmo Bastion, Triq Il-Mediterran ⓣ 243776;
ⓦ www.mxp.com.mt. On the hour: July–Sept daily 11am–1pm; rest of year Mon–Fri 11am–4pm, Sat & Sun 11am–2pm; Lm2.50.
A film documentary covering seven thousand years of Maltese culture. It's professionally made, with good shots of the island's landscapes, but unfortunately only dips a toe into Maltese history.

housed the mentally ill. The original **Great Ward** of the hospital, 153m long and adorned with elegant crossbow arches that rise to meet in an X, survived the aerial bombardment, but is now used for private receptions and banquets, and, sadly, is closed to visitors.

FORT ST ELMO

Map 2, M3. Triq Il-Mediterran. Sat 1–5pm, Sun 9am–5pm; Lm1. Optional guided tours (free).

Fort St Elmo occupies the tip of Valletta's peninsula, accessible at the point where Triq Ir-Republika meets the perimeter road Triq Il-Mediterran. It was built by the Knights in six months in 1552 in order to forestall an imminent invasion by the Turks, and was dedicated to St Elmo, patron saint of mariners. Its star shape, which was designed to provide a defence umbrella of crossfire, gives it a mysterious and elegant look; the walls rise sharply, their angles acute. When the Turks finally invaded in 1565 (see p.336), they bombarded the fort with cannon fire from three sides, but it still took them four weeks to capture it and its six hundred defenders.

During Valletta's construction in the 1570s, the fort was enlarged and incorporated within the city fortifications. In 1775 a handful of priests captured the fort to force Grand Master Francisco Ximenes de Texada to make economic concessions, but they were quickly subdued and their leaders executed. In World War II, the fort took the bomb that caused the war's first six casualties. It is now home to Malta's Police Academy, and is open for visits only at weekends.

Through the entrance gate of the complex, a path winds through the fortifications into a square, overlooked by the loggias of the two-storey barracks and once the scene of the Knights' military parades; every Sunday at 11am, a colourful and historically accurate re-enactment of the parades is held here. It's worth joining the informative **guided tours**, which start on the hour from the south side of the square near the small Renaissance **chapel**, notable both for its intricate barrel-vaulted stone ceiling and for a figurine of St Anne embracing Mary and Jesus. This figurine was originally carried in the Knights' flagship in Rhodes, to serve as protector of the fleet; during the Great Siege of 1565 it was hidden in a well for safekeeping.

From the chapel, stairs wind up to the **parapets** of the fortifications. Heading clockwise, you'll spot holes lining the walls above the entrance gate through which muskets were fired: during the Great Siege, the Knights took advantage of the fort's star shape to provide a gauntlet of crossfire, a technique employed so effectively that each time the Turks tried to storm the fort they found themselves hemmed in and under attack from all sides. If you look closely at the opposite walls of the dry moat, you'll see that they're riddled with marks made by the lead pellet fire of the Knights. The next section of the wall peers over the north flank of the fortifications at the **barracks** below, which were built in 1760 in the ditch outside the perimeter wall; they famously featured in the prison scenes of the 1978 film *Midnight Express*, and are still occupied by squatters, who moved in after filming.

A flight of stairs leads you to the next section of walls, atop the **Cavalier**, perched high up at the mouths of both Grand Harbour and Marsamxett Harbour. Looking south, across the mouth of Grand Harbour, you can see the skeletal hulk of Fort Ricasoli, the largest ever built by the Knights, which is now abandoned and crumbling. Northwards, the view extends to Sliema and beyond, and inland, your gaze slides up the long Triq Ir-Repubblika, past the City Gate to the heights of Mdina across the island. A plaque here commemorates those who died when the first bomb of World War II landed on the Cavalier's roof.

The War Museum

Map 2, L3. Fort St Elmo. Mid-June to Sept daily 7.45am–2pm; rest of year Mon–Sat 8.15am–5pm, Sun 8.15am–4.15pm; Lm1.

A southern corner of the fort, with its own entrance, has been converted into the small and rather lacklustre **War Museum**. The star exhibit is the George Cross that was awarded to the Maltese population as a whole in 1942, but among the displays of militaria is the jeep used by General Eisenhower during Operation Husky and one of the three Gloucester Gladiator biplanes (now without its wings) that amounted to Malta's air defences in 1939.

THE MANDERAGGIO DISTRICT

Map 2, I4–J4.

Occupying the northern corner of Valletta is the old, semi-abandoned slum district of **Manderaggio** (Il-Mandraġġ), named after the galley port that the Knights tried, and failed, to carve out of the rocky coast hereabouts. The area is demarcated on two sides by the sea, and on the other two by Triq It-Teatru L-Antik (Old Theatre St), running northwest–southeast, and Triq Id-Dejqa (Strait St) running northeast–southwest. Up to the 1960s, these alleys bustled with the activity of blacksmiths and bakers, and had their fair share of sleazy bars – especially in Triq Id-Dejqa – where prostitutes served British sailors. The area was dirty and overpopulated; some residences were even hewn underground, and from Marsamxett Harbour you can see the mouths of some underground dwellings breaching Valletta's fortifications like caves high up on a cliff face. Evelyn Waugh found the Manderaggio so forbidding that he was too scared to visit the area after dark, describing the place in his 1930 book *Labels* as "the most concentrated and intense slum in the world". These days, many buildings are abandoned, their interiors too cramped for habitation and the area too depressing in its state of semi-ruin. Old people and some families, struggling on low incomes, are the only ones left in the neighbourhood.

From the perimeter road Triq San Bastjan, round a couple of corners, **Triq Il-Punent** heads up into the heart of the Manderaggio. It opens into a small square where a monument commemorates the late-eighteenth-century figure Father Mikiel Xerri who, along with others, plotted to ambush the French within Valletta; all 34 of them were shot in Misraħ San Ġorġ in 1799. On the west side of the square is the prominently spired **Anglican Cathedral** (1839), built at the expense of Queen Adelaide (widow of King William IV), who was shocked, as she convalesced in Malta, at the absence of an Anglican church. Behind the Neoclassical, colonnaded facade is a bare, whitewashed interior; there are now only three services a week for a dwindling congregation of elderly expats, and the cathedral's empty, close-packed pews only add to the atmosphere of abandonment.

Behind the Anglican Cathedral, at the corner of Triq Il-Punent and Triq It-Teatru L-Antik, you can see a surviving example of a **niche**, holding a figure of a saint, that was added to comply with the knights' planning decree that every corner house in Valletta should have some sort of decoration. The rows of enclosed balconies along the Baroque buildings here, painted green, create a harmonious pattern that have ensured they are among the most photographed subjects in Malta.

OUR LADY OF MOUNT CARMEL

Map 2, I4. Triq It-Teatru L-Antik. Daily 7am–9pm; free.

On Triq It-Teatru L-Antik stands the massive church dedicated to **Our Lady of Mount Carmel**, originally built in the 1570s, then bombed in World War II. Its postwar rebuilding took twenty years, and the Catholic Church took the opportunity to reassert its authority, working in domineering Baroque-style architecture and adding a fat dome to top the spire of the Anglican Cathedral nearby. Dome and spire now blend together to form a classic feature of Valletta's skyline.

The interior of the church is unusually bare, the globigerina limestone unpainted, and marble used only to girdle a few columns. The unadorned, egg-shaped dome is dizzyingly high, with the joints between its blocks creating crazy patterns of detail over the interior surface.

THE MANOEL THEATRE

Map 2, I5. Triq It-Teatru L-Antik ☎ 246389, ⓦ www.teatrumanoel.com.mt. Guided tours Mon–Fri 10.30am & 11.30am, Sat 11.30am; Lm1.65.

About 20m south of the Carmelite church, and only a couple of blocks behind Misraħ San Ġorġ, sits the **Manoel Theatre**, one of Europe's oldest working theatres. Grand Master Antonio Manoel de Vilhena personally funded the construction of this small, six-hundred-seat venue in 1731; today, after restoration, it serves as Malta's prestigious National Theatre, hosting performers of world renown. The only way to visit – aside from attending a performance – is to join a guided tour.

Wholly built from timber, the intricate interior is ringed by boxes, with those reserved for dignitaries finished in gold. Its small size and unusual oval shape help to generate a warm intimacy that is best experienced by attending a performance. Two underground reservoirs perfect the acoustics, which are so precise that orchestra conductors have to stand to one side of the stage: if they're

THE MANOEL THEATRE

at stage-centre, their page-turnings can be heard around the auditorium.

Alongside the theatre is a small **museum** of costumes, scores and other memorabilia from past performances.

Every Wednesday between October and May there is a free lunchtime concert of classical music in the foyer of the Manoel Theatre, from 12.30 to 1.00pm.

Floriana

The quiet suburb of **FLORIANA** lies west of Valletta at the neck of the Mount Sciberras peninsula. It is named after Pietro Paolo Floriani, the seventeenth-century engineer who designed the tiered fortifications that expanded Valletta's original *enceinte*, and was intended to contain Valletta's growing population safely in the face of the continuing threat of an Ottoman invasion. For the most part it's a pretty soulless place, but it's nonetheless worth a detour to wander through tranquil gardens to the **Floriana Lines**, the tiered fortifications that seal off the Sciberras Peninsula from the rest of the island.

THE GRANARIES AND AROUND

Map 2, E9.
Floriana begins where Valletta ends, and there is no discernible boundary between the two. From the City Gate bus terminus, head away from Valletta along **Triq Sarria**, keeping the eagle-topped column of the **RAF Memorial** – commemorating World War II casualties – on your left.

THE FLORIANA LINES

In the 1630s, as the Turks expanded their fleet, the Knights feared an attack, and so commissioned Pietro Paolo Floriani, engineer to the pope, to assess Malta's defence readiness.

In 1635, Floriani proposed a line of fortifications across the neck of the Sciberras Peninsula – enclosing Valletta and in effect creating a new suburb, Floriana – so that Malta's entire population could be crammed behind the fortifications in the event of an invasion. Critics pointed that these **Floriana Lines** were too ambitious and too expensive, but work nonetheless began in 1635. By 1650 the fortifications were almost complete, and already girdled the new district of Floriana.

In 1670, Count Valperga suggested strengthening the whole structure by means of the **Floriana Hornwork**, a horn-shaped head of fortifications jutting out from the southwest corner of the Floriana Lines. Crowned by bastions, the Floriana Hornwork was armed with cannon with a range extending across the inner creeks of the Grand Harbour out to the Corradino Heights. This, and **Portes Des Bombes**, the sole gate through the fortifications, were completed in 1716 and proved the ultimate deterrent: the Turks never attacked, principally because of the virtual impossibility of breaking through the fortifications.

Beyond the memorial and the multistorey car park, Triq Sarria opens on the left into a rectangular square larger than a football pitch, with the rebuilt, lacklustre Neoclassical **St Publius Church**, rebuilt after World War II damage, at the far end. Publius, claimed to be the former Roman governor, was ordained by St Paul in 60 AD as the island's first bishop.

In chambers tunnelled underneath the square the Knights stored Malta's two-year grain supply, hence the square's title of **The Granaries**. The globigerina limestone roof of the

Granaries give the square a neat, planned look, its flatness punctuated by the stone lids of the chambers. The square with benches along its edges is pleasantly sunny and open, but on the eve of general elections the square becomes a venue for political rallies, with 100,000-strong crowds cheering their politicians' rhetoric.

Across Triq Sarria from the Granaries, **The Mall** was originally constructed by Grand Master Jean Paul de Lascaris Castellar (1636–57) as a pitch for the ball-game *palla a maglio* (from which London's Pall Mall is named) but has since been refashioned into a small, sparse garden of stunted trees. At the head of the Mall stands the **Independence Monument**, a bronze erected in the 1990s to symbolize freedom.

Triq Sarria continues past St Publius Church to the small **Sarria Church**, a curious domed cylinder that was designed in 1676, most likely by Mattia Preti, to a commission by Grand Master Nicolas Cotoner. Opposite it rises the **Wignacourt Tower** (1615), which marks with a fountain what was once the terminus of the Wignacourt Aqueduct that channelled spring water to Valletta from Girgenti on Malta's west coast.

ARGOTTI GARDENS AND ST PHILIP GARDENS

Map 1, J5. Triq Sarria. Daily 7.30am–dusk; free.

Behind the Wignacourt Tower at the southwestern end of the Mall is the entrance to the **Argotti Gardens**, originally the private retreat of the knight Ignatius de Argote De Gusman. In 1805, Malta's first professor of natural history, Carolus Hyacinthus, converted the area into public botanical gardens, a rather overstated title for this fanciful collection of exotic plants, everything from monumental ficus trees to prickly pears and aloe vera. The garden squats on the parapet of the Floriana Lines; peer over the balustrades to see the fortifications fanning out in both directions.

On a lower level atop St Philip Ravelin – a triangular horn that is part of the Floriana Lines – is the separate **St Philip Gardens**, adorned with citrus groves, climbing vines and bougainvillea. The garden is dominated by the Wignacourt Fountain, built by Grand Master Manoel Pinto de Fonseca in the eighteenth century, as a replica of the original that was erected in Misraħ San Ġorġ in 1641 to christen the Wignacourt Aqueduct. From here opens the best view of the Floriana Lines, its tiered walls of ravelins, bastions, curtains and fortifications fanning north and south. To the south, you can glimpse the **Portes Des Bombes**, a pompous early-eighteenth-century Baroque gate of three arched doors that still punctuates the main road entering Floriana and Valletta.

ARGOTTI GARDENS AND ST PHILIP GARDENS

The Three Cities

Across from Valletta and Floriana, **Vittoriosa**, **Senglea** and **Cospicua** occupy two narrow peninsulas which jut out into the waters of the Grand Harbour. Known rather grandly as the **Three Cities** – a flattery invented by Napoleon in the vain hope that it would instil a sense of unity among these fiercely town-proud working folk – the three retain a romantic, medieval urban fabric that makes them a pleasure to wander through, and there's a scattering of individual sights around which to construct a walking tour.

These small towns share a welter of names that can get confusing. The three are frequently referred to in road signs and casual conversation by their original, pre-sixteenth-century names of **Birgu** (Vittoriosa), **L-Isla** (Senglea) and **Bormla** (Cospicua), and you may also hear locals referring to the three collectively as "Il-Cottonera", after the semi-circular **Cottonera Lines** of fortifications which comprise their land defence.

Most sights are concentrated in Vittoriosa, and date back to its heyday when the Knights settled in **Fort St Angelo** in 1530, before they built Valletta. The grand **Inquisitor's Palace** – which saw service until Napoleon put paid to the Inquisition – is a major highlight, and the **Collachio**, the quarter once reserved for the Knights, retains its medieval charm. Both Cospicua and Senglea were flattened by bombing in World War II and have less to recommend them; the former boasts the **Margarita Lines**, one of two concentric lines of fortification (the other being the Cottonera Lines) which sealed off the Three Cities from landward attack, while the latter's **Ġnien Il–Gardjola**, at the head of the peninsula, offers a waterfront view that puts the grand into the Grand Harbour.

East of Vittoriosa is a separate attraction, the British-built **Fort Rinella**, which is home to one of the world's only surviving Armstrong 100-ton guns.

There is no accommodation in the Three Cities, and, until the Waterfront Regeneration Project is complete (see p.93), you'll also find very few places serving food or drink. If you're exploring the whole area, you'd do well to bring along picnic supplies.

Some history

Although there is some inconclusive evidence of prehistoric settlement, much of the history of the Three Cities has been intimately linked with that of the Grand Harbour. **Fort St Angelo**, which was built some time before 1200 at the head of the peninsula to guard the Grand Harbour, gave rise during the Middle Ages to **Vittoriosa**, along with Mdina one of Malta's first settlements, which developed alongside the castle under the name *Borgo*, or suburb. ("Borgo" became corrupted in Maltese to **Birgu**, a name still informally used today.) During the medieval era, Birgu's *castellan* (governor) enjoyed independence from the Universita, or ruling council, of Mdina and presided over a booming seafaring town that was home to merchants from as far afield as Pisa, Genoa and Venice.

When the Knights arrived in Malta in 1530, they made Fort St Angelo their headquarters, girdled Birgu with fortifications and founded a new town on the neighbouring peninsula, naming it **Senglea** after Claude de la Sengle, Grand Master at the time. The town of **Bormla** developed outside the walls of Birgu and Senglea as overspill. After success in the Great Siege of 1565, Birgu was renamed Vittoriosa (meaning victory) and Bormla rechristened Cospicua (referring to its conspicuously exposed position outside the fortifications).

Even after the Knights moved from Vittoriosa to Valletta in 1571, the Three Cities held their own thanks to their two deep creeks where ships could berth in sheltered waters – **Dockyard Creek** between Vittoriosa and Senglea (preferred haven for the Knights' fleet) and **French Creek** west of Senglea. In the 1670s the Knights started work on Malta's largest project of military architecture, the **Cottonera Lines**, a wall of fortifications several kilometres long named after the Grand Master of the day, Nicolas Cotoner, that was to encircle the land front of the Three Cities. It was a task that took the Knights 54 years to complete.

When, in the eighteenth century, Malta became the headquarters of the British **Royal Navy**'s Mediterranean fleet, the Three Cities saw greater prosperity with more docks being built in Dockyard Creek. During the Navy's peak periods of demand – principally in times of conflict (the Crimean War, for example) – up to twelve thousand people were employed in the dockyards, which reinforced their status as the mainstay of the local economy. In **World War II**, the Axis powers heavily bombed the dockyards and the Three Cities themselves suffered from a continuous rain of stray ordnance: Senglea was virtually razed to the ground in this way.

After World War II, as the British defence budget was drastically cut and thousands of dockyard workers were made redundant, the bottom fell out of the local economy. Since then, the government has poured subsidies into the dockyards (see box on p.105) to little effect: today, the Three Cities have Malta's highest unemployment rates, crime rates and illiteracy, and the island's worst housing stock. Recently, the government has begun trying to lift the area out of its economic and social depression by handing parts over to private tourism companies. The epicentre of the **Cottonera Waterfront Regeneration Project** is Dockyard Creek, between Senglea and Vittoriosa, where a new yacht marina is planned and where historic harbourfront buildings will be converted into offices, apartments, a hotel and casino, and shops and restaurants. It remains to be seen, however, whether the project will tangibly benefit the local economy.

Vittoriosa

VITTORIOSA, also known by its old name of **Birgu**, is a slow-paced, working-class town where life revolves around the handful of old hole-in-the-wall cafes in the church square, **Misraħ Ir-Rebħa** (Victory Square). The shaded, meandering streets are lined by romantic Baroque townhouses, prime among which is the sombre **Inquisitors' Palace** in Triq L-Mdina Il-Kbira, an imposing Baroque building that was seat of the Inquisition until 1798. **Fort St Angelo**, the bulwark at the tip of the peninsula that defines Vittoriosa's history, and the **Maritime Museum** on the western waterfront are other draws, but just as attractive is the prospect of an afternoon wander in the tranquil, shaded alleys of the **Collachio**, the Knights' quarter.

Arrival and orientation

Buses #1, #2, #4 and #6 from Valletta take about half-an-hour to reach Vittoriosa's bus terminus, which is located at the neck of the peninsula just outside the **Three Gates**. There's a small **car park** outside the same gates.

As Vittoriosa is less than 1km in length and half that at its widest point, everything is within easy walking distance of the bus terminus. The main street is **Triq L-Mdina Il-Kbira**, which runs north from the Three Gates to the central square, **Misraħ Ir-Rebħa**. Alleys fan out on either side, and streets from the square head north to Fort St Angelo.

THE THREE GATES

Map 3, F7–F8.

Cut west across the bus terminus to reach the first of the **Three Gates** that provided the sole entrance to Vittoriosa through the fortifications before the walls were breached for vehicle access via Triq L-Mdina Il-Kbira. The exuberantly Baroque **Advanced Gate**, first of the three, built in 1722, gives into an elegantly restored courtyard overlooked by buildings burrowed into the fortifications, now converted into government offices. Across the courtyard the north-ernmost door leads into a recently renovated World War II **bomb shelter** (usually Mon–Fri 7.30am–4.30pm; free), a maze of claustrophobic tunnels that lead to larger rooms pickaxed into the limestone. Continuing north takes you over a bridge spanning the dry moat between two sets of bastions, and through the **Couvre Porte**, the second gate of the three that opens into another courtyard, a bare stone affair with worn-out stairs heading up to the ramparts. Across this courtyard is the third, **Main Gate**, on the other side of which is Triq L-Mdina Il-Kbira, the main road leading into the town.

THE INQUISITOR'S PALACE

Map 3, G6. Triq Il-Mdina Il-Kbira. Daily: mid-June to Sept 7.45am–1.30pm, rest of year 8.15am–4.30pm; Lm1.

Some 80m inside Vittoriosa along Triq Il-Mdina Il-Kbira stands the **Inquisitor's Palace**, a large Baroque building that up until 1798 housed the tribunal and prisons of the Inquisition. The palace was originally built as law courts in the thirteenth century during the rule of Roger the Norman, a role it continued to serve until 1571, when the Knights moved to Valletta. In 1574, when the Inquisition set up shop in Malta, the Knights handed the building over, but although they officially supported the Inquisition, they refused to submit to prosecution. Indeed, on several occasions rebellious Knights broke into the prisons to free their mistresses or fellow Knights, and on one occasion a group of Knights plotted to throw the Inquisitor from the fortifications (see p.339). In 1798, Napoleon finally banished the Inquisition from the Maltese islands. The present building, most of which is open for visitors, was remodelled and enlarged following damage in the earthquake of 1693, and has been beautifully restored. Don't let the bare entrance foyer mislead you: the palace, and its art collection, is worth at least an hour of your time. Pick up a floor-plan at the entrance.

The ground floor

The most engaging aspect of the **ground floor** is the roofed flanks of the courtyard, which have the oldest ribbed cross-vaults in Malta, a rare example of the kind of Gothic architecture the Knights imported from Rhodes and their chief engineer there Niccolo Flavari. The courtyard leads to a garden, on the west flank of which is a row of prison cells; you have to bend double to squeeze into these dim, malodorous dens, still redolent with fear after two centuries of disuse.

The upper floor

The **upper floor** of the palace has a sombre, melancholy atmosphere. The staircase from the main entrance and foyer leads into the **Chancery**, boasting a vaulted timber ceiling and the coats of arms of Malta's sixty-three Inquisitors. A door leads to the Baroque **Chapel**, small and oddly plain. As you face the chapel, the door on your left leads to the garishly coloured **Waiting Room**, its faded blue walls topped by a belt of Baroque designs; a closed door here, barring further access, leads to the Inquisitors' winter apartment. On the opposite side of the Chancery is the pink **Audience Hall**, with two painted columns compositionally supporting a band of Baroque motifs frescoed on one wall near the ceiling. It's a dim and dull room, and the two windows painted on the opposite wall fail to provide much cheer. Next door is the austere **Tribunal Room**; the Inquisitor's throne is incorporated into a monument of wooden crownwork, while the accused sat on a low stool in the middle of the room. Behind the prisoners' stool is a half-sized door, designed in order to force even the most recalcitrant heretics to bow to the Inquisitor. Beyond the Tribunal Room is the Inquisitors' cool and breezy summer apartment, unfortunately closed to visitors.

THE COLLACHIO

Map 3, G6.

The old **Collachio**, or Knight's Quarter, lies east of Triq L-Mdina Il-Kbira, covering the area from the fortifications north to Misraħ Ir-Rebħa. This is the most attractive part of Vittoriosa, with winding, pedestrianized alleys and carefully restored buildings, and is a perfect place to lose yourself on a warm afternoon. In the Knights' old power-base of Rhodes, the Collachio was cloistered by high perimeter walls, but in Vittoriosa it was marked only by stone bollards and locals enjoyed open access to the area. Bottled up in the quiet, shaded streets, the Knights had some years to muse on the claustrophobia of their new headquarters – one reason why they later designed Valletta's streets as a regular grid. In Triq Ħilda Tabone sit three Knightly *auberges*, converted, with few alterations, from townhouses – the Auberge de France, Auberge d'Allemagne and Auberge d'Auvergne et Provence. None, unfortunately, is open to the public. In nearby Triq Il-Majjistral, the **Auberge d'Angleterre**, with the vernacular simplicity of a farmhouse and a noticeable lack of escutcheons, is now Vittoriosa's public library (Mon–Fri 8am–5pm).

FORT ST ANGELO

Map 3, D2. Triq Il-Palazz tal-Gvernatur L-Antik. Usually Sat 10am–2pm; check times with tourist office. Lm0.50.

From the Inquisitor's Palace, head north along Triq L-Mdina Il-Kbira and across the main square Misraħ Ir-Rebħa into Triq La Vallette, flanked by unattractive postwar apartment blocks. At the end of the road, turn right into Triq Il-Palazz tal-Gvernatur L-Antik, which ends at the gate of **Fort St Angelo** at the very tip of Vittoriosa's peninsula. This large, impressive stronghold, with a Cavalier towering over its entrance gate, is Malta's oldest fort, and has come to stand as a monument to, and symbol of, the island's militaristic past. Although two decades of governmental indifference has left the fort crumbling, it remains highly impressive as a demonstration of the Knights' supreme power; you can only truly grasp the scale of their architectural achievement from within the walls of the fort.

The origins of Fort St Angelo are unknown, but it definitely existed by 1200 AD. In 1283, when an Aragonese armada destroyed the Angevin fleet in the Grand Harbour, the defenders retreated to the safety of the fort, then called

Castrum Maris, the Castle by the Sea, and withheld a siege for a full seven months. When the **Knights** arrived in Malta, they adopted the fort as their headquarters, enlarging it, building the Cavalier, deepening the moat and improving the fortifications, which resisted Turkish attempts to breach them with explosives during the Great Siege of 1565. After the Knights' departure to Valletta in 1571, Fort St Angelo lost its prominence.

When the **British** arrived, the Royal Navy took tenure of the fort and, in 1933, listed it as the ship HMS *St Angelo*, stuck a ship's mast on top, and converted it into a shore establishment. To create more living space, the Navy built a string of one-storey barracks that invade the ramparts on the east side of the fort and a tarmac road – alien elements that stick out sorely in this medieval building. In **World War II**, Fort St Angelo took 69 bombs that caused only a few scratches on its solid upper coralline limestone walls, and the Royal Navy remained in residence until 1979. At a NATO meeting held in the fort shortly before the British withdrew, a Turkish delegate joked, "I believe I am the first Turk that has penetrated this far." In 1999, following a series of complex diplomatic negotiations, the Knights were granted the right to use the upper part of the fort as a base (aside from their Rome headquarters) for their charitable works. They had staked a claim to be handed the entire fort in perpetuity, but were eventually forced to settle for a 99-year lease (see p.340). The order has now begun to restore its part of the fort, which includes the **Magisterial Palace** and **Chapel of St Anne**, while the semi-ruined lower sections are open to the public.

The best way to get a feel for the fort's impenetrability is to follow the tarmacked road which loops from the entrance over the ramparts. At the northern tip of land, where the road loops sharply, is the **sentry post**, a pillbox that has a commanding view over the Grand Harbour.

Continuing along the road takes you past the old **barracks** with their windows and doors kicked in and their walls cracking, then on to the top of the **Cavalier**, its ambience ruined by an abandoned swimming-pool. A ramp near the main entrance leads down to a series of chambers in the lower part of the fort beneath the road that served as **dungeons** and ammunition stores; they are, however, pitch-dark inside and you'll need a torch to explore.

ST LAWRENCE CHURCH

Map 3, F6. Triq San Lawrenz. Daily 6am–noon & 4–6pm.

Back in the centre of Vittoriosa, just west of Misraħ Ir-Rebħa, is the **St Lawrence Church**, set across from the waterfront on a high parapet and evocatively reflected in the harbour waters. The original building was one of the earliest medieval parish churches in Malta, said to have been built by Roger the Norman after he seized the island from the Arabs in 1090 and reinstituted Christianity. When the Knights arrived in 1530, they made it their conventual church and used it to store the art treasures that they had brought from Rhodes. Two years later, fire damaged the church and destroyed most of the artwork inside. The present church was designed by the Baroque trendsetter **Lorenzo Gafa** in 1681, with a richly decorated exterior; Gafa's elegant dome was destroyed by a World War II bomb and rebuilt to the same design, embellished with braids of stonework, although his skill is demonstrated best by the building's compositional harmony.

The **interior**, which is constantly being tinkered with, is disappointingly gloomy, with the wine-hued marble that covers the walls enhancing the dimness. The altarpiece, **Mattia Preti's** largest painting, shows St Lawrence being roasted; it evokes a sense of fearful claustrophobia tempered only by the saint's face that, instead of manifesting pain, is set with conviction.

From the western shore of Vittoriosa, and the eastern shore of Senglea just across Dockyard Creek, you can negotiate with local boatmen for an impressive tour of the Grand Harbour by **kajjik** (an open wooden boat similar to a Venetian gondola). Duration – and price – are up to you, but Lm5 per half-hour is a good rule of thumb.

THE FREEDOM MONUMENT

Map 3, E6.

In front of the St Lawrence Church is a rugged hillock topped by the **Freedom Monument**, commemorating March 31, 1979, when Prime Minister Dom Mintoff lowered the British flag and raised the Maltese one. This was Mintoff's day: he had fought for a Malta free from military alliances for half his lifetime, so it seemed fitting that he was the one who designed this monument, which depicts a British navy officer bidding farewell to a Maltese peasant. The artificial hillock of stone boulders and pockets of soil that root Aleppo pines, prickly pears, capers and aloe vera expresses an egalitarian vision of a rustic, rural Malta.

This wharfside is the epicentre for the **Cottonera Waterfront Regeneration Project**, currently taking shape and expected to be complete by 2005. Historic shoreline buildings are being converted into hotels, cafés and restaurants, and pontoons are being laid for a yacht marina. It remains to be seen whether the development will suit the medieval cityscapes of domes, towers, fortifications and Baroque buildings, but the fact that the government gave the go-ahead for the project without first commissioning a survey of the major archeological remains that, it's suspected, are buried on the seabed and are likely to be disturbed by an alteration of currents, does not bode well.

THE MARITIME MUSEUM

Map 3, E5. Ix-Xatt Tal-Birgu. Daily: mid-June to Sept 8am–2pm; rest of year 8.30am–4.30pm; Lm1.

From the Freedom Monument, turn north along the promenade at the water's edge. Some 50m beyond a stone gate bearing the escutcheon of the British Royal Crown is the entrance to the **Maritime Museum**, formerly the naval bakery supplying the entire Mediterranean fleet; the building's colonnaded portico is distinctly British.

This small, modern museum has an interesting collection of well-displayed exhibits grouped by era in a hall on the upper floor, from Roman anchors and *amphorae* to an eighteenth-century model of one of the wooden *luzzu* fishing boats that ferried passengers between Malta and Gozo until the early nineteenth century. Displays from the era of British rule, which lie near the entrance, consist mainly of photographs and models of ships, but also include a machine from 1840 that powered the revolving beam of a lighthouse, and navigation aids such as compasses, hourglasses, maps and logbooks. The section encompassing Knightly exhibits is larger, and takes in a peculiar 1574 instrument for navigation at night, weights used by customs officials in the eighteenth century, various cannons mounted on galleys, and models of many types of boats used by the Knights, from a ceremonial barge to an eighteenth-century galley.

Cospicua

COSPICUA (aka **Bormla**) occupies the ground at the head of Dockyard Creek, south of both Vittoriosa and Senglea. It developed before and after the 1565 Great Siege as overspill from its two neighbours, but was extensively bombed in World War II. Characterless rebuilding has left it clustered haphazardly around its parish church on the shores of Dockyard Creek, and aside from viewing the town's concentric rings of fortifications, there's little to aim for on the walk between Vittoriosa and Senglea.

From the **Three Gates** at the southern entrance to Vittoriosa, Ix-Xatt Ta' Bormla heads south and down the hill into Cospicua's centre, where the parish church towers over the road alongside a striking monument of an angel brandishing the British Crown and the Latin cross which commemorates World War II victims. Some 400m south of the church, at the head of the creek, is Misraħ Gavinu Gulia: from here, Triq San Pawl heads north up the hill into Senglea (see p.103), while Triq Il-Ġdida heads 200m south to **St Helen's Gate**, the opening that pierces the **Margarita Lines**, the arc of fortifications built by the Knights in the mid-seventeenth century which corrals Cospicua.

THE COTTONERA LINES

Map 1, SL.

Some 200m south of St Helen's Gate on Triq L-Immakulata is the Polverista Gate, which penetrates the **Cottonera Lines** (1670), the most ambitious military engineering project the Knights took on in Malta. Grand Master Nicolas Cotoner backed the project, but almost every engineer in Europe criticized it for being too ambitious and too magnificently Baroque; the fortifications also had to cope with maintaining regular height over an irregular ground of hillocks. Despite the carping, the project succeeded; the heavy, semicircular wall, about 20m thick, envelopes the Three Cities on their land front to this day. If you stand facing the exterior of the Polverista Gate, you get a view of the wall fanning out on either side, zigzagging to create triangular bastions designed for a 260° sweep of fire; the wall is studded by eight of these triangular bastions and two demi-bastions where it connects with the fortifications of Vittoriosa and Senglea. These days, squatters have burrowed unlikely homes into the great walls.

Senglea

SENGLEA (otherwise known as **L-Isla**) squats on the tongue of land west and parallel to Vittoriosa, separated from its neighbour by Dockyard Creek. It was founded by Grand Master de la Sengle in 1552 to relieve overcrowding in Vittoriosa and to corral the rural population within fortifications. Since then, the town has been almost completely rebuilt on two occasions – after the Great Siege of 1565 and again after World War II. Aside from the historic **Malta Drydocks** on the western French Creek, Senglea offers only two minor sights, both of them situated along the main **Triq Il-Vitorja** that runs along the length of the town – the Kristu Redentur statue in Our Lady of Victories Church, and the photogenic vista of the Grand Harbour from the sentry post at the head of the peninsula.

Bus #3 to and from Valletta stops in Misraħ L-4 Ta' Settembru, halfway along Triq Il-Vitorja in the centre of Senglea.

On the Dockyard Creek waterfront in Senglea, the
simple *Alice Springs Kiosk* (Map 3, C5; daily 9am–10pm),
serves up fast food and fish-and-chips.

OUR LADY OF VICTORIES CHURCH

Map 3, D7. Misraħ Papa Benedittu XV. Daily 6–11.45am &
4–6.45pm; free.

From Misraħ Gavinu Gulia, Triq San Pawl heads uphill
and, as Triq Il-Monsinjur Panzavecchia, passes through
Senglea's fortifications and into Misraħ Papa Benedittu XV,
a square dominated by **Our Lady of Victories Church** –
so named to commemorate victory in the Great Siege.
During World War II, the Luftwaffe destroyed the church
since it obstructed their aircraft from effectively dive-
bombing the dockyards; after the war, it was completely
rebuilt. The imposing but architecturally uninspiring exterior prefaces a sumptuous interior, complete with blood-
red velvet curtains and massive altar, but the church is
famous for its statue of **Kristu Redentur**, which attracts
thousands of pilgrims annually from all over Malta and
which is believed to have miraculous healing powers. The
statue, a moving depiction of a bloodied Christ collapsing
on all fours under the burden of the cross, nestles in a red-
velvet niche in a chapel reached through a doorway to the
right of the altar. All ages and classes of people trickle into
the chapel every day to pray for divine healing.

At the very tip of land, 600m northwest of Our Lady of
Victories Church, is the small garden of **Ġnien Il-Gardjola**.
At the far end, an elegant little hexagonal sentry post juts out
over the Grand Harbour, giving grand panoramic views.

THE MALTA DRYDOCKS

Although the **dockyards** in French Creek on the west side of Senglea were started by the Knights and expanded under the British, their prosperity only peaked in **World War II**, when they employed twelve thousand people (and were the target of tons of Luftwaffe bombs). By 1958, with defence spending slashed, the British government decided that it was "no longer possible to justify the maintenance by the Admiralty of their naval yard in Malta". **Dom Mintoff**, then deputy Prime Minister, raised objections, and the British realized that axing the yard's nine thousand jobs would be asking for trouble. The dockyard was privatized instead, but following the discovery of financial irregularities, the British government rescinded the contract in 1962. Five years later, the Maltese government saved the workers from redundancy by nationalizing the yard under the new name of the **Malta Drydocks**. Nonetheless, financial problems remained, as subsidies drained the national coffers: by 1974, the yard was Lm12 million in debt. Under threat of closure, performance slowly improved and, when the yard made its first, marginal profit, Mintoff introduced Malta's only experiment of full worker participation – which failed in the face of genuine lack of business, gross overstaffing and over-time irregularities.

The yard stumbled on through subsequent decades and is still in operation. In 1997 MLP Prime Minister **Alfred Sant** alienated the workers by putting professional managers in charge and trying (but failing) to introduce diversification. The present PN government is careful not to stir the wrath of the yard's workers, whose numbers have now shrunk to three thousand: to buy industrial peace, over Lm10 million in subsidies is pumped into this obsolete industry every year.

Fort Rinella

Map 1, L4. St Rocco Rd, Kalkara. Daily: June–Sept 9.30am–1pm;
Oct–May 10am–4pm; Lm1.

North of the Three Cities in the town of **KALKARA**, at
the mouth of the Grand Harbour, sits **Fort Rinella**, the
twin of Fort Cambridge in Sliema (which is now a nightclub in the grounds of a luxury hotel) – both were designed
to protect the sea routes into the Grand Harbour. Fort
Rinella was erected by the British in the 1870s specifically
to operate the **Armstrong 100-ton gun**, the largest gun
ever made, of which this specimen and another in Gibraltar
are the sole survivors. The recent, sensitive restoration of
Fort Rinella by the historic care foundation Fondazzjoni
Wirt Artna makes this one of the most pleasant and informative attractions in the Valletta area, with a detailed tour
of the fort (included in the admission fee) that illustrates the
building's history and function. It's served by **bus** #4 from
Valletta, which runs via Vittoriosa's bus terminus; from the
bus stop it's a signed ten-minute walk to the fort.

The huge Armstrong gun – painted pale yellow for camouflage against the background of limestone – was designed
so that its shells could pierce the steel plates of ships, and it
commands the highest point in this low-lying fort. The gun
was manufactured in England and the operation to transport it to the fort proved a mammoth task: on the best days,
the gun inched ahead just 75 yards along a specially laid,
reinforced road that is now buried beneath the town. A
coal-fired mini-power station in the fort's basement powered the whole intricate operation of firing the gun without human intervention: rail barrels carted the gunpowder
and shells onto a steam-propelled lift; the gun was wheeled
towards the lift and the gunpowder and shell fed into the
barrel; and then the gun was turned into position and fired.

It was fired just forty times, on the last occasion in 1905.

The fort itself is a rare example of **Victorian military architecture** in Malta; particularly striking is the way the stones that form the exterior walls were deliberately left in a rough, seashell-like finish. You can wander round it independently, or join the tour to see the interior – sleeping quarters, common room and kitchen – which has been accurately and evocatively re-created with props and period furniture. A handful of smaller guns that were intended to defend the fort from invasion are also on display.

FORT RINELLA

Sliema and St Julian's

Sprawling along the coast north of Valletta, the towns of **Sliema** and **St Julian's** comprise a new, cosmopolitan urban centre that has superseded Valletta in terms of nightlife and entertainment. Sliema is a middle-class town of high rises skirting the eastern shore of Marsamxett Harbour and stretching along the northeast coast to **Balluta Bay**, where it gives way to its neighbour St Julian's, which is ranged around the picturesque, *luzzu*-dotted **Spinola Bay**. Both are a cross between residential towns and tourist resorts, where you can find the island's highest concentration of cafés and restaurants (see p.256), some of its finest accommodation (see p.239) and excellent transport connections – making this area the best base from which to explore Valletta and the rest of the island while remaining in touch with nightlife. **Paceville**, a district within St Julian's, is where most of Malta's clubs and bars are located (see p.283), every weekend pulling in thousands of young revellers. The wide promenade that skirts the coastal **Tower Road** is the locals' destination of choice for the evening *passiġġiata*.

During the **Knights'** rule, the deep and sheltered Marsamxett Harbour – less well-defended than the Grand Harbour – often provided shelter for the armadas of Ottoman invaders. In 1551, Dragut sailed into Marsamxett before giving up his attempts to take Malta and heading for Gozo, while the Ottoman fleet also found refuge here in the Great Siege. The harbour's defences were given their due by the Knights in the eighteenth century when they erected **Fort Manoel** on Manoel Island and **Fort Tigne** at Tigne Point at the tip of the Sliema peninsula. The **British** built four additional forts to guard the northern sea-routes into the Grand Harbour in the nineteenth century: Fort Cambridge and **Sliema Point Battery** in Sliema, Fort Spinola in St Julian's and Fort Pembroke.

At the time, Sliema and St Julian's consisted mainly of open fields behind the clusters of fishermen's hamlets on the numerous sheltered bays along this coast. By the mid-nineteenth century, the **British** had started building summer houses and villas on the coast, and the Maltese bourgeoisie slowly followed suit. After World War II people from the towns around the Grand Harbour began relocating here to escape the overcrowded conditions, and the construction of hotels began in earnest as part of the drive to build a **tourist industry**; the ensuing boom made Sliema Malta's first resort town.

These days, the building boom stumbles on despite the increasingly vociferous protests of the residents; in an economy that thrives on property speculation, at any given time a couple of hotels and high-rises are under construction – while over twenty percent of Malta's housing stock remains vacant. The result is that ranks of high-rises tower claustrophobically over narrow streets, and the area's infrastructure is strained, with traffic jams common and parking near-impossible.

ARRIVAL AND ORIENTATION

From Valletta's bus terminuses, **buses** #62, #67 and #68 (every 10min) wind along the coast through Msida, Gzira and Sliema before terminating on the fringes of Paceville, north of Spinola Bay in St Julian's. Half-hourly bus #60 from Valletta heads to the centre of Sliema near the police station and the post office, up the hill from the area opposite Manoel Island on the shore of Marsamxett Harbour known as the **Sliema Ferries**. A more scenic route from Valletta is the **ferry** from the Manderaggio to the Sliema Ferries (daily 9am–7pm, every 30min; Lm0.30; takes 5min).

There's a small **bus terminus** (Map 4, K8) at the Sliema Ferries from where bus #70 goes to Buġibba, bus #645 to Ċirkewwa (for the Gozo ferries), bus #70 to Rabat, bus #65 to Mdina, and bus #652 to Għajn Tuffieħa and Golden Bay (all Lm0.40).

Drivers will have a frustrating time finding somewhere to park, especially during shopping and office hours; your best chance is to use the multistorey **car park** on High Street in Sliema (Map 4, K7).

Sliema

An address in **SLIEMA**, especially in the heart of the action along the coastal **Tower Road** (Triq It-Torri), is the aspiration of the young Maltese middle-classes: right in the centre of the newest urban areas, close to nightlife and Malta's best shopping, Tower Road's luxury apartments enjoy unparalleled sea-views, with the beach only a few metres away. But Tower Road is plagued by endless traffic,

BOAT TOURS

Informative guided **boat tours** of Marsamxett Harbour and the Grand Harbour depart from the **Sliema Ferries** several times a day (Lm6.25), operated by Captain Morgan Cruises, based at Dolphin Court, Tigne Seafront, Sliema (☎ 343373 ⓦ www.captainmorgan.com.mt). They take about an hour, and give an impressive, sea-level view of the fortifications and the imposing scale of the harbour.

In addition, Captain Morgan and a smaller company, Hera Sails (Abate Rigord St, Gzira; ☎ 319581), offer a host of other worthwhile boat tours, for broadly similar prices, all departing from the Sliema Ferries. Trips to the **Blue Lagoon** in Comino (daily; Lm6.95), and **cruises** around the three Maltese islands (Mon, Wed & Fri; Lm15.95) are both all-day affairs with lunch included, while there's also a complete 24-hour **overnight package** aboard the luxury vessel *Fernandes II* (Lm69.95), departing every Friday at 6.30pm and including a free bar, evening meal, breakfast and an en-suite cabin. Other worthwhile options include **sunset cruises** every Sunday at 7.30pm (June–Sept; Lm18.95) that head to St Paul's Islands and include an onboard barbecue.

Alternatively, you can charter a yacht, complete with skipper, from Captain Morgan for cruises ranging from one day or night to several days; check the details at ⓦwww.yachtcharter.com.mt.

and has a schizophrenic saw-toothed profile and an unfinished feel as the redevelopment of townhouses into apartment blocks and hotels continues unabated; the streets are dusty from construction sites, while the growls of digging machines and clanks of cranes are everyday background sounds – along with techno music blaring from car stereos. Many of Malta's foreign residents choose to live in Sliema, and thousands of young Northern Europeans also lodge here with host families while they study English. When the

SLIEMA

blistering heat of summer days abates, young people crowd the **cafés** that line Tower Road, and streams of pedestrians converge on the promenade for the evening *passiġġiata*. Aside from strolling Tower Road, the only target to aim for in Sliema is the dilapidated **military architecture** occupying Tigne Point to the southeast of the town centre.

Sliema has over six hundred commercial outlets; its **shopping district** (see p.319) of international chains of designer clothes shops and home-decor stores – not to mention offshore financial companies and plenty of media outfits – comprises a small triangular area northeast of the Sliema Ferries, demarcated by Bisazza Street, Tower Road and Triq Ix-Xatt Ta' Tigne (more popularly known by its old name, The Strand). South of Sliema Ferries lies Gzira, a working-class town notorious for its drug peddling and prostitution, and Msida, an unremarkable residential town clustered round Msida Creek at the inner mouth of the harbour, where over six hundred yachts berth in Malta's largest **yacht marina**.

TIGNE POINT

Map 1, K4.

From the Sliema Ferries, head southeast along Triq Ix-Xatt Ta' Tigne towards **Tigne Point**, the outcrop of land that forms the lip enclosing Marsamxett Harbour from the north. It is littered with the detritus of military structures and forts erected by both the Knights and the British, all of which are now shuttered and abandoned; you can snoop around the barracks and the fort, and pause to enjoy the picture-perfect view of Valletta, but there's not much else to occupy a visit.

As the street swerves north from the coast, turn right opposite the football ground into a driveway flanked by the complex of former **British army barracks**, identifiable from their characteristic colonnaded porticos, and on to the remains of **Fort Tigne**. Built in the 1790s, the diamond–

MANOEL ISLAND

Manoel Island (Map 1, J4) juts into Marsamxett Harbour about 1km southwest of the Sliema Ferries. Tragically, both the historic buildings on the little island are in a sad state of ruin, and you may find that access is restricted while the area undergoes long-term redevelopment.

Fort Manoel, built between 1723 and 1726 on the east flank of the island, is a classic square fort with corner bastions and bomb-proof Cavaliers that accommodated five hundred troops. In the eighteenth century, the Knights built the **Lazzaretto** on the south shore of Manoel Island as a quarantine station. In World War II it housed the Royal Navy's submarine flotilla, and so was showered with bombs by the Axis powers – which accounts for its present state, a roofless skeleton towering directly over the water. Its neighbour Fort Manoel also suffered several direct hits, but the indifference of the British and then the Maltese authorities, more than the bombs, led to the tragic deterioration of the fort; the crumbling shell of the building, attacked by both sea-spray and vandals, is full of rubbish and daubed with graffiti, and its stone motifs and chapel have been dismantled and looted.

A large development project currently underway, the **Manoel Island and Tigne Point Project**, is transforming the little island. Expected to be completed by 2010, the development is a cross between a resort and residential sprawl, incorporating a yacht marina, hotel, apartments and amenities on Manoel Island and a tower block at Tigne Point. The developers have signed an agreement with the government to restore Fort Manoel and the Lazzaretto, granting public access to these sights and the island's coast.

MANOEL ISLAND

shaped fort was considered faultless in design by the British army, though they made various modifications to it throughout the nineteenth century to keep its weaponry up-to-date with military technology. At the beginning of the twentieth century, the Royal Navy installed a weapon beneath the fort that was all the more insidious for being concealed: a torpedo that could be fired through a tunnel just below the water towards a ship breaking into Marsamxett Harbour. Sadly, the area has now become an illegal rubbish tip for rubble from construction sites and old household appliances. Parts of the site are being re-developed, and access may be restricted (see box overleaf).

The rewarding highlight of Tigne Point is the **view** of Valletta across the harbour, particularly at sunset when the weathered fortifications and facades are lit with the auburn rays of the sun, and the medieval vista of the town cloistered behind its walls conjures up the glory and chivalry of the Knights. The spire of the Anglican Cathedral pierces the sky, with behind it the Baroque dome of the church of Our Lady of Mount Carmel, the highest building in Valletta.

ALONG TOWER ROAD

Map 1, J4.

From the Sliema Ferries, **Tower Road** heads north across the neck of the Tigne Point peninsula, emerging on the northeast coast at Għar Id-Dud, the starting-point for a promenade that winds all the way west to Spinola Bay. Nowhere in Malta is the **passiġġiata** (strolling along the seaside promenades) more popular than here. At dusk hundreds of people – both local residents and those who come from other parts of Malta – swagger along the promenade to savour the silky summer evenings, chat with friends and pause for an ice cream or *imqaret* (deep-fried date pastries) and a soft drink.

At the next corner north of Għar Id-Dud stands the **Sliema Point Battery**, built by the British in 1876 and separated from the road (and promenade) by a dry moat. It's a small square fort, and Malta's only Gothic Revival military building; now converted into a restaurant, its interior has been altered and only the shell survives.

Beyond the battery begins a rocky belt sandwiched between Tower Road and the sea. This is a convenient **beach** for locals and visitors alike, but is often crowded and dirty in summer. Like most beaches in Malta (see p.308), it's informally and roughly segregated into various groupings.

Ferro Bay, between Sliema Point Battery and Surfside, attracts hundreds of visiting teenage English-language students and is also a popular gay meeting-point (see p.306). Local families occupy the hundred-metre stretch on either side of **Surfside** (a private lido where it costs Lm2 to rent a sun lounger and have the facility of a shower). Further on, below the next bend in Tower Road, is **Exiles**, where Sliema's yuppies and lost hippies hang out, their focal point being the *Exiles Barbecue Shack* where the jukebox incessantly blares rock and techno. Beyond Exiles and Tower Road is the **Peace Promenade** garden, a strip consisting of a small playing-area for children, flowerbeds and fountains, its far edge marking the end of Sliema and the start of Main Street, St Julian's.

St Julian's

ST JULIAN'S stretches north across Spinola Bay and St George's Bay before giving way to the sprawl of Pembroke in the northeast. Its only sights are the impressive Art Nouveau **Balluta Buildings** in Balluta Bay, and **Spinola**

Bay itself, with its traditional fishing boats around the coast. **Paceville**, Malta's nightlife district, is the pulsating heart of St Julian's, the district that defines the town.

Over the past decade St Julian's has grown into a **resort** with Malta's densest concentration of hotels; upmarket places ring the coastline from Spinola Bay to St George's Bay, while in from the sea are less-expensive hotels and self-catering apartments. The latest addition to St Julian's resort-style development is the controversial *Portomaso*, an upmarket complex on the coast east of Spinola Bay comprising Malta's tallest building (a glass office-block), a *Hilton* hotel, hundreds of luxury apartments and a yacht marina created by dynamiting what was once a public beach; the complex sparked protests and hunger strikes by some environmentalists, not least for breaching the ruins of the historic Fort Spinola and annihilating the breeding grounds of a type of alga.

BALLUTA BAY

Map 4, D4.

The pleasant **Balluta Bay** is a marked by a small triangular piazza studded with Judas trees and outdoor seating for a handful of mediocre restaurants. On the south side of the bay stands the 1950s **Carmelite Church** flanked by the Carmelite Convent; the church's interior is relatively bare, but its exterior is a rare example of Gothic Revival (see p.375). Behind the piazza, the bay is dominated by the monumental **Balluta Buildings**, an apartment-block erected in the 1920s that is Malta's best example of Art Nouveau. With its buttresses framing the facade with two huge arches, its intricate motifs of angels, and its terraced profile, the whimsically creative Balluta Buildings lends an ornate feel to an otherwise architecturally bland area.

Across the square survive two of the early **villas** that

once housed the bourgeoisie and British bureaucrats on the shorefront of Sliema and St Julian's, designed in a hybrid of Baroque and Neoclassical. Set behind front gardens and dominated by towering Norfolk Island pines, both are listed buildings – the only reason why they've been spared from the claws of the bulldozer.

SPINOLA BAY

Map 1, A1–B1.

The next bay northwest of Balluta Bay is the kidney-shaped **Spinola Bay**, still partly occupied and used by fishermen: their moored *luzzus* (wooden fishing boats) clutter the bay. Beyond the orbit of the promenade, where fishermen work in front of their boathouses, the bay is lined with apartment blocks and restaurants, and always bustling. Amid the haphazard development of shoebox apartments, the *luzzus* lend character to Spinola Bay, painted in neon green, blue, red and yellow, and decorated with Baroque designs and the much-photographed **Eyes of Osiris** – carved on their bows to ward off evil, bad omens and bad luck while the fishermen are at sea. At night, the lights emanating from the restaurants shimmer on the water and bring out the boats' colours in a quaint and romantic scene.

PACEVILLE

Map 1, I3.

Just over 100m north of Spinola Bay, the main Triq San Ġorġ (St George's Rd) heads on to **Paceville**, Malta's nightlife district. In an area of less than one square kilometre, demarcated by Triq San Ġorġ to the west, Triq Dragunara to the north, Triq Il-Knisja to the east and Triq Gort to the south, dozens of bars and clubs (see p.283) rub shoulders at ground level, with high-rise resort-style apartment blocks rising overhead. During the day the area is shabby and the streets dirty, and its highlights a handful of souvenir shops, but at night, particularly on winter weekends and every night in summer, Paceville comes alive with thousands of young people and all the streets are congested with traffic. There's a merry and boisterous mood, loud music blaring from the open bars and people spilling onto the streets to avoid the crowds and the heat indoors.

Buses #62, #67 and #68 from Valletta, and #65 from Buġibba, drop you at Paceville's small bus terminus on Triq Sant' Andrija just off Triq San Ġorġ. On weekend nights, buses shuttle to and from Valletta until 2am.

Fort Madliena

Map 2, H4. Triq Il-Madliena, Madliena. Sat 3–5pm only; free guided tours on the hour.

Fort Madliena formed part of the defence arrangement created by the Victoria Lines – the wall that effectively dissected Malta east to west along the escarpment known as the Great Fault (see Contexts, p.374). Built in the 1870s, the pentagonal fort (along with another two forts on the Victoria Lines) was designed for active defence; additionally, its guns protected the sea approach to the Grand Harbour. Its ramparts are at ground level to make it unnoticeable to anyone approaching the Victoria Lines or enemy ships plying the coast. These days the building is the headquarters of the voluntary rescue organization **St John's Rescue Corps**, whose members provide the guided tour that fills in the history of the building.

The dilapidated fort is situated on the crest of a hill in **MADLIENA**, an exclusive residential area of sparse villas some twenty-minutes' uphill walk from the nearest stop on bus #627 from the Sliema Ferries; get off on Triq Sant' Andrija, at the first bus stop beyond the *Forum Hotel*, where St Andrew's gives way to Madliena. From here, head west up the slope into Triq Il-Prekursur, then north into Triq Il-Madliena that leads on for about 500m to the fort.

Although the fort itself is a minor sight, the highlight of a visit is the extraordinary **panorama** from its ramparts, some 400m above sea level. To the west you can see the most intact stretch of the **Victoria Lines** winding into the steep-sided gorge Wied Id-Dis. South is the urban sprawl of St Julian's, Sliema and their satellites, while to the north is a view all the way to Gozo across the artificial hill of the Maghtab Landfill.

FORT MADLIENA

Mdina, Rabat and central Malta

West of Valletta, the city suburbs and a jumble of towns southwest of Sliema and St Julian's give way to agricultural land which rolls across the centre of the island before climbing to Mdina. This ancient city and its neighbour Rabat sprawl on the craggy highlands a few kilometres in from the southwest coast. West of Rabat, meandering valleys gnaw into the plateaux of garigue, eventually reaching Dingli Cliffs, Malta's highest point at 253m, where the land tumbles dramatically into an inky blue sea.

The web of fields, divided by rubble walls, that splay in all directions from Rabat and Mdina pay homage to traditional, non-intensive local farming methods that produces the delicious Maltese tomatoes, expanses of cereals, potatoes for export, melons, watermelons and strawberries. The warm, shimmering air is tinged with drying hay, and the treeless landscape unfolds towards calm, undulating horizons. To the north of Rabat, beyond Mosta, the land slides down the escarpment of the Great Fault, which divides Malta east to west and is traced by the defensive wall called the Victoria Lines (see p.374).

Built on a ridge and ringed by fortifications, aristocratic **Mdina** is one of Malta's major highlights. This small, winningly attractive, Baroque walled town was the island's first urban settlement and its capital until Valletta took over in 1568. You can detect its medieval history beneath the Baroque makeover that has survived, and its maze of narrow, twisting alleys have kept modernity at bay. With just four hundred inhabitants and virtually car-free, at night it falls deathly quiet. A wander here to soak up the atmosphere is unmissable.

Located next to Mdina, **Rabat** started to take shape in the Middle Ages as overspill, and has now grown into a major town. The remains of a Roman villa are incorporated into its Museum of Roman Antiquities, while in the town centre is a church built atop a cave where St Paul is said to have preached. Rabat's most affecting sight is a dual set of medieval Christian catacombs, complete with original skeletons. The Grand Masters' country retreat of Verdala Palace nestles in the lush Buskett Garden, south of the town.

In **central Malta**, midway between Rabat and Valletta, lie the elegant **Three Villages** of Attard, Balzan and Lija, filled with charming villas and Baroque townhouses that once belonged to nobles and knights. The three have retained an aura of gentility and wealth, and can boast a scattering of attractive churches and palaces that make for an interesting half-day. Northwest of the Three Villages is **Mosta**, a characterless town hemmed in by agricultural land to the east and the Great Fault to the west, that nonetheless justifies a detour in order to lay eyes on the mighty Mosta Rotunda, said to be Europe's third-largest church.

Mdina

As you approach **MDINA**, some 12km west of Valletta and almost in the centre of Malta, the land all around opens into a checkerboard of fields cut by rubble walls, with the Baroque dome of Mdina's cathedral punctuating the skyline ahead. The town lives up to the promise of that first glimpse: it's a marvellously atmospheric place, built out of yellowish limestone on a bluff overlooking central Malta and the northeast coast, and still girdled by weathered fortifications (in Arabic, a *medina* is a walled town). This was the island's medieval capital, and ever since Grand Master Antonio Manoel de Vilhena's extensive Baroque regeneration in the early eighteenth century, it's been left virtually untouched. **St Paul's Cathedral**, with its museum, is a major highlight, and the Baroque **Magisterial Palace** boasts a grand exterior and courtyard but an altered and simplified interior. Among the host of other handsome patrician townhouses, most of them bedecked with elaborate details such as ornate door-knockers and facade stone-carving, the **Palazzo Falzon** stands out as the town's best-preserved medieval building, with parts surviving from its eleventh-century Norman original.

Mdina is popularly referred to as the **Silent City** on account of its tiny population and its winding alleys that are too narrow for motor traffic; even today, the town has no cultural or social life to speak of, and all the cafés are shut by 7pm. The only people you're likely to see are day-trippers, the only shops souvenir shops. With that in mind, the way to get under Mdina's skin is to linger until the sun has set and the tourists, the touts and the horse cabbies have gone home. At dusk, Mdina's medieval past hangs thick in the air, and after dark, roaming through the web of alleys in and out of the eerie shadows created by traditional streetlamps, it's easy to see that the town was designed in order to confuse an invading army.

Some history

Mdina became Malta's first urban centre – and its default capital – during **Phoenician** rule (800–480 BC); under the **Romans** it remained at the centre of political and cultural life, producing textiles that were famous throughout the empire. But it was probably the **Byzantines** who built the city's first perimeter wall, smaller in scale than the present fortification but encircling an area twice as large, extending southwest to where Rabat's St Paul's Church stands today. After the **Arabs** took Malta in 870 AD, they redrew the boundaries of the city and rebuilt the fortifications which are extant today, reducing the city's size for a tighter defensive capability. Subsequently, the Maltese dialect corrupted the Arabic name *Medina* to Mdina.

After the **Norman Conquest** in 1090, Roger the Norman annexed Malta to Sicily within the Norman Kingdom, and this period saw the Siculo-Norman **nobility** – Malta's feudal overlords who wielded control of the cotton-based economy – build their palaces in Mdina; an ecclesiastical hierarchy involving the absentee Sicilian bishops established its authority, and the city's first cathedral was erected. On the heels of widespread abhorrence of the corrupt feudal lords, in the late fourteenth century the **Aragonese** set up in Mdina the **Universita**, Malta's self-rule government which controlled provincial affairs, including the administration of justice. In 1429, a year after Alfonso V of Aragon named Mdina *Città Notabile* (Noble City) in a gimmick to inspire loyalty, the local militia at Mdina and Fort St Angelo repelled an 18,000-strong invading army of **Hafsid Saracens** from Tunisia. In 1492, along with the rest of the Spanish dominions, Mdina lost its thriving **Jewish** community – mostly

MDINA

physicians, artisans and barbers – expelled en masse by Ferdinand II.

When the Knights arrived in 1530, they ceremonially received the keys to Mdina from the nobles, but chose Vittoriosa on the coast as their strategic base instead (see p.93). In 1568, when the new city of Valletta became the capital, the Knights rechristened Mdina as the **Città Vecchia**, or Old City. Noble families stayed on in Mdina, even though the Universita's jurisdiction was being whittled down to municipal affairs only. In 1693 an **earthquake** damaged almost half of the city, following which the nobility and ecclesiastical authorities embarked on a slow rebuilding programme. In 1723 Grand Master Manoel de Vilhena launched a more ambitious **redevelopment** drive: he built the Magisterial Palace, moved the Main Gate further east, reinforced the fortifications and improved the urban fabric.

Mdina stormed out of political oblivion during the **uprising** against the French in 1798. French troops stationed in Mdina were looting Catholic treasures from the churches and selling them at auction in Pjazza San Pawl to raise funds for **Napoleon**'s expansionist ambitions. As the troops set about pillaging the Carmelite Church, the locals' simmering grudges suddenly erupted into an angry riot. Mobs slaughtered the French garrison and within two days fanned the fire of revolt throughout Malta. During the subsequent two-year French blockade, Mdina became the capital of the insurgents (see p.342).

In 1818 the British governor Sir Thomas Maitland abolished the Universita, which had survived largely as a symbolic nod to tradition. These days, with nobility no longer officially recognized, many of Mdina's buildings have been converted into restaurants or tourist attractions.

MDINA

ARRIVAL AND ORIENTATION

Mdina is served by **buses** #80 and #81 from Valletta, #65 from Sliema Ferries, and #86 from Buġibba's bus terminus, all of which terminate on Triq Is-Saqqajja (Map 5, H6), 200m southeast of Mdina on the northeastern edge of Rabat. From the bus stop, it's a five-minute stroll northwards to Mdina's Main Gate. If you're driving, aim for the car park flanking Triq Is-Saqqajja just outside the Main Gate.

Mdina is tiny, barely 400m from end to end. It is divided by **Triq Villegaignon** that runs from the Main Gate in the south wall to the northernmost tip of the bastions. All the principal sights are on, or just off, this street, including the central town square **Pjazza San Pawl**, location of St Paul's Cathedral and the Cathedral Museum. However, the whole of Mdina is packed with beautiful architecture, even though most of the townhouses aren't open to the public. We've put together a looping half-day walk through the town, starting at the Main Gate and exiting through the **Greeks' Gate**, in the south wall 200m west of the Main Gate.

While strolling, it's impossible to evade the touts drumming up business for Mdina's audiovisual shows and theatrical "experiences" of history – all of which are tourist traps whose advertising promise much but deliver little.

THE MAIN GATE

Map 5, G5.

At the head of the stone bridge that spans the dry moat on the south side of the walls, Mdina's **Main Gate** is a Baroque stone archway constructed in 1724 as part of Grand Master Antonio Manoel de Vilhena's restoration programme. He shifted the gate east – you can still see the outline of its predecessor to one side – so that it would lead directly to the planned Magisterial Palace and open onto Pjazza San Publiju, the square giving access to Triq Villegaignon. Vilhena's coat of arms and stone-carved triumphal motifs top the gate. Three stone statues of Mdina's patron saints (St Paul, St Publius and St Agatha) crown the internal facade of the gate.

THE MAGISTERIAL PALACE

Map 5, G4. Pjazza San Publiju. Daily: mid-June to Sept 8am–2pm; rest of year 9.30am–4.30pm; free.

The Main Gate opens onto **Pjazza San Publiju**, a small square marked, on the left side, by the **Torre dello Standardo**, a watchtower built by Grand Master Vilhena in 1750 to send up smoke and fire signals to Valletta in the event of invasion; it now serves as Mdina's police station.

Opposite the tower, dominating the east side of the square, is the **Magisterial Palace** (sometimes known as Vilhena's Palace or Palazzo Vilhena), the fourth of the palaces built throughout the island by Grand Master Manoel de Vilhena in 1724. Designed by the French architect Charles François de Medion, it shows influences of French Baroque, particularly in the courtyard in front of the building, a feature alien to most Maltese Baroque designs (which placed the courtyard at the centre). The palace itself is set on two floors around a second central courtyard; Vilhena spent the summers here away from public life in Valletta, and his bust and coat of arms dominate the building's facade. While the exterior of the building looks like a large Baroque townhouse, the interior was altered when the British converted the palace into a hospital, after which more damaging alterations continued until the palace was re-opened in 1973 as the **National Museum of Natural History** (daily: mid-June to Sept 8am–2pm; rest of year

8.30am–4.30pm; Lm1), a tedious and eminently missable collection of motheaten odds and ends.

CORTE CAPITANALE

Map 5, G4. Misraħ Il-Kunsill Città Notabile.

A small square opening diagonally east of Pjazza San Publiju, named Misraħ Il-Kunsill Città Notabile, shelters, on its south side, the **Corte Capitanale**, a wing of the Magisterial Palace that served as Mdina's Court of Law until the abolition of the Universita in 1818. The stone-balustraded balcony protruding over the door is known as the **Herald's Loggia**, after the custom of the town crier's ceremonial announcements from the balcony. Trumpets would blast to attract attention, then the town crier would loudly proclaim the decrees and laws established by the Universita. These days, the building is only occasionally open to the public for temporary exhibitions on Mdina's history and culture, set up in an elegant barrel-vaulted hall that is the best-preserved section of the Magisterial Palace.

FROM PJAZZA SAN PUBLIJU TO THE CATHEDRAL

Triq Villegaignon, Mdina's main street, runs from just north of Pjazza San Publiju to Pjazza San Pawl, home of St Paul's Cathedral (see overleaf), and on to the northern walls. It's narrow and shaded, sandwiched between high Baroque and medieval townhouses, and always bustling with visitors browsing in the souvenir shops and horse-cabbies touting for business. The southern 100m of the street is marked by a handful of whistle-stop sights.

At the southernmost end of Triq Villegaignon is the small **St Agatha's Chapel** (Map 5, G4), dedicated to one of Mdina's patron saints. Originally built in 1410, it was destroyed by the 1693 earthquake and redesigned by

Lorenzo Gafa in the same year. A metal grille now barricades the chapel, but you can peek into its diminutive interior, which is uncharacteristically restrained for Malta's Catholic shrines. Legend has it that Agatha found refuge in Malta in 249 AD, having fled from Sicily to escape persecution for refusing to marry the Roman governor of Catania. She returned to Sicily in 251, whereupon the Romans cut off her left breast and roasted her to death. The chapel's altarpiece triumphantly commemorates the martyrdom of the saint.

Next door to St Agatha's Chapel rise the high walls of the **Nunnery of St Benedict** (Map 5, G4). This cloistered Benedictine convent was built in 1418, and is home to twenty nuns who are forbidden from ever leaving; the only males allowed inside are doctors, builders and whitewashers. An open door set into the nunnery wall leads to **St Benedict's Church** (daily 7am–3pm), a small and austere chapel that features an uninspiring Mattia Preti altarpiece of the Madonna with saints.

Next door to the nunnery is **Casa Testaferrata** (Map 5, G3) the palace of the noble Testaferrata family from medieval times. The present owner and occupier is the Marquis de San Vincenzo Ferreri, whose title was bestowed by King Philip of Spain in 1716. It's a striking house with a red door framed by two columns that support the balcony, and a facade that rears over the street.

ST PAUL'S CATHEDRAL

Map 5, G2. Pjazza San Pawl. Mon–Sat 9.30–11.45am & 2–5pm, Sun 3–4.30pm; free.

In the heart of Mdina is Pjazza San Pawl, a large square dominated by the magnificent **St Paul's Cathedral**, principal focus of a visit to the city. An earlier cathedral was built here shortly after the end of Muslim rule in 1090, but was ruined in the 1693 earthquake, after which the ecclesiastical authorities grabbed the opportunity to replace it with something grander. They bought and cleared some houses in front of the site to create an open square, and commissioned the Maltese architect **Lorenzo Gafa** to design the new cathedral. It took almost a decade to build, and was inaugurated in 1702.

The cathedral's monumental presence dominates Mdina's skyline. Its heavy Baroque facade is panelled by vertical bands interspersed among horizontal stone lips and scrolls, leading up to two ornate belfries. The elegant octagonal **dome** – Gafa's architectural masterpiece – rises above the cathedral and the city, and is visible for miles around. Its compositional balance is outstanding, the sixteen pilasters framed by twin panels leading to stone scrolls, the eight windows recessed. The upper part of the dome is draped by ornately carved locks of curly stone rising towards the graceful lantern.

If the Co-Cathedral in Valletta celebrates the Knights, the simpler Mdina cathedral is the shrine of the ecclesiastical authorities. Its floor-plan, in the form of a Latin cross, comprises a vaulted nave flanked on each side by three side-altars, with enclosed, harmoniously designed chapels on both sides of the chancel.

The interior

The musty **interior**, its pews cleared, looks much larger than the exterior suggests. The floor of the nave is a faded patchwork of variegated marble **tombstones** commemorating prominent churchmen and Mdina's nobility. The three ceiling **frescoes** are the work of the Sicilian brothers Vincenzo and Antonio Manno, simple yet moving portraits done in the 1790s depicting St Paul preaching to congregations of crowds. Attached to the piers dividing the nave from the aisles are five **monuments**, bronze busts with

ST PAUL'S CATHEDRAL

marble plinths commemorating five notable Maltese bishops, including Fabrizio Sciberras Testaferrata, who later became a cardinal, and Mikiel Gonzi, the authoritarian bishop who resisted Prime Minister Dom Mintoff's attempts to limit the church's extra-legal privileges.

With a few exceptions, the **side chapels** are modest affairs, and artistically unremarkable; their tombs were reserved for bishops. Originally, the altarpieces of the side altars were painted by Mattia Preti's students under the master's direction; all fail to meet Preti's high standards, so much so that the three on the left aisle were replaced by more powerful works by Roman artists in the nineteenth century. Clockwise from the main entrance, these are the *Annunciation* by Domenico Bruschi, the *Madonna and the Guardian Angel over Valletta* by Pietro Gagliardi, and the *Pentecost* by Francesco Grandi. Moving clockwise, the three on the opposite side of the nave, which are the originals created by the anonymous Preti students, are pedestrian portraits of *St Publius*, *St Gaetano* and *St Luke*.

The paintings that originally covered the interior of the dome were ruined by humidity over the centuries and repainted by the Italian artist **Mario Caffaro Rore** in 1955; in them, Jesus Christ presides over several saints, including St Peter and St Paul. The large, dramatic paintings behind the altar are the work of Mattia Preti – the **altarpiece** depicting the *Conversion of St Paul*, and the painting on the apse above of *The Shipwreck of St Paul*.

The two highly decorated side-chapels flanking the altar have an intimate and holy atmosphere, and are mostly the creation of the Maltese artist **Francesco Zahra** (1710–73), at the apex of his career. The various lunettes and cupola paintings in both chapels are Zahra's masterworks, a powerful set grouped under the themes of the *Triumph of the Eucharist* and *Triumph of the Cross*. Left of the altar, the **Chapel of the Blessed Sacrament** has an intricate inlaid marble floor by

Zahra (who also created the chapel's gilded gate) and a simple fifteenth-century icon of the Virgin and Child. To the right of the altar, the **Chapel of the Cross and the Relics** also has a similar gate and marble floor by Zahra, as well as a seventeenth-century wooden crucifix by the Italian Franciscan monk Fra Innocenzo da Petralia.

On the feast of the Conversion of St Paul (held on the first Sun after Jan 25), on June 29 and on Christmas Day, a magnificent set of fifteen **silver statues** that originally belonged to the Knights are displayed on the main altar. These are the church's most prized possession, auctioned off by the French in 1798 and bought back by the ecclesiastical authorities in a move which virtually bankrupted the cathedral treasury.

THE CATHEDRAL MUSEUM

Map 5, G3. Pjazza Ta' L-Arċisqof. Mon–Fri 9am–4.30pm, Sat 9am–2pm; Lm1.

Facing the south wall of the cathedral is the small Pjazza Ta' L-Arċisqof, which holds the Diocesan Seminary, built in 1733–40 but disused for much of the twentieth century until its opening in 1969 as the **Cathedral Museum**. It's a large Baroque building set on two floors around a central courtyard, with a facade sporting a concave balcony with balustrades supported by two grand Atlantean sculptures. The museum fills both storeys but you can get around it in under an hour. Notes accompany the exhibits, highlights of which include an excellent collection of Dürer woodcuts and a fifteenth-century Spanish polyptych of St Paul.

The upper floor

Through the entrance hallway, a marble staircase leads to the **upper floor** where you're greeted by a bust of Grand

Master Antonio Manoel de Vilhena. The first hall is dedicated to **Catholic art**; highlights include a striking eighteenth-century ivory cross by Maltese artist Francesco Bologna, various heavily embroidered seventeenth-century ecclesiastical vestments, and Fra Salvatore di Bisignano's embossed Choral Books (1576), which open to the size of a coffee table. The hall leads through to a simple oval **chapel**, built *in situ* during the original construction. The French artist Antoine de Favray, famous for his evocative portraits of Grand Masters, painted the technically proficient but emotionally mute *Annunciation* altarpiece in 1749, and the inlaid cabinet opposite the altar displays a Romanesque chalice dating from the twelfth century and an intricately enamelled Byzantine altar stone.

The next hall through the chapel's second door displays paintings, woodcuts and copperplates from the sixteenth to the eighteenth centuries that were donated by the Maltese Count Saverio Marchese (1757–1833), a lifelong collector who procured some of the paintings from Count Francesco Seratti in Florence. In a series of 53 small and superbly executed woodcuts and copperplates, Albrecht **Dürer**'s refined technique is best illustrated by his outstanding *St Jerome*.

The adjacent hall has been left bare, both to reveal its chessboard floor of marble – parallel rows of inlaid tiles that create soothing tableaux of perspective – and to draw attention to the **Polyptych of St Paul**. Created in Spain and attributed to Luis Borrassa (who died in 1425), the polyptych formerly hung above the altar in the Cathedral until it was replaced by Preti's painting in 1682. In this well-crafted work, stirring in its deceptive simplicity, St Paul is enthroned at the centre of the polyptych brandishing a sword and the Bible, surrounded by panelled paintings re-creating episodes of his life.

A neighbouring **loggia** looking over the courtyard is lined with 33 sculptures in light tan and fragrant olive wood by the contemporary Maltese artist Anton Agius. The pieces comprise abstracts of human and animal figures; provocative and mystic, the finishing lines are both vague and convoluted.

The ground floor

On the ground floor, **Room II** displays the archives of the Inquisition between 1574 and 1798, as well as the genealogical tables of the Knights that proved their sixteen lines of nobility. **Room III** celebrates Malta's national poet Dun Karm Psaila, who wrote the national anthem – the lyrics are inscribed on a marble plaque here – and who was elevated to sainthood by Pope John Paul II in May 2001. **Room IV** displays intact Roman and Punic pottery unearthed in Mdina and Rabat, including a copper urn that was found overflowing with Byzantine and Islamic golden coins. A large **numismatic** collection is arranged in glass cabinets, dating from Carthaginian coins of the fourth century BC to modern examples minted in the 1980s.

THE BISHOP'S PALACE

Map 5, H2. Pjazza Ta' L-Arċisqof.
On the east flank of Pjazza Ta' L-Arċisqof, wedged between the Cathedral Museum and the cathedral itself, is the **Bishop's Palace**, residence of the Archbishop of Malta since its construction in 1722 (and so closed to the public). Lorenzo Gafa designed the building in a way that would present a Baroque continuity to the cathedral, with panelling on the facade and a door that is the same shape as the cathedral's door. But since the palace perches on the town's fortifications, the design had to be slightly altered as stipulated by the Commissioners of War and Fortifications, whose brief specified smaller windows, a reduction in the

THE BISHOP'S PALACE

height of the building (which led to a mismatch of the stone scrolls which Gafa intended to be on the same level as those of the cathedral) and the removal of porch steps to facilitate the quick deployment of artillery.

NORTH OF PJAZZA SAN PAWL

Map 5, F2.

North of Pjazza San Pawl, **Triq Villegaignon** continues to Pjazza Tas-Sur, tucked inside the northern walls of the town.

On the left of the street, opposite Pjazza San Pawl, is the large medieval **Palazzo Santo Sofia**, recognizable for its flat, imposing facade, cut by an alley that creates an arched gateway straddled by the upper floor. Its ground floor is the oldest structure in Mdina, surviving from 1233. The palace is a prime example of rare Siculo-Norman architecture – a hybrid of Sicilian peasant farmhouses and Norman influence – that survives in a handful of palaces in Mdina and Vittoriosa. One characteristic feature is the two-light windows on the upper floor: these are double-arched windows divided by a column, whose arch narrows to a pitched apex. The main door on the ground floor also has the same pitched peak, plus the metal studs and exposed hinges reminiscent of Gothic architecture.

Towering above the next corner is the **Carmelite Church** (open erratic morning hours only), part of the Carmelite Convent complex. The Carmelites, a Sicilian order, came to Malta in 1370; this church was designed by Francesco Sammut and built between 1630 and 1690. Its facade is embedded and hidden in the square perimeter wall of the complex, and as you step in, the bustle of the street gives way to an incense-laden hush. The hollow interior, its pews cleared, rises sharply to the apex of its dome, and in its unusual oval shape, the main altar is only slightly more prominent than the other six side-altars; the interior feels hollow and rises sharply to the apex of its dome. Stefano Erardi (1630–1716) painted the *Annunciation* of the main altar, a sober canvas that fits the dim, sombre church.

PALAZZO FALZON

Map 5, F2. Triq Villegaignon. Mon–Sat 10.30am–1pm & 2.30–4.30pm; Lm0.75.

A few metres short of Pjazza Tas-Sur, on the right-hand side of Triq Villegaignon, stands the **Palazzo Falzon**, sometimes known as the Norman House. A two-storey house around a central courtyard, it dates to 1495 and is the finest surviving example of Norman architecture in Malta, its upper floor sporting the characteristic two-light windows. It was originally the residence of the Aragonese Vice-Admiral Falzon; in 1530, when the Knights arrived in Malta, Falzon hosted Grand Master L'Isle Adam for his first eight days on the island. You can still see the memorial coat of arms belonging to L'Isle Adam in the courtyard.

Left intact by its absentee landlord, the **interior** boasts heaps of fine carpets, medieval armour, old paintings and furniture, and collections of traditional tools. The building is a study in medieval architecture, its simplicity full of character and charm.

PJAZZA TAS-SUR AND AROUND

North of Palazzo Falzon, Triq Villegaignon opens into the small **Pjazza Tas-Sur** (aka Bastion Square; Map 5, F1), nestling behind the fortifications. It's a pleasant space shaded by ficus trees and backed by characterful houses, with a bench-filled parapet set on the ramparts. This is one of Malta's highest points, and the vista from the parapet takes in a full third of the island: terraced fields step down from the foot of the fortifications below towards the central agricultural plains and on to the conurbation of the northeast coast, from the Three Cities to the south to Buġibba in the north. Some 50m east of the square, you can enjoy the panorama from the Fontanella Tea Gardens (see p.264).

West from Pjazza Tas-Sur is Il-Wesgħa Ta' Sant' Agatha, from where Triq L-Imħażen heads southwest into a little-visited quarter of Mdina. At the end of the street, which is lined with Norman-style townhouses, you'll come to Mdina's second gate, **Greeks' Gate**, (Map 5, E4) a simple stone archway named for an enclave of Greek inhabitants during Phoenician rule.

Rabat and around

The town of **RABAT**, contiguous with Mdina to the south, grew in the shadow of its more illustrious neighbour. Before the Arab invasion in 870, Mdina and Rabat formed one settlement, with a defensive perimeter wall probably built by the Byzantines that encompassed the whole of Mdina and extended to what is now the centre of Rabat. When the Arabs tightened the fortifications, they named the cluster of houses that now stood outside the fortifications *rabat*, an Arabic word implying a suburb. In the Middle Ages, Rabat emerged as a distinct town with its own parish.

Most of Rabat's sights date to this medieval period and are concentrated in the town centre, a mere five-minute walk south of Mdina. **St Paul's Grotto**, below the church of the same name, is the cave where St Paul is said to have lived and preached outside the confines of Mdina during his three-month sojourn in Malta. Recognition of the site's importance dates to the seventeenth century, when the Knights constructed a complex of chapels and the **Wignacourt College Museum** to cater for the pilgrims that visited the grotto. Round the corner from the town square, underground Christian burial shrines **St Paul's Catacombs** and **St Agatha's Catacombs** are as claustrophobic as they are dramatic. It's also worth making time for sights around the town, including the verdant woodland of **Buskett Gardens** and the rugged **Dingli Cliffs** on the south coast, Malta's highest point.

Rabat is a distinct town of some 13,000 people, who have an accent discernibly different from that of other parts of Malta. The town is surrounded by a rural belt of valleys and some of Malta's best agricultural land, from which it benefits in the form of boisterous farmer/hunter **cafés**, which characteristically feature caged finches and hunting memorabilia, and serve up Malta's best *pastizzi* (see p.257).

At *L-Imnarja*, the feast of St Peter and St Paul
every June 29, Rabat hosts a farmer's fair at Buskett;
medals are awarded and there's plenty of rabbit
dishes and home-made wine to sample.

THE MUSEUM OF ROMAN ANTIQUITIES

Map 5, D5. Il-Wesgħa Tal-Mużew. Daily: mid-June to Sept 7.45am–2pm; rest of year 8.15am–5pm; Lm1.

Directly outside Mdina's Greeks' Gate, 200m west of Main Gate, is the well-signed **Museum of Roman Antiquities**. The Neoclassical building sits over the remains of a Roman villa built around 50 AD and unearthed – complete with intact floor mosaics – in 1881. This is one of 25 Roman villas found throughout Malta that served as the homesteads of large agricultural estates, probably involved in producing olive oil. The museum's highlight is undoubtedly the fine mosaic floor of the villa's peristyle, preserved *in situ*, but there's little else to see.

The **ground floor** exhibits include Roman amphorae, an olive press, and pieces of columns, statues and fragments of mosaics unearthed from Roman villas elsewhere in Malta. In the **basement**, the peristyle of the original villa is dedicated to remains found on site: some of the original columns that framed the peristyle survive, and the mosaic floor displays a three-dimensional geometric pattern executed with fine detail. There are more fragments of mosaics arranged around the corridor that skirts the peristyle. The two statues here are of Emperor Claudius (41–54 AD) and his mother Antonia; their presence indicates that this villa belonged to a leading figure at the top of the hierarchy of Roman rule on the island. A smaller room off the main hall displays a handful of rough-cut marble **Islamic tombstones** excavated from the graveyard that was dug into the ruined villa by the Arabs in or just after the ninth century.

ST PAUL'S CHURCH AND GROTTO

Map 5, D10. Triq San Pawl. Daily 9am–5pm; free.

Heading south from the Museum of Roman Antiquities into **Triq San Pawl** brings you into the church square at the centre of Rabat, which is dominated by **St Paul's Church**. It's built on top of **St Paul's Grotto**, a natural cave where St Paul (see p.158) is said to have been interned during his three-month stint in Malta in 60 AD, while awaiting his transfer to Rome to stand trial. Ever tireless, Paul is supposed to have used his time in the grotto delivering sermons and conducting baptisms. A church is known to have existed on the site by 1372, while the present Baroque building was designed by the Knights' resident engineer Francesco Bounamici in the eighteenth century and funded by Grand Master Alof de Wignacourt.

For a shrine with such a lengthy history, the interior is relatively bland, set on bare stone and lacking the atmosphere of Malta's finest churches. Its only noteworthy features are the three altarpieces by renowned Maltese artists – from bottom to top, a clichéd *St Paul's Shipwreck* by Stefano Erardi (1630–1716), a calculated, reserved *St Publius* by Mattia Preti (1613–99) and an abstract *Eucharist* by Francesco Zahra (1710–73). Near the main entrance, stairs lead down to the small, dampish **grotto**, which is adorned with an unremarkable marble statue of St Paul made by Melchiorre Gafà in 1718, a silver model of a galley donated by Grand Master de Moyana in 1960, and four lamps gifted by Pope Paul VI. Even the trickle of pilgrims seem to have lost any interest in the place.

THE WIGNACOURT COLLEGE MUSEUM

Map 5, D10. Pjazza San Pawl. Mon–Sat 10am–3pm; Lm0.50.

Across the street from St Paul's Church is the entrance to the **Wignacourt College Museum**, originally built by Grand Master Alof de Wignacourt in 1617 as a hostel for pilgrims visiting St Paul's Grotto. The simple Baroque building has the appearance of a convent inside, with long, wide corridors, branching rooms and internal chapels. The collection, though, is disorganized and unlabelled, a repository for anything of marginal historic interest, from traditional tools to church vestments, portable organs to a small collection of Punic-Roman pottery.

The only part of the museum worth attention is the display of 49 wooden models of the **medieval chapels** that dot Malta's countryside, showcasing their architectural variations (see p.369). An extensive World War II **air-raid shelter** – which once protected five hundred people – is another, incongruous highlight, tunnelled beneath the museum building (there is a better air-raid shelter in Mġarr; see p.171).

ST PAUL'S CATACOMBS

Map 5, C11. Triq Sant' Agatha. Daily: mid-June to Sept 7.45am–2pm; rest of year 8.15am–4.15pm; Lm1.

Southwest of the church square, Triq San Kataldu then Triq Sant' Agatha lead you to **St Paul's Catacombs**, a maze of early Christian burial chambers dug in the fourth and fifth centuries. This underground cemetery is set on a number of different terraced levels, with around one thousand sarcophagi occupying every conceivable space. Its execution is highly sophisticated, with different types and sizes of graves, all of which have headrests cut into the stone. If you plan to visit just one set of catacombs, head on to St Agatha's Catacombs down the road (see opposite), where the skeletons are preserved *in situ* and there's a detailed guided tour.

Down the entry staircase are two rooms divided by a column. On the right is a primitive **chapel** used for burial ceremonies, where a stone-cut altar is discernible, while to the left are two round **agape tables**, circular tables surrounded by semicircular benches: this is where the congregation gathered to pray, mourn and feast after the deceased was laid to rest.

From here, there is no easily pinpointable way to tour the labyrinthine passageways of the catacombs, which are lit with electric bulbs; all of them end in a blank rock wall, so the best way is simply to roam around the small, mazey corridors, constantly doubling back on yourself. Formerly, the occupied sarcophagi were covered by stone slabs; now they are uncovered and it's possible to discern the various types of graves: a **loculus** is a small rectangular recess cut into the walls of a passageway, generally used for infants and children; **arcosolium tombs** are dug directly into the ground of passageways and small room openings; while **canopied table tombs** consist of a series of graves dug alongside each other about a metre above the floor, on shelves framed by arches (some of these accommodated two bodies).

ST AGATHA'S CATACOMBS AND MUSEUM

Map 5, B13. Sqaq Sant' Agatha. Mid-June to Sept Mon–Sat 9am–4.30pm; rest of year Mon–Fri 9am–noon, Sat 9am–12.30pm; Lm0.50.

A 150m walk southwest of St Paul's Catacombs is a sign-posted alleyway leading to the entrance of **St Agatha's Catacombs and Museum**. St Agatha (see p.128) is said to have hid in the crypt for a few days in 249 AD, when she had fled Roman persecution in Catania. The crypt and the catacombs – which consist of five hundred graves (two hundred for adults, three hundred for children) – were used over a period stretching from Byzantine rule in the fourth century through to the seventeenth century. There is an informative **guided tour** of the catacombs that convenes for each handful of visitors, approximately every half-hour.

The tour starts in the **crypt**, which has several well-preserved frescoes: the earliest three, nearest the door, are Byzantine representations of the *Madonna*, *St Agatha* and *St Paul*. The remainder date to the fourteenth and fifteenth centuries; Gothic in style, they depict, with raw emotion, St Agatha in various poses. Off the main crypt is a smaller chapel dedicated to the Madonna. From the crypt, the tour winds clockwise through the **catacombs**, from the early Christian section to a second-century pagan burial chamber, complete with the original, almost intact skeletons in open sarcophagi. Next is a sixth-century Christian burial chamber planned around a small, oval chapel with a primitive altar and a fresco altarpiece imbued with symbolism – the shell represents heaven, the pigeons the soul, and the tree life.

In an outbuilding is a small, haphazard archeological **museum** covered by the admission fee to the catacombs, but which is of limited value and interest.

THE DOMINICAN MONASTERY

Map 1, F6. Triq Ġorġ Borg Olivier. Daylight hours, free.

From St Paul's Church, Triq Il-Kulleġġ heads south to join Triq Il-Buskett; across the junction rises the high forbidding wall of Rabat's **Dominican Monastery**. The Dominicans arrived in Malta from Sicily in 1450 and chose this site for their convent, located over the cave dedicated to Our Lady of the Grotto. The grotto became a venerated pilgrimage site in the Middle Ages following an improbable tale woven by a local hunter, who, sheltering from the rain, claimed he had a vision of the Madonna. Some elderly locals still congregate here every afternoon to say the rosary. The original convent buildings of 1462 were renovated and expanded, with the addition of a larger church, in 1683. Ottoman troops occupied the convent for a few days in 1551, and in 1798 it was seized by French soldiers and held for two years. Today there are just twenty monks left, whose living quarters span the upper floor. The public have access to the courtyard and cloister, and the convent church.

The main door is left ajar, and through it is a large, square **courtyard** around which the convent is built on two floors. The architecturally elegant **cloister** that surrounds the courtyard is the main focus of a visit; it has a ribbed, barrel-vaulted ceiling while balustrades and loggias overlook the courtyard of orange trees and crossing stone pathways. All these elements combine in rhythmic patterns of composition to create a subtle harmony. A door (also ajar) leading off the west flank of the cloister leads to the sacristy and on to the **church** dedicated to Our Lady of the Grotto. Its interior is simple and bathed in light; near the front door a staircase leads down to the original **grotto**, now decorated as a separate chapel.

AROUND RABAT

To the southwest, the fringes of Rabat peter out into farm-houses nestling in green valleys. A short way south of the town, **Buskett Gardens** is Malta's only mature woodland, originally established by the Knights as part of the hunting grounds of the magisterial Verdala Palace (which is sadly closed to visitors indefinitely). Other sights around Rabat include the **Clapham Junction Cart Ruts**, a dense network of prehistoric tracks whose purpose is still a mystery, and, beyond, the sheer drop of the **Dingli Cliffs**.

Verdala Palace and Buskett Gardens

Map 1, F8. Triq Il-Buskett.
The grand **Verdala Palace** and its hunting grounds of **Buskett Gardens** lie 4km south of Rabat centre, accessible by following Triq Il-Buskett to its end or by taking bus #81 from in front of the Dominican Monastery.

- -
Dingli Cliffs, on the south coast about 4km southwest of Rabat, reached on bus #81 from Triq Il-Buskett, is Malta's highest point at 253m. A country road runs along the windswept clifftop, where the drop to the crashing waves is dizzying and the vista dramatic – not least at sunset.
- -

Designed by Ġirolmu Cassar, who was responsible for many of Valletta's most charming buildings, **Verdala Palace** was built in 1586 by Grand Master Cardinal Hugues

THE "CART RUTS" MYSTERY

About 550m west of Buskett, a signposted secondary road peters out at a rugged rocky plateau surrounded by fields. The area, crisscrossed by sets of parallel pairs of ruts furrowed into the rocky surface, most about 30cm deep by 60cm wide, comprises the densest network of such ruts in Malta, and was named by British archeologists the **Clapham Junction Cart Ruts**, after the similarly intricate web of rail lines at Clapham Junction station in South London.

The cart ruts pose an archeological puzzle, since no satisfactory explanation exists as to their origin. Ruts are found all over the Mediterranean, but they are more numerous in Malta than elsewhere. The most accepted theory, though hazy, is that they were made by wheeled carts during the Bronze Age (2300–800 BC). However, the ruts have no apparent destination or pattern. Some of them peter out, others disappear into the sea or halt at cliff-edges. Even the surface of Filfla, a tiny islet off Malta's south coast (see box p.187) is covered in these cart ruts. The mystery is deepened by the fact that in some places multiple sets of ruts cross over one another.

The debate on the possible date and origin of the cart ruts continues. The book *Echoes of Plato's Island*, published by the Prehistoric Society of Malta in 2000, expounds the theory that Malta is the surviving tip of Atlantis, and uses the fact that the cart ruts jump off cliffs, go underwater and cover Filfla as proof that Malta was a much larger island in the Neolithic era; the claim runs that it was reduced to its present size by the catastrophic earthquake Plato describes in his tale of Atlantis, which also caused the abrupt end of the Neolithic era (see p.329).

Loubenx de Verdalle as a country retreat, becoming Malta's second magisterial palace after Valletta's Grand Master's Palace. These days, it's the summer residence of the

President of Malta and is closed to visitors, but you can get a glimpse of its exterior rising above the lush grove of Aleppo pines that nestle around the building: it's a large, square palace with the high, stout walls of a tower, surrounded by a shallow, dry moat and four partly embedded corner turrets defining the structure.

Immediately west of Verdala Palace, a left turning snakes down to the bottom of the valley, the heart of **Buskett Gardens**. This is an extension of the palace's gardens – a woodland created by Grand Master Jean Paul de Lascaris Castellar in the seventeenth century as hunting grounds for the Knights, who released wild boar and deer here. It's Malta's only surviving mature woodland, a dense web of Aleppo pines, Mediterranean oaks, olives and carobs, with pathways weaving enticingly through the undergrowth of ivy. With the barrenness of much of the rest of the island, these gardens can get crowded with weekend picnickers and strollers. In autumn, the area is popular with birders, attracted by the migrating birds of prey – especially honey buzzards and harriers – that roost in the trees. Unfortunately, hunters are equally attracted to the gardens, even though they lie outside legal hunting areas; scuffles between birders and hunters are frequent.

Fomm Ir-Rih Bay

Map 1, C6.

On the coast some 8km northwest of Rabat is **Fomm Ir-Rih Bay**, as dramatic as it is bleak. It's not easy to find, and needs at least a half-day to justify the effort, but is one of Malta's wildest and most beautiful spots. No public transport runs even close, confining you to driving there or tackling the long hike (1hr 50min).

From Rabat's church square follow the signs to **Baħrija**, a small village just over 5km west of Rabat. Keep heading

AROUND RABAT

along Baħrija's main street, which dissects the village, and beyond the village take the first right, then right again. Here the landscape is rutted by a series of valleys and terraced cliffs, with "**RTO**" splashed everywhere in white paint (standing for "Reserved To Owner", put up by hunters and trappers to keep competitors and hikers alike out of their territory; see p.365). After the road slopes down into a valley, take the next right, a dirt road that ends in a clearing on the southern flank of the bay, from where a footpath meanders to the pebbly shore.

Owing to its relative inaccessibility, Fomm Ir-Riħ Bay (its name means "the mouth of the wind"), cut into the cliff and backed by gutted clay slopes, is generally quiet, the haunt of a some peace-seeking lovers and a handful of nude bathers. On calm days it is a tranquil cove of clear-blue sea and rocky boulders dotting the shallows, offering good **snorkelling** both in terms of variety of marine life and the underwater scenery.

Central Malta

Lying midway between Rabat to the west and Valletta (see p.41) and Sliema (see p.108) to the east is one of the most densely populated areas of Malta, a string of villages that have become subsumed into a suburban girdle around the capital. The three genteel, close-knit communities of **Attard**, **Balzan** and **Lija** together make up the **Three Villages**, set amidst open fields and offering addresses that are as highly desirable today for Maltese high society as they were in the seventeenth century. With public transport linking the three with Valletta and Mdina, it's easy to devote a pleasant half-day to strolling around the area, taking in the series of elegant parish **churches** and fine old townhouses, along with the splendid formal **gardens** of San Anton Palace. Few tourists bother to visit, adding to the villages' allure. Mosta, a short distance northwest of the Three Villages, is a busy young town that has little character, but is worth the bus-ride from Valletta to see the bulbous **Mosta Dome**, claimed to be Europe's third-largest church.

THE THREE VILLAGES

None of Malta's towns are as pleasant to wander through as the **Three Villages**. The new streets are wide and clean, the houses fronted by small gardens, the air fragranced by sweet-smelling foliage, while in the old town centres, the narrow, shaded lanes meandering between Baroque townhouses are a watercolourist's delight.

On what was a fertile agricultural plateau, the prospect of wide-open spaces and no limitations on the size of dwellings explains why the Three Villages attracted the bourgeoisie, who built Baroque houses surrounded by copses and large gardens. Grand Master Antoine de Paule started the trend in the 1620s when he built **San Anton Palace**, the third magisterial palace after Valletta's Grand Master's Palace and Verdala Palace. Others followed suit, and the Three Villages developed into wealthy, independent parishes. Today, despite their appealingly rustic moniker, the three are affluent and uncharacteristically spick-and-span suburbs, characterized by detached villas set well back from quiet streets. All, though, still feature a core of shaded alleys clustered quaintly around medieval parish churches. We've outlined here a **walking tour** that starts in the centre of Attard, continues past the San Anton Palace to Balzan, and ends in the middle of Lija; all three villages are well-served by buses from Valletta. Although there's only a kilometre or so between each village centre, you'll be hard-pushed to determine where one community ends and the next begins.

Attard

Map 1, H6.

A small, quiet pedestrianized square, Pjazza Tommaso Dingli, in the southeast corner of **ATTARD** is the setting for Dingli's own, beautiful, Renaissance **St Mary's Church**, designed in 1613. Buses #80 and #81 from Valletta stop at the junction of Triq Il-Belt Valletta and Triq In-Nutar Zarb, from where it's a short walk along Triq Il-Belt Valletta to the piazza. The square complements the harmonious lines of the church, which was designed on the form of the Latin cross. Its delicately stone-carved temple-like exterior is most striking, with three domes painted a deep pomegranate red, the middle one larger than the side two, and two standard belfries.

From the square, Triq Il-Kbira swerves northeast, past the police station, and then divides. Taking the left fork, Triq Sant Antnin, takes you to a crossroads, beyond which you can trace the high perimeter wall of **Villa Bologna**. This is one of Malta's largest villas, whose garden, only partially visible through the gates, occupies a whole block. The aristocrat Nicola Perdicomati Bologna built the villa in 1745 as a wedding present for his daughter; it was also the home of Lord Gerald Strickland, prime minister from 1927 to 1932. It's still privately owned, and is closed to the public.

San Anton Palace and Gardens

Map 1, H5. Triq Lord Strickland, Attard. Palace: no public access. Gardens: daily 7am–dusk; free.

Beyond Villa Bologna is a right turn into Triq Lord

Strickland, which leads to the entrance to the grand **San Anton Palace and Gardens**, at the corner with Triq Birkirkara. The large garden, with its towering, mature trees and various fountains, is enclosed behind high perimeter walls; it has the delight and intimacy of a private garden-turned-public, plus the added bonus of relatively few visitors.

The French Knight Antoine de Paule built a private house here in 1620. When he was elected Grand Master in 1623, de Paule enlarged both the house and its gardens, re-christening it **San Anton Palace**, the third magisterial palace. In its day, the palace had a full complement of servants, from valets and grooms to bakers and falconers, and even a clock-winder and rat-trapper: Grand Masters liked to spend lazy days in the lush tranquillity of San Anton, where they entertained guests and held state dinners. Emmanuel de Rohan Polduc, Grand Master from 1775 to 1797, spent his days at San Anton and only retreated to his palace in Valletta at night for security reasons. The palace continued to serve as the private residence of Malta's governors, and even played host to the Duke and Duchess of Edinburgh on their sojourn in 1876–77. Today, it's the official residence of Malta's president, and is consequently off-limits, but the garden has been open to the public since 1882.

San Anton Garden is laid out on a grid-pattern of cobbled paths: the main path crosses the garden from the street entrance on the east side over to the palace grounds in the northwest. Every transverse intersection of the paths is decorated by a stone fountain and pond – five in all – which are home to turtles as well as the usual ducks, swans and goldfish, and the garden bristles with towering trees, especially palms, oaks, ficus, cypresses and citrus groves. It's a lovely spot, with rustic stone benches around the ponds and stone-cut irrigation canals running alongside the paths.

THE THREE VILLAGES

Balzan and Lija

Map 1, H5.

From the gates of San Anton Garden, backtracking to Triq Sant Antnin and then heading right into Triq Il-Kbira brings you to the central square of the quiet village of **BALZAN**, overlooked by its **Parish Church of the Assumption**, built when Balzan became an independent parish in 1665. The church is modest by Maltese standards, but forms an attractive central feature in a town square ringed by Baroque townhouses.

The route from Balzan to its upmarket neighbour **LIJA** is convoluted, but short (only about ten minutes). From Balzan's church, retrace your steps along Triq Il-Kbira and take the first right into Triq Santa Marija. Head right (north) into Triq Il-Barriera, and when this street opens into Triq Mifsud Bonnići, continue right (north) then left (west) into Triq Ramiro Barbara. Another right turn north into Triq Il-Kbira will lead you to Lija's central square, **Misraħ It-Trasfigurazzjoni**.

Lija is renowned for its huge *festa*, held on the weekend closest to August 6 and featuring the largest fireworks display in Malta.

On the square is the **Lija Parish Church**, dating from the 1690s. It is a large and dramatic building, but otherwise unremarkable, raised on a platform and framed by two plinths.

North of the square, Triq Sir Ugo Mifsud Bonnići leads to Lija's **Old Parish Church** of St Saviour, a modest early-sixteenth-century rectangular building topped by one of Malta's earliest domes, which forms a stylistic bridge from vernacular medieval chapels with their pitched roofs to later, grander churches of the Baroque period.

MOSTA

Map 1, G5

Lying about 3km west of the Three Villages, **MOSTA** is built on an escarpment above the Great Fault, which runs to the west of the town. A somewhat characterless urban sprawl, Mosta is nonetheless squarely on the tourist trail for its nineteenth-century parish church of Santa Marija, which is known to one and all as the **Mosta Dome**. Visible from vantage points all over Malta, it's undoubtedly impressive, but the feverish hype surrounding it says more about the Maltese awe of anything gigantic than about its true artistic importance.

Buses #43, #44, #45, #49, #50, #58 and #86 from Valletta drop off on Mosta's Pjazza Rotunda, home of the dome.

The Mosta Dome

Pjazza Rotunda. Daily 5am–noon & 3–8pm; free.

Even before it had got off the drawing-board, the **Mosta Dome** at the centre of the town was courting controversy. The architect Georges Grognet de Vasse designed the church with a circular, instead of a more usual cruciform, floor-plan – and so an invitation to lay the foundation stone was snubbed by the archbishop, who muttered that the church reminded him of a mosque. Building began regardless in 1833 around Mosta's old parish church, which was left intact to be used as scaffolding; some 27 years later, the dome was complete, and the old church was dismantled. The controversy surrounding the building continues, however. It is claimed that this is Europe's **third largest dome**, behind the Pantheon and St Peter's in Rome – although measuring domes is an inexact science, and Hagia Sofia in Istanbul and the new church at Xewkija on Gozo (see p.206) have both staked claims to the title.

The church's **facade** mimics the Pantheon, with a portico featuring twin rows of six columns; two belfries stick up awkwardly against the bulk of the dome. Sixteen windows and a lantern-light illuminate the **interior**, with its coffered ceiling of gilded stone-carved flowers set on a blue background swirling around the yawning inner face of the dome and a floor of inlaid marble, also in a geometric pattern. The famous Maltese artist **Giuseppe Cali** painted the murals above the side altars at the beginning of the twentieth century, but sadly Cali's work here is too high up to display his abilities to any effect.

Left of the altar, the sacristy is dedicated to recounting, in pictures and rambling text, what has been dubbed the **Miracle of St Mary**. In World War II, as a congregation of three hundred people waited for Mass under the dome, a Luftwaffe bomb pierced the ceiling and skittered along the floor. When it failed to explode, the parishioners put the episode down to divine intervention.

The northwest

A n absorbing combination of full-scale resort towns and sandy beaches within easy reach of little-visited rural tracts, and significant historical sights alongside tourist tack, **northwest Malta** is an exercise in contrariety. The area boasts Malta's most scenic landscapes, a series of rugged, humpback ridges of garigue – the Wardija, Bajda, Mellieħa and Marfa ridges – rolling into wide valleys patchworked with agricultural fields that deliver some of the island's choicest produce.

The **northwest tip** – three spits of land jutting into the Mediterranean and sloping gently down to the water at two twin bays – sees some of the island's heaviest tourist traffic. Most of the holiday trappings are concentrated around the calm waters of St Paul's Bay on the northern coast, where back-to-back hotels and rows of multistorey apartment blocks make up the bulk of **Buġibba**, on the eastern side of the bay. Malta's only true sun'n' sea resort, it's popular with British package tourists, and has several rocky lidos from which to swim as well as a glut of rather tacky restaurants and bars. The apartment blocks have also marched south along the bay, engulfing the former fishing village of **St Paul's Bay**, more quiescent than its neighbour and boasting a couple of intriguing historical sights linked to the **shipwreck of St Paul**, which is said to have taken place here in 60 AD. Rising up from the west side of the bay, the Mellieħa Ridge holds the primarily residential town of **Mellieħa**, a place of pilgrimage for its **medieval shrines**, which are said to have healing powers. Beyond the town proper, apartment blocks have spilled down the hills to colonize the rims of **Mellieħa Bay**, Malta's largest and most popular sandy beach.

The opposite shore – the northeast coast – is Malta's least populated area, punctuated by a series of inlets and beaches that cut through the headlands jutting into the sea. The only town of any size is mildly diverting **Mġarr**, but the real draw here are some of the island's most dramatic sandy **beaches**: **Golden Bay** and the neighbouring coves of **Ġnejna** and **Għajn Tuffieħa**. Inland, the area is dedicated to agriculture rather than recreation; Pwales Valley, its parcels of agricultural land and concentration of greenhouses extending all the way to St Paul's Bay, is particularly fertile, but other than a visit to the absorbing re-creation of an air-raid shelter at Mġarr, there's little to draw you away from the coast.

The area covered in this chapter is relatively small, and you can see all the sights in a day via the **buses** that run between the resorts and along the northwest coast; the only exceptions are Mġarr and Ġnejna Bay, which are connected by buses from Valletta; from Buġibba, you have to detour via Għajn Tuffieħa for Mġarr. If you're planning on nighttime excursions to St Julian's or Paceville (see pp.115 and 117), though, you're best off **renting a car**, as taxi rates are a rip-off hereabouts.

BUĠIBBA

Occupying a cone-shaped peninsula on the eastern side of St Paul's Bay, the sprawling resort town of **BUĠIBBA** was inhabited during the Neolithic era, and was fortified by the

Knights, but it consisted largely of open fields until the 1960s. During the 1970s and 1980s, Maltese speculators, bewitched by the lucrative earnings from early tourism, developed Buġibba with heady recklessness. There was no unifying vision and little cohesive planning to the building programme, with multistorey apartment blocks and hotels erected in the shortest time possible to monumentally ugly effect. Aesthetics were always an afterthought, and it was only in the 1990s that belated beautification efforts began – the area now boasts smooth tarmacked roads, neat pavements, plenty of palm trees and an attractive pedestrianized centre. The upside of all this development is that Buġibba boasts plenty of accommodation options in all categories, and serves as a convenient, lively base from which to explore the northwest.

Buġibba's **bus terminus** (Map 6, D4) is on Triq It-Turisti, about a ten-minute walk northeast of Bay Square. Bus #58 shuttles between here and Valletta, but the rest of the services are tailored around the main sights: #48 to Ċirkewwa via St Paul's Bay and Mellieħa; #51 to Għajn Tuffieħa and Golden Bay; #86 to Rabat and Mdina; #427 to Marsaxlokk; and #627 to Sliema and the Three Cities.

Picturesquely situated, with views out to sea, **Bay Square** (Map 6, B5) is the pedestrianized heart of Buġibba. It's a sunny, pleasant plaza fringed by several bars, whose outdoor chairs and tables are perfect for watching the world go by. The web of streets surrounding Bay Square, especially west towards the aptly named **Triq It-Turisti** Map 6, D5–E4 (Tourist St), are usually jammed with cars, strolling holiday-makers and hordes of persistent time-share touts, while souvenir shops are back to back with car rental agencies and tour operators offering all kinds of manufactured excursions round the islands. The bars along here, including

BUĠIBBA

some cheap imitation British pubs, are largely rather tawdry, however, and amid the rows of uninspiring pizza-pasta-steak houses, only a handful of restaurants stand out.

On the other side of the coast road that skirts the town (Islets Promenade), the narrow rocky shoreline slopes gently towards the water, and serves as the main local **bathing** spot. Though the rocks are sharp and uncomfortable, and the waves sometimes wash up unsightly flotsam, the sea offers an inviting variegation of blues; some of the cleaner stretches are good for snorkelling, and all manner of water sports are on offer. For a more comfortable day by the sea, head to one of various **lidos** that punctuate the shoreline. The best options are those maintained by the *New Dolmen Hotel*, on the Islets Promenade side of the bay (Map 6, C2), and, on the opposite side of the shore along Dawret Il-Qawra, the *Suncrest Hotel* lido (Map 6, G2). For Lm2, you get the luxury of a sun lounger, umbrella and use of showers, the bar, and platforms and ladders to get in and out of the water.

ST PAUL'S BAY

Working southwest around the bay, Buġibba meshes almost imperceptibly into the small town of **ST PAUL'S BAY**, a ribbon of development that skirts the coast towards the inner mouth of the bay proper and erupts into a mass of apartment blocks on the opposite side of the bay. At the beginning of the twentieth century, St Paul's Bay was inhabited by a fishing community of less than two hundred inhabitants, and though a small fishing fleet is still based here, lending a picturesque aspect to the place, tourism is the main earner today, and the town has a part-residential, part-resort feel. With only a handful of bars and restaurants, St Paul's Bay is Buġibba's modest sister – minus the congestion and the touts. Although there are no sandy beaches, the horseshoe-shaped, pebbly **Mistra Bay** to the north offers inviting azure sea and good snorkelling.

As the place where St Paul's ship ran aground in 60 AD (see box overleaf), the town holds a soft spot in the Maltese psyche. He's said to have scrambled ashore at **St Paul's Shipwreck Church**, whereupon he thanked the Maltese for his life by miraculously removing the venom from the islands' snakes forever. Saintly myths notwithstanding, there's little other than the **Wignacourt Tower** to explore. The only one of the Knights' defensive towers open to the public, it's also unique in holding the island's sole exhibition on Maltese military architecture. Otherwise, the best plan is to soak up the scene – a refreshingly peaceful alternative to the chips-and-vinegar seaside tack of Buġibba.

St Paul's Bay is a ten-minute walk along the waterfront Dawret Il-Gzejjer west of Buġibba; buses #49 and #86 from Valletta and #427 from Sliema both call at a stop in front of St Paul's Shipwreck Church.

St Paul's Shipwreck Church

Map 7, I4. Triq Il-Knisja. Daily 6.30–8am & 6–8pm; free.
Right at the waterfront, the small **St Paul's Shipwreck Church** was originally erected in the early fourteenth century. Grand Master Alof de Wignacourt's attempts to elevate the church's appearance during the seventeenth century – enlarging it and surrounding it with a raised, arcaded portico and adding a bald and tiny belfry – made it neither attractive nor prominent, however, and it hardly lives up to the hype that surrounds it. The entire building was flattened by a stray World War II bomb in any case, and today's building is a mere reconstruction. It's a simple stone struc-ture, and the diminutive interior is largely bare, with bland stone altar with a motif of the Maltese Cross carved on its

ST PAUL'S SHIPWRECK

Given Malta's Catholic sensibilities – 99 percent of islanders follow the faith, and 70 percent attend Mass every Sunday – it's hardly surprising that the biblical story of **St Paul's Shipwreck**, the single event that's said to have first brought Christianity to Malta, is still a prominent feature of the local calendar, with the February 10 anniversary a public holiday.

Though it's a myth (there are only a few pieces of circumstantial evidence, and historians agree that he's more likely to have been stranded in Kefallinia, Greece), the story goes back to Luke's biblical account of the wreck detailed in the Acts of the Apostles. The account took place during St Paul's journey from Jerusalem to Rome, where he was to stand trial for heresy. The ship met a fierce storm (seen in a premonition by Paul, who prophesied that all 146 passengers would survive the wreck), and ran aground on the rocky shore of what's now St Paul's Bay. After the passengers scrambled ashore, local people helped them to gather wood to build fires. When a snake bit St Paul on the wrist, and he survived unscathed, the locals concluded that he must be a **saint**; he's later said to

face, and an uninspiring altarpiece depicting St Paul with his hands thrown up in glory.

Wignacourt Tower

Map 7, H4. Triq San Ġeraldu. July–Sept Mon–Sat 9am–1pm; Oct–June Mon–Fri 9.30am–4pm & Sat–Sun 9.30am–1pm; free.

A couple of minutes' walk east of the St Paul's Shipwreck Church, beyond the small, laid-back fishermen's cove, Triq San Ġeraldu branches left along the coast toward where the prominent **Wignacourt Tower** erupts. Built in 1609 to guard the entrance into St Paul's Bay, it's one of the largest have miraculously removed the venom from Maltese snakes forever (and there are no poisonous snakes in the islands today). For three days after the wreck, then-Governor **Publius** accommodated St Paul in his country villa, during which time he healed Publius' terminally ill father. Publius immediately converted to Christianity (he was later made Malta's first **bishop**, an unlikely proposition for a Roman governor), and the rest of the population soon followed suit, a devotion that's still unshaken some 2000 years later. St Paul himself is said to have spent three months hunkered down in St Paul's Grotto in Rabat (see p.138), healing the sick and **baptizing** a deluge of converts.

Maltese are zealously proud of the fact that their Catholic roots go directly back to St Paul; he's the island's patron saint, and there are shrines and pilgrimage sites dedicated to him all over the island. Maltese schools still present the shipwreck as fact, a rather flagrant attempt to rewrite history to justify the Catholic Church's cultural domination. In the bay itself, there are two commemorative **statues** of St Paul: one on St Paul's Islands at the mouth of the bay, and another serving as an underwater attraction for divers.

of the chain of defence towers around Malta's coastline, and it served as a prototype for subsequent larger versions, such as St Mary's in Comino (see p.233). A squarish, boxy design, its walls rise solidly to four turrets that are partly embedded into the structure and jut above the four corners.

Wignacourt Tower has two floors to explore. The entrance on the **ground floor** was cut through during British rule; originally, a staircase led to the drawbridge and doorway on the first floor. The lower room, with a fine barrel-vaulted ceiling, holds a small permanent **exhibition** on the Knights' military architecture in Malta. Prints of the original designs and wooden or plaster models of the coastal

ST PAUL'S BAY

forts and the larger defence structures such as the Floriana and Cottonera Lines (see pp.87 and 102) are accompanied by detailed descriptive panels which breathe life into the displays. Reachable via a spiral staircase, the **first floor** room holds a re-creation of the living quarters of the **Capomastro** (master bombardier), who was in charge of the tower with the assistance of two gunners. The original stone cooking hearth remains, and plain period furniture – a bed, table and benches – have been installed, as well as militaria from cannonballs to lances, muskets and swords. Stairs lead to the roof where you can see one of the two original **cannons**, and enjoy the calm vista of St Paul's Islands at the mouth of the bay.

MISTRA BAY

Map 1, D3.

On the opposite side of St Paul's Bay to the town, **Mistra Bay** is a small, horseshoe-shaped inlet that offers azure-green sea and good snorkelling. The shoreline, however, consists of a strip of pebbles backed by the road that skirts the bay, while the only building in the area is a rather uninspiring pizzeria. Mistra lies at the head of a shallow valley bristling with bamboo; to the northeast, it's backed by terraced fields stepping up to the Mellieħa Ridge; to the southwest, there's a rocky headland smothered with scrubby maquis vegetation which serves as a popular playground for amateur rock climbers. A few small boats anchor in the bay, and the cove never really gets busy owing to the discomfort of lying on pebbles or cramped rocky surfaces.

The best way to get to Mistra is via the #648 bus; the route starts at Buġibba's bus terminus and follows the coast road round the bay (the #44 and #45 from Valletta, and #645 from Sliema also run here). Get off at the first bus stop beyond the last houses of St Paul's Bay town, where the signposted side road to Mistra Bay branches off from the main. From here, it's a fifteen-minute walk to the bay.

MELLIEĦA

Map 1, C3.

The northernmost town in Malta, **MELLIEĦA**, about 5km northwest of St Paul's Bay, spreads over the Mellieħa Ridge, its string of holiday apartments and exclusive villas clinging limpet-like to the slopes and cliffs. Although settlements have existed here since prehistoric times, Mellieħa's geographical vulnerability (northern Malta was never fortified to the extent of Valletta or Sliema) ensured that the area was never heavily populated until the Knights offered the mantle of protection in the seventeenth century, via the construction of coastal towers and forts. Since then, the population has grown steadily, but Mellieħa remained relatively isolated until the advent of the motor car, and local people still retain a separate dialect. These days – the onslaught of tourism notwithstanding – many remain tied to their rural roots, subsisting largely on farming, hunting and fishing.

The last thirty years have seen an influx of tourists, though, and on the fringes of the largely anonymous residential sprawl, several hotels and apartment blocks have sprung up to cater for them. The narrow, sloping Triq Ġorġ Borġ Olivier defines the town centre, and holds a smorgasbord of small shops and restaurants, including two of the best places to eat in the islands. At its north end, Triq Ġorġ Borġ Olivier opens into Misraħ Iż-Żjara Tal-Papa, home to the many buildings of the **Mellieħa Parish Church Complex**, the town's only historic sight. This attractive cluster of medieval chapels, partly hewn into the rock, are topped by a modern parish church that stands on a bluff like a space shuttle ready for takeoff. North of town, the land rolls down to **Mellieħa Bay**, a large and attractive sandy beach that suffers from overcrowding in summer. To the west, the Mellieħa Ridge's mysterious valleys and garigue plains offer excellent rambling possibilities.

As Mellieħa is rather remote, you'll end up going to Buġibba if you're planning on seeing the northwest's sights by public transport. The #648 bus from Buġibba's terminal runs along Triq Ġorġ Borġ Olivier where it opens into Misraħ Iż-Żjara Tal-Papa in the town centre, as do buses #44 and #45 from Valletta, and #645 from Sliema – before continuing to Mellieħa Bay and on to Ċirkewwa for the Gozo ferries.

Grotto of Our Lady

Triq Ġorġ Borġ Olivier. Daily 8am–6pm; free.

Across the street from the bus stop on Triq Ġorġ Borġ Olivier, an unmarked doorway opens onto a staircase cutting through a small, ivy-clogged valley to the rock-cut chapel called **Grotto of Our Lady**. Legend has it that a Sicilian wine merchant paid for the structure to be dug into the side of the valley in the twelfth century, though no-one's sure why he chose this spot. Inside, the only decoration under the slightly pitched roof is an unremarkable **statue of the Madonna** enclosed by a metal grille; this, as well as the waters of an underground **spring** that was struck during construction and rerouted through the chapel, are said to have miraculous healing powers; in the twentieth century, a group of worshippers swore that they witnessed the Madonna gesture the shape of a cross. Many still have faith in the redemptive properties, and the multiple candles left by believers give off a somewhat surreal light.

The Sanctuary and Church of Our Lady

Daily 8am–noon & 4–6pm; free.

At the north end of Misraħ Iż-Żjara Tal-Papa, passing

MELLIEĦA

under the Monumental Arch – a stone Baroque construction dating back to 1716 – takes you into the small **Sanctuary** complex. Just through the arch is a lovely courtyard that forms the heart of the complex, decorated by a crude statue of the Madonna at its centre, and with a simple yet charming one-storey vernacular building on the right flank built in the eighteenth-century to lodge pilgrims. On the left is the **Church of Our Lady of Mellieħa**, an elegant structure embedded into the rockface. The entrance leads to the small sacristy, and on the left you can see the **Crypt**, a small cave dug in the sixteenth century as a shrine and now converted into a kitchen for the parish priest. On the right, a tunnel heads into the church proper – it's lined with votive offerings from people allegedly healed by the power of the church's fresco. Having mutated from the Crypt as an extension to the original shrine, the church was enlarged twice: half of it burrows into the rock, while the rest is constructed; the built part, which includes a large belfry, meshes seamlessly into the rockface. The dimly lit interior is beautiful in its crude simplicity: the walls are covered with marble, cut along the cross-section to reveal streaky, rippling veins, while the **altar** is framed by two marble columns and an arch topped by a crescent of gold mosaic. Until recently, the **fresco** that makes up the altarpiece, depicting the Madonna cradling Jesus in her arms, was thought to have been painted by St Luke in 60 AD – the reason for its supposed healing powers. However, recent studies have dated the fresco to the thirteenth century.

Mellieħa Parish Church

Daily 6–8.30am & 5–7.30pm; free.

At the north head of the Sanctuary courtyard, a second archway and staircase leads to the **Mellieħa Parish**

Church. Built on a bluff between 1881 and 1898, and dedicated to the Birth of Our Lady, it's a prominent feature of the Mellieħa skyline. Imposing it may be, but architecturally it's pretty dull, a lean structure with belfries and a dome, the panels of its facade finishing in decorative scrolls. The airy interior is set on bare stone, the panelled piers topped by a smattering of flowery, Baroque motifs. You can get a rather more diverting sight by walking behind the church, where there is a small garden perched atop the Mellieħa Ridge: the view takes in Mellieħa Bay and the span of Marfa Ridge.

Mellieħa Bay

Map 1, B3.

Malta's most expansive sandy beach, **Mellieħa Bay** is about 2km from the town centre via Triq Il-Marfa, which strikes off Triq Ġorġ Borg Olivier. Around a kilometre long, the sandy beach is backed by the road, and there's plenty of space to park. It's Malta's most popular strip of sand, particularly favoured by families owing to the sandbank that makes the water ankle-deep one hundred metres into the sea, as well as being the only beach in Malta that's patrolled by lifeguards, and though attractive, it's very crowded during the summer. A few hotels have grown round the edges of the bay, and it's well served with facilities: watersports equipment, umbrellas and sun loungers for hire, and several kiosks that offer drinks and bland pizzas, fries and burgers. In the evenings, the beach is usually dotted with hundreds of smoking barbecues – a favourite Maltese pastime – and an appetizing smell of grilled meats envelopes the bay.

Bus #648 runs from Mellieħa town centre to the bay.

POPEYE'S VILLAGE

Map 1, B3. Daily: Oct–March 9am–5pm; April–Sept 9am–7pm; adults Lm2.75, children Lm1.75.

Just under 2km west of Mellieħa Bay, and reachable via a secondary road that swings off the Mellieħa bypass (which loops around the town's western outskirts), the well-signposted **Popeye's Village** is little more than the detritus of the film set constructed for the Robert Altman film *Popeye, the Movie* – a commercial flop starring Robin Williams that was made here in 1979. The ubiquitous advertising and pervasive signage might lead you to believe that Popeye's Village is a sight you can't miss: on the contrary, it's essentially a tourist scam. After the film was shot and the set had destroyed the banks of the once-beautiful Anchor Bay, a local entrepreneur put up a gate and started charging an entrance fee to see what is, twenty years on, the sagging, cracking and peeling cluster of wooden houses that made up the set. To make matters worse, a small sandy beach that survived Hollywood's bulldozers has now been concreted over.

If your children nag you into squandering the entrance fee, you get to dawdle through the semi-ruined houses and take snapshots standing next to crude wooden casts of Popeye and the rest of the characters, or play for half an hour in a small field that's misleadingly called a "fun park". Worse still, there are plenty of opportunities to shell out further on tacky souvenirs. If you want to cast a passing glance over the place but don't want to pay the fee, carry on past the entrance, following the farmers' road for about 50m to the edge of the cliff overlooking Anchor Bay, from where there's a good view of the village below – it looks more attractive the further you stand away from it.

POPEYE'S VILLAGE

AROUND THE MARFA RIDGE

North of Mellieħa Bay, the road that skirts the bay climbs to the **Marfa Ridge**, a rugged crest of garigue interspersed by groves of trees planted during a 1970s reforestation drive. The road, which continues to Ċirkewwa (where the Gozo ferries dock), divides the Marfa Ridge southwest from northeast; dominating the southwest peninsula is the fairy-tale-looking Red Tower, surrounded by some fabulous seacliff scenery at windswept Ras Il-Qammiegħ; the northeast side of the peninsula, L-Aħrax Tal-Mellieħa, is less visually attractive, but does hold a couple of decent beaches.

If you're not walking from Mellieħa, you can take bus #648 from Buġibba, or the #45 from Valletta and #645 from Sliema; alight at the bus stop by a junction just above Mellieħa Bay (look out for a Catholic niche dedicated to the Madonna at the side of the road). From here the peninsula is easily explorable on foot.

The Red Tower and Ras Il-Qammiegħ

From the bus stop above Mellieħa Bay, the **Red Tower** (Map 1, B3) is easily visible to the west, accessible via a secondary road that branches off the main road to the southwest. Erected in 1649 as St Agatha's Tower, its current name derives from the dried-blood paint job on the exterior walls. It's a boxy construction with a framework of four mini-towers at each corner; from a distance, its saw-toothed roof parapet and sooty-red colour lend a whimsical aspect, but up close, it looks stoutly impenetrable. The Knights installed cannons and stationed soldiers here, making it the main hinge of defence in this part of the island. The British kept the tower active, and during World War II it served as a signalling station. These days, two Maltese army personnel monitor seacraft passing through Maltese waters, and as such, the Red Tower is not open to the public.

The side road to the tower continues west along the crest of the ridge until it peters out completely about 2km on near the edge of the cliff at Ras Il-Qammiegħ – the views on both sides are worth the trek. The road cuts through thyme-scented garigue, a windswept, scrubby landscape dotted with the stone huts of bird trappers and hunters. Groups of young people sit around picnicking on weekends, and it's a popular spot for strolling lovers. At the head of the ridge, the **Ras Il-Qammiegħ** cliffs (Map 1, A3) plummet down dramatically to steep slopes of clay; at the base, gigantic boulders tumble towards a purple-blue sea. Facing south, you see the craggy meander of the cliffs and inlets that characterize the area's coastline; facing north, you can pick out Comino and Gozo.

Paradise Bay

Map 1, A2.

The small sandy beach of **Paradise Bay** snuggled into an inlet enclosed to the north by the Ċirkewwa promontory (a spit of land where ferries depart to Gozo). Far more scenic, and boasting clearer seas than Mellieħa Bay, it's the best place to swim hereabouts, with a sunrise-coloured swath of sand nestled between the stands of bamboo that stretch down the cliff. The sea is an inviting turquoise, and there's some good snorkelling to be had along the rocky boulders that stretch either side of the beach. There's a car park at the top of the cliffs, and a bar that serves palatable refreshments as well as staging boisterous afternoon **beach parties** for Malta's energetic ravers. On summer Sunday afternoons the excellent DJ-mixed music ranges from Balearic tunes to rhythmic Latin and house. If you're after peace, Sundays are best avoided, but like all Malta's sandy beaches, Paradise Bay is pretty crowded throughout the summer.

Bus #648 from Buġibba, as well as the #45 from Valletta and #645 from Sliema, will drop you at the start of the path to Paradise Bay (ask the driver), from where it's a 1.5km walk to the beach.

L-Aħrax Tal-Mellieħa

Map 1, B2.

The area northeast of the road that divides the Marfa Ridge is known as the **L-Aħrax Tal-Mellieħa** – which translates as "the wilds of Mellieħa", an apt title for an area that attracts some of the island's most unruly characters. It's largely comprised of sparse, scrubby woodland, forested in the 1970s, now being slowly eroded by slash-and-burn farming or hunters making way for trapping sites. The only reason to visit is for the pair of small **beaches** on the northern shore, facing Comino.

To get to the beaches, follow the road that strikes off to the northeast from the bus stop at the junction above Mellieħa Bay. The more westerly of the two, **Ramla Bay** is reachable via the first left fork, a distance of just over 2km. It's a mildly attractive crescent-shaped bay with a strip of sand and a shallow swell, quiet on weekdays but invaded by hordes of loud Maltese families on weekends. For more privacy, you can pay Lm2 to use the **lido** (for this you get a sun lounger and access to a bar) of the *Ramla Bay Hotel* on the western flank of the bay. Beyond the eastern shore, the bay is tempered by the growing tentacles of the shanty settlement centred around the next beach, Armier Bay. As Ramla Bay is sporadically contaminated by sewage, you might want to check pollution levels with staff at the headquarters of the Malta Tourism Authority (☎224444) before heading there.

What was once a beautiful beach, **Armier Bay** (some 3km from the bus stop and reachable from the third left fork in the road) has been ruined by ramshackle squatter settlements clustered round the bay; the five hundred or so concrete shacks have all been built here illegally on public land in the last forty years. In the 1990s, the government attempted to bulldoze the settlements on various occasions, but the squatters blockaded the roads with cars and, following tense showdowns, the authorities and the cordons of police backed off. These days, the government seems to be dealing with the shantytown by official blindness: on maps, the anonymous town is left blank, and not even the streets winding through the settlements are marked or named. As the waters of the bay are contaminated by **sewage** from the shacks, it's not a place to come for a swim, but it does provide access to some of the best **scuba diving** in Malta – a safe 1km away from the shore.

GĦAJN TUFFIEĦA AND GOLDEN BAY

Map 1, B5.

Across the coast from St Paul's Bay, and reachable via a road that winds along Pwales Valley 5km west of St Paul's Bay, **Għajn Tuffieħa** and **Golden Bay** are twin sandy beaches separated by a gently rounded peninsula. A combination of easy access – they're both on main roads and are served by bus #51 from Buġibba, #47 from Valletta (via Mġarr) and #652 from Sliema – and stunning natural beauty make these some of Malta's most attractive and, consequently, popular beaches, perfect for a relaxing day by the sea. Both have adjacent car parks at the top of the cliffs, and kiosks offering refreshments on the shore.

The more southern of the two, **Għajn Tuffieħa** is enclosed by dramatic cliffs and clay slopes, its small, crescent-shaped sandy shore reached via a flight of stairs from the car park. It typically attracts image-conscious twenty-something Maltese, and it's an experience of brief designer swimsuits and flashy sunglasses, awash with the pungent smell of suntan oil; you'll feel at home sunbathing topless here. Just south of the bay proper via a footpath that winds along the shore, there's a smaller sandy cove that has become Malta's unofficial **nude beach**. For more on Malta's nude beaches, see p.310.

Golden Bay, the north beach, is partly spoiled by the development that envelops the bay: a road runs down from the main to the side of the beach, where it opens into a tar-macked car park, and the ambience is partly ruined by the unsightly, worn-out multistorey block of the *Golden Sands Hotel* that erupts over the cliff. Nonetheless, the large swath of sand is unusual in its crimson tinge, and the headlands dramatic. Golden Bay gets more crowded than Għajn Tuffieħa during the summer, attracting a mix of young Maltese and hotel residents, and the full range of water sports are on offer.

MĠARR

Map 1, D5.

A few kilometres inland and southeast of Għajn Tuffieħa, the small town of **MĠARR** is very much cut off from any of its neighbours, surrounded by the rural land that makes this Malta's least populated region. As you approach, passing through fields webbed charmingly with rubble walls, Mġarr suddenly bursts onto the horizon: its ugly egg-shaped parish church rising at the centre of anonymous concentric suburbs. First settled in the 1850s, the town is home to a mostly farming community who grow all manner of produce in the surrounding land – particularly strawberries, shielded by the low-lying plastic tunnels that are ubiquitous hereabouts. Tractors trundle through the streets and trucks

MĠARR

loaded with produce on the way to the market are a common sight. The town goes to sleep with the roosters, and has no cultural or social life to speak of – the only reason to visit is to tour the well-preserved **Mġarr Air Raid Shelter** in the town square. You also have to pass through the fringes of the town to get to **Ġnejna Bay**, 3km to the west, a scenic sandy beach at the mouth of a valley that's been partially claimed as Malta's best-known **gay beach**.

Bus #47 from Valletta calls at the Mġarr town square, before continuing to Għajn Tuffieħa. An alternative route from Buġibba is to take the #51 to Għajn Tuffieħa, then connect with #47 on its way back to Mġarr.

Mġarr Air Raid Shelter

Il-Barri Restaurant, Wesghat Il-Ġublew. Tues–Sat 9am–2pm, Sun 9–11.30am; Lm1.

Pickaxed into the globigerina limestone, the **Mġarr Air Raid Shelter** covers an area of 225 square metres, and provided protection from World War II bombs for all two hundred of Mġarr's residents in a claustrophobic, underground hive of rooms and tunnels – an atmosphere evocatively re-created by the shelter's careful restoration. The entrance is through *Il-Barri Restaurant* at the north side of the town square. Before you enter the shelter proper, a six-minute video commentary about the war sets the tone, with period footage of bomb raids. You then go into the long main tunnel, from where rooms housing the displays branch off; an audio commentary details shelter life in general. Waxwork props of wounded people pepper the corridors, while individual rooms are re-created using period furnishings: **family rooms** with bunk beds, kerosene stoves and candles, and a **classroom** fitted out with benches, desks and blackboards. The furniture is covered in veils of damp mildew and the walls beaded with condensed

MĠARR

water. At the centre of the complex is a secondary tunnel that served as a **clinic** for the wounded.

WORLD WAR II'S SUBTERRANEAN LIFE

When it became clear to the British authorities that Malta's strategic position would make it a target for heavy bombing during World War II, the decision was taken to create a network of subterranean **shelters** – this foresight proved crucial in 1941–42, when the island suffered the uneasy distinction of being the most heavily bombed country involved in the conflict.

At the outbreak of the war, Malta's inhabitants had climbed down wells, cowered underneath tables or crowded into caves to protect themselves from air raids. Such makeshift refuges offered only superficial protection, though, and in 1940, the shelter-building programme began. Pickaxes were moulded at the dockyards and an army of diggers deployed to gouge the 841 public shelters that accommodated some 170,000 people. Ten thousand bunk beds were installed, and each shelter had a classroom, a clinic and a chapel.

Those who were better off either dug their own **private shelters** underneath their houses (and invited their neighbours to join them), or got government permits to buy their own enclave in public shelters – paying Lm20 to Lm30 (about one-third of the average annual salary) to have their own private room. For everyone, though, life in the shelters was **claustro-phobic**, the thin, damp and warm air providing the ideal conditions for diseases to attack the already emaciated population. In a bid to halt the spread of contagious diseases, the wounded were kept apart from the healthy, and children separated from adults.

Today, some of the shelters are used as water reservoirs, but most are closed up – in some town squares you can still spot the former entrances, now sealed by concrete slabs.

MĠARR

ĠNEJNA BAY

Map 1, C5.

Some 3km down a winding valley road west of Mġarr's town square, **Ġnejna Bay** is a large, scenic beach where you could easily spend a day, losing track of time as you explore its clear, calm water. There are no public transport connections, but the road is well signposted and there's a car park backing onto the sand. Nestled in a trough at the mouth of a valley that bristles with bamboo, it's a dramatic spot, with clay slopes and crumbling cliffs rising up sharply from the relatively small patch of dull-orange sand, while a Knightly coastal tower guards the bay from its vantage point at the edge of a rocky bluff. Though it's popular with Maltese families during the summer, when water-sports operators offer canoes and jet-skis for rent, it's largely off the tourist trail. A kiosk sells refreshments and snacks all year round.

About 500 metres north, along a meandering coastline not visible from the main beach (but in the same bay), a rocky plateau surrounded by inviting azure sea serves as Malta's only **gay beach** (see p.306). The watersports centre operates an informal speedboat shuttle service, costing Lm2 for drop-off and pick-up.

The southeast

Although the **southeast** – the chunk of land east of an imaginary line drawn between the Three Cities and Dingli Cliffs – constitutes about a third of Malta's landmass, it's one of the island's least-developed regions, home to only a handful of scattered sights. The area is peppered with working-class towns that have a haphazard and dusty feel, squatting in the shadow of obnoxious car dumps, industrial estates, tarmac plants, a waste recycling plant and the Delimara Power Station at Marsaxlokk. It's not a particularly attractive region overall, but its highlights – the **Hypogeum**, a hallucinatory Neolithic underground necropolis and place of worship, and the other three **Neolithic temples** of Tarxien, Ħaġar Qim and Mnajdra – are an absolute must-see. Listed by UNESCO as World Heritage Sites, these impressively colossal circular temple complexes are the oldest built structures in the world, and rank among the globe's most important ancient monuments. Aside from the temples, **Wied Iż-Żurrieq** is worth an afternoon for its spectacular scenery of seacliffs and gorges, and those with a paleontological bent will enjoy perusing the collection of ancient remains displayed at the expansive **Għar Dalam Cave**.

The southeast's sights are scattered around the area, and you'll need to take separate bus journeys from Valletta to see them (though the #38 covers both Ħaġar Qim and Mnajdra as well as Wied Iz-Żurrieq). Although the important sights are well signposted, the tourist infrastructure in the southeast consists of only a handful of accommodation options, virtually no nightlife and a largely mundane eating scene, save for a handful of excellent fish restaurants at Marsascala and **Marsaxlokk** to the extreme southeast. The latter is still the home port for Malta's largest fishing fleet, and conveniently close to the swimming spots of the **Delimara peninsula**: bathing holes cut into attractive white cliffs, lapped by clear blue water.

The underdevelopment of the southeast, coupled with the proliferation of ugly industrial buildings, reinforces Malta's socioeconomic north–south divide: the southeast is more working class while the north is more conservative; culturally, the southeast is less affluent and educated. This anomaly has led to simmering antipathy, and in the politically tumultuous 1980s it provided a stage for often violent **political hostilities**: a series of bombings culminated in the ambush of PN supporters by gun-toting Labour thugs on the Tal-Barrani road (near Marsaxlokk) in 1987. Nerves have been lulled in the 1990s following a growing awareness that more investment needs to be pumped into the region, but the locals, however, retain a touch of proud defiance in reaction to what they perceive as a north-centred political and cultural elite.

ADDOLORATA CEMETERY

Map 1, J6. Triq Il-Labour. Daily 7am–5pm; free.
Malta's largest burial ground, designed by Maltese architect Emanuele Luigi Galizia and consecrated in 1869, **Addolorata Cemetery** is set on the outskirts of the town of Marsa, just inland from the inner creeks of the Grand Harbour. While it's hardly one of the island's major

highlights, there's some interesting Gothic Revival architecture to admire, and the lush landscaping makes it a pleasant place to wander for an afternoon. To get there, take buses #1, #2, #4 or #6 from Valletta and alight outside the Malta Shipbuilding Company in Marsa Industrial Estate – the cemetery is across the road.

Ranged up a hillside, with its entrance and incline facing north, Addolorata is a pretty spot, with erect, cone-shaped cypress trees partly screening the elaborate tombstones stepping up the slope towards the dramatic pinnacles of the Gothic Revival chapel. Characteristically caked in marble, the tombstones commemorate the family title of each grave (each is owned and reserved for members of the extended family), and many are topped by stone angels with their wings hunched protectively. Well-to-do families have their graves enclosed in Neoclassical and Baroque temples, with the family's name engraved above the door; many of the names are Italian, illustrating the cultural affinity to Italy amongst Malta's higher classes before World War II.

From the entrance, a path meanders past grave after grave, all overhung by cypress, olive and carob trees and Aleppo pines, towards the **Gothic Revival chapel**. The interior is closed to the public, but the ornate exterior is worth admiring: all trimmings and crannies, and a facade that tapers to a pointed pinnacle, punctuated by attractive stained-glass windows. Beyond the chapel, a now nondiscernible section of land along the cemetery's western flank formed part of what was known as **"the dump"** during the 1960s. Formerly outside the cemetery walls, it was the burial place for members of the Labour Party who were interred without Catholic consecration after Archbishop Mikiel Gonzi excommunicated Labour party members following party leader Dom Mintoff's manoeuvrings to whittle down the legal prerogatives of the clergy (for more on this, see Contexts, p.355). The dump was redeemed and incorporated into the Addolorata Cemetery when the Labour Party and the Catholic Church signed a truce in 1969.

TARXIEN

Map 1, L6.

About 3km southeast of the Grand Harbour, Tarxien is a tightly-built residential town splayed around its parish church, hemmed seamlessly by a smorgasbord of other similar towns, and with little to distinguish it from its neighbours. The streets are confusingly similar, girdled by monotonous terraced townhouses, some weathered and some new, and the only reason to visit Tarxien is to see the **Hypogeum** and **Tarxien Temples**; the former, particularly, is one of the world's most impressive archeological monuments. Both can be visited in a single trip that will take the best part of a day, including travel. The constant stream of visitors to the Hypogeum over the last 75 years has led to a fast rate of **deterioration**. In the 1990s, local authorities embarked on a sophisticated restoration project that entailed redirecting sewage pipes and rainwater culverts in the area, knocking down some buildings, and installing sophisticated equipment to calibrate the various gases in the air. **Visiting** arrangements are now governed by the Hypogeum's calibrated climate, regulated to ensure that carbon dioxide levels don't exceed a set threshold. Only seventy visitors are allowed per day, and all must join an hour-long guided tour in groups of ten; you have to buy a ticket in advance from the **reception** of the Hypogeum to ensure a visiting slot days in advance.

From Valletta, take buses #8, #11, #15, #26, #27 or #29 and alight at Tarxien's town square. The Hypogeum is a ten-minute walk along Triq Ħal Luqa heading south past the church, then right into Triq Iċ-Ċimiterju. For the

Tarxien Temples, another ten-minute walk, double back in Triq Ħal Luqa, walk towards the church, then east into Triq Sammut and right in Triq It-Tempji Neolitiċi.

For more on Malta's Neolithic temples, see Contexts p.328.

The Hypogeum

Triq Ic-Ċimiterju. Daily 9am–4pm; Lm3.

An extensive and underground burial shrine spread over three levels, the **Hypogeum** is one of the oldest and most impressive monuments of the ancient world. It was built between 3600 and 2500 BC, and was still a work in progress when Malta's Neolithic settlers disappeared without trace (for more on this, see the box on p.180). Builders stumbled on the Hypogeum in 1899 while digging the foundations of a house, but only reported the discovery in 1902 when the building was completed, probably to ensure that the government did not appropriate the land. Excavations began the following year under one Fr Emmanuel Magri, but after four years of meticulous work, he died suddenly in Tunisia. His notes were never recovered, but Sir Temi Zammit, then curator of Valletta's Museum of Archeology, took over in 1907 and published his report three years later. He estimated that 7000 bodies were buried here, which works out to only seven interments per year, suggesting that the Hypogeum was a privileged burial place, reserved for shamans, priests or priestesses only. Artefacts such as stone mallets, green-stone necklaces, and the famous sleeping lady exhibited at the National Museum of Archeology in Valletta (see p.55) were also unearthed.

The Hypogeum is unlike any other architectural structure, and you really do have to see it for yourself to appreciate the profound, sacred atmosphere created by its spatial arrangement and architectural elements. It has a surreal feel and many people swear they feel an abstract form of undefined energy when inside. Even after spending three years meticulously excavating the remains, Zammit concluded that "an air of profound mystery pervades the place".

Conducted by trained personnel, the informative, detailed **tours** take in the first and second levels. The **first level** is a jumble of ruins save for the intact entrance trilithon – two upright megaliths and another lying on top to make a doorway, which normally would have stood beyond the **threshold**, a sort of porch-like megalith that signified the portal from the physical world to the divine one. Things get more exciting in the **second level** where there are representations of the spiral, painted in red ochre, which symbolized the Neolithic peoples' worldview of cyclical continuity. You pass lobed chambers that served as graves, and an incomplete section that illustrates how the complex was dug out, generation after generation, by first boring holes into the rock with deer antlers, then knocking off chunks of rock between the holes using stone mallets, and finally polishing the walls. In the **Oracle Room**, where a painting of a tree is thought to symbolize the tree of life, guides point out the Oracle Hole – an opening in the wall which, when spoken into, amplifies a baritone voice into an echo that booms through the complex. After passing through more trilithons, you get to the Hypogeum's highlights – two small central rooms known as the **Holy of Holies** and the **Main Chamber**. These were obviously used for some sort of ceremonies, the specifics of which are unknown. The rooms are connected via a trilithon, and feature cantilevered steps to the ceiling as well as various round windows opening into smaller lobed chambers. These two rooms give you an idea of how the outdoor temples' interior chambers looked when

TARXIEN

NEOLITHIC CULTURE AND GODDESS WORSHIP

With 23 major Neolithic temples and two underground burial shrines, Malta was of major importance during Europe's Neolithic era. In 3800 BC, when the temple-building era began, Malta's Neolithic peoples created the first known **architectural civilization**, and although the temples have been the subject of intense scrutiny by generations of scholars, what little has been pieced together has deepened the puzzles and mystique of the Maltese islands' Neolithic peoples. In recent years, American archeologists Marija Gimbutas and Christina Biaggi have proposed the idea that the temples were created by **matriarchal, goddess-worshipping societies**, eventually subdued by warring tribes with male Gods that swept Europe east to west. The theory asserts that the "fat ladies" found in the temples are representations of fertility goddesses, and that the temples themselves were modelled on the ladies' rotund outlines. In this way, the Neolithic peoples expressed their ideas by spatial and artistic **symbolism** – the contextual symbolism archeologists employ to figure out what went on. As well as using red ochre (symbolizing the blood stream as the life stream) and carving spiral motifs throughout the temples, they are thought to have performed elaborate burial rituals, painting the dead with red ochre to catalyse their rebirth and placing offerings in the graves. In one grave at the Xaghra Stone Circle (see p.220), a mother was buried cradling her baby in her arms; in another a dog was buried with its owner.

Although the Goddess theory is resisted by many archeologists, who accuse its proponents of a covert **feminist** agenda (the debate continues to rage on), the temples have become something of a pilgrimage spot for Goddess-worshipping women and New Age bleeding hearts. They come to experience an alleged **energy** within the temples that has been assigned to the ley lines – invisible conduits of electromagnetic energy – which are said to flow through all Neolithic sites – this energy is said to be especially concentrated in Malta. Several tour operators offer pilgrimages, and the best are listed below.

Edge of Wonder Tours, PO Box 6181, Albany, CA 94706, USA ⊤ 510/524-4183 ⓦ www.edgeofwonder.com.
Once-yearly twelve-day tours by Jennifer Berezan include lectures, yoga, meditation, and ceremonial rituals of dancing and purification. All-inclusive tariff, including four-star accommodation and flights from the USA, is US$2200.

Goddess Tours to Malta, PO Box 388, Portsmouth, NH 03802, USA ⓦ www.goddesstourstomalta.com.
Several tours each year, ranging from five to eleven days, offering an overview of Malta's history with a special focus on Neolithic culture, with workshops and lectures on reviving Neolithic wisdom. The all-inclusive cost, excluding airfare, for an eleven-day tour is about US$1885.

In the Lap of the Goddess, 7638 58th Ave NE, Olympia, WA 98516, USA ⊤ 360/455-4701 ⓦ www.femininematrix.com.
Danica Anderson, a psychotherapist, organizes one yearly tour focusing on healing, therapy, workshops and rituals of reconciliation and purification in the temples. The all-inclusive price, including five-star accommodation and airfare, is US$2000.

OTS Foundation, PO Box 17166, Sarasota, FL 34276, USA ⊤ 941/918-9215 ⓦ www.otsf.org.
Linda Eneix organizes several annual two-week tours open to participants older than 55 years, focusing on archeology and including lectures and field trips. The all-inclusive tour, including four-star accommodation and airfare from the USA, costs US$2520.

NEOLITHIC TEMPLE TOURS

they were intact – one of the rewards of visiting the Hypogeum. An egg-shaped architectural masterpiece, the Main Chamber boasts three trilithon doorways and polished walls, and its concave, protracted walls play tricks on perception.

Tarxien Neolithic Temples

Map 1, L6. Triq It-Tempji Neolitiċi. Daily: mid-June to Sept 8am–2pm; Oct to mid-June 8.15am–4.30pm; Lm1.

The largest and most architecturally advanced temple complex in Malta, the **Tarxien Neolithic Temples** were among the last batch built on the island, constructed between 3000 and 2500BC. Evidence of fires here suggests that Bronze Age peoples used the buildings as a crematorium, but it seems that after this time, the complex lay buried under an accumulation of rubble until it was discovered by a farmer in 1914, when he investigated the large rocks that kept ruining his plough. Although the site is in a state of semi-collapse today, you can still see the impressive bottom third of the original building which, when intact, stood some 23m high. But the ruins are pretty poorly illustrated, and you'll have to use your imagination to fully appreciate the ceremonial rituals that took place here, and the monumentality of the original, intact structure.

The complex, made up of globigerina limestone megaliths, is comprised of three intermeshed temples; you enter through the massive trilithons of the **South Temple**. In the first chamber to the right is an altar with spiral reliefs and a niche where Sir Temi Zammit, who excavated the site, found the flint knives and animal bones that served as definitive proof that animal sacrifices were performed here. The room also holds a replica (the original is in the National Museum of Archeology in Valletta) of what's left of the largest "**fat lady**" found anywhere in the world;

when whole, it towered 2.5m high. Past the room, a passageway, studded with holes that are thought to have been used for tethering animals, leads to the **Middle Temple**, the largest of the three with three pairs of small, symmetrical chambers. The inner two are marked by a knee-high stone slab wedged in the passageway, smothered with variations of the spiral motif: this is thought to mark the threshold into the inner sanctum of the temple, probably reserved only for priests or priestesses. If you look closely, you can also see the fading motifs of marching bulls and goats carved on the megaliths, though the significance of these isn't known. The Middle Temple leads to the **East Temple** of which only the bottom foundation stones survive.

ĦAĠAR QIM AND MNAJDRA NEOLITHIC TEMPLES

Map 1, I9. Daily: mid-June to Sept 8am–2pm; Oct to mid-June 8.15am–4.30pm; Lm1.

On Malta's southern coast, some 10km south of Valletta, the **Ħaġar Qim** and **Mnajdra** Neolithic temple complexes are set on a ruggedly scenic garigue plateau that falls down to the areas' dramatic seacliffs, a thyme-scented, windswept and open setting unchanged since the Neolithic era. The complexes are within a kilometre of each other, and both were progressively constructed and used between 3600 and 2500BC.

Throughout the 1990s, the government attempted to turn the area into an **archeological park**, but bird trappers squatting on public land here threatened to blow up the temples if they were evicted – they partly defaced Mnajdra's facade with splashes of black paint, and the government backed down. In April 2001, the government finally designated the site as an Area of Archeological Importance, barring all non-archeological related activity, but when the bird trappers were served an eviction notice, they carried out their threats by **vandalizing** one of Mnajdra's temples, toppling some sixty megaliths. Thankfully, archeology students visiting the site on the night of the attack disrupted the perpetrators from completing what would have otherwise been the full destruction of Mnajdra; at the time of writing Mnajdra was **closed** indefinitely for restoration.

Bus #38 from Valletta drops you outside the gate to the temples.

Ħaġar Qim

The least understood of all temples in Malta, **Ħaġar Qim** is a circular complex consisting of four temples and two opposite entrances – the one nearest the gate, through which you enter, and the back entrance along the passage that dissects the temple. When intact, this was a round, imposing structure on the shallow crest of the plateau which was visible from afar: today, the heavy facade of the front entrance and some of the massive, upright megaliths that survive give you an idea of its former grandeur. The temple is in a semi-ruined state, and its design detracts from the paired-apses of the other temples in Malta. The spaces and chambers open into each other in an intricate jumble of rooms, but the understanding of these spatial arrangements, and their ceremonial significance, is close to nil. The most significant relics found in Ħaġar Qim were the "fat lady" figurine of a naked woman that archeologists dubbed the **Venus of Malta** on account of her handsome proportions; the Venus is exhibited at the National Museum of Archeology in Valletta (see p.55). There is some inconclusive evidence that the layout of the passageway from front to back is aligned with the northern and southern maximum declinations of the full moon, an event that occurs every 18.6 years.

Mnajdra

Reachable from Ħaġar Qim via a five-minute walk along a gently inclining path, **Mnajdra** consists of three temples, known as East, Middle and South. Together, they form a continuous concave facade, and it's thought that the arena-like space created by the concave facade would have been where the common people congregated whilst priests or priestesses conducted the ceremonies inside. The **East Temple** on the eastern flank is the smallest and most primitive, and only the outline of its foundations survive. The **Middle Temple**, which bore the brunt of the damage following the recent attack by vandals, is fairly bare, its interior formed by two pairs of chambers – uniquely, it has two entrances at the front. The **South Temple** is the most intact of any on the Maltese islands – only the upper crest of its megalithic roof has collapsed – and is also the most elegant. Small, intimate spaces, the chambers symmetrical, and the passageway megaliths are pitted dramatically, the stones fitting together seamlessly. The temple has two pairs of chambers; beyond them is the inner lobe, which forms the head and inner sanctum of the temple. Mnajdra's South Temple is the only one that has been proven to be aligned to sunrise on the **solstices** and **equinoxes**. The latter events – sunrises on September 23 and March 21, when the shaft of sun breaking through the entrance trilithon falls evocatively on the innermost shrine – are greeted by groups of New Age types dancing and chanting outside the temple, and holding thanksgiving rituals that include sage-burning for purification and offerings of bread or pomegranate. As you step into the first chambers, the **Oracle Hole** is to the right: a small window that opens into a cubicle, whose doorway is at the other end of the wall, and is thought to have been the seat of a special person who perhaps passed messages or mantras, or interpreted epiphanies during ceremonies. Uniquely within Malta, the three altars in the inner chambers are propped on round, tapered stones that Marija Gimbutas has suggested mimic the frontal shape of a female crotch, symbolizing that the path to the divine is through the feminine.

WIED IZ-ŻURRIEQ AND BLUE GROTTO

Map 1, I9.

About two kilometres southeast of the entrance to Ħaġar Qim and Mnajdra temples, the road snakes down to the tiny fishing settlement of **WIED IZ-ŻURRIEQ**, enclosed by a deep gorge and lying at the mouth of a creek. The gorge and cliffs here are an arresting sight, and the rocky coast provides a peaceful spot from which to enjoy the vista; 6km offshore, the tiny islet of **Filfla** emerges through the haze. Also offshore of here are a handful of excellent **scuba diving** sites (see p.311). Flanking the creek are the police station, based in one of the Knights' coastal towers, and the cluster of boathouses, souvenir shops and rather tacky restaurants that make up the settlement.

There's little to keep you in Wied Iz-Żurrieq, though it's an appealing place to while away a couple of hours, Many people join one of the ten-minute, round-trip boat excursions to the Blue Grotto, offered by a handful of touts that patrol the village. About a kilometre south of the creek, the **Blue Grotto** itself is a huge domed cave opening at sea level, and fronted by a buttress eroded into the rocks; the sea in the cave has a lovely azure colour, but the tour is pretty disappointing, offering only a fleeting glimpse of the cave, which has a distinct aroma of engine oil thanks to the volume of boats passing through. If you don't fancy a boat trip, you can still see the Blue Grotto by peering down the cliff where the side road climbing from Wied Iż-Żurrieq joins the main.

Wied Iz-Żurrieq is served by bus #38 from Valletta.

FILFLA'S STORM PETRELS

Six kilometres offshore of Wied Iz-Żurrieq, **Filfla**, a bleak unin-habited islet about the same size as a couple of tennis courts, houses a large colony of **storm petrels**, and is regarded by birders as one of the most important seabird breeding sites in the Mediterranean.

Filfla was first recognized as a breeding colony in 1863, when naturalist C.A. Wright reported seeing Cory's shearwa-ters and storm petrels trapped in mist nets put up by fisher-men, who used the birds' feathers on fishing lines and the flesh for bait. For some time in the twentieth century, the British army used Filfla as a target for **bombing** practice, which reduced its size by half. In 1971, local ornithologists pleaded with the British to halt the bombing in view of the bird populations; that same year, the army, which was winding down its Malta operations anyway, relented.

Ironically, though the bombing devastated Filfla itself, it did leave rubble scree that provided additional **nesting crevices** for storm petrels. Thrush-sized and sooty black except for a white band on their tails, **storm petrels** are secretive birds. During the mating season, adults spend the day at sea gorging on small fish and plankton, and return to their nests at night to feed their young on regurgitated seafood. When the fledglings leave the nest, the parents spend the winter at sea – often getting as far as the Atlantic Ocean – and only return to land during the mating season. One bird ringed by ornithologists in 1969 was retrapped 21 years later, still healthy and mating.

Since 1987, Filfla has been a **nature reserve**, and you need clearance from the Department of Environment (T 231895) to visit, but bear in mind that the petrels are very secretive and hard to spot.

FILFLA'S STORM PETRELS

GĦAR DALAM CAVE

Map 1, L7. Triq Iż-Żejtun, Birżebbuġa. Daily: mid-June to Sept 8am–2pm; Oct to mid-June 8.15am–5.15pm; Lm1.

Some 6km east of Wied Iz-Żurrieq, and reachable via bus #11 from Valletta, is **Għar Dalam Cave**. Discovered in 1892, the 145m-deep natural cavern, excavated the same year and again in 1922, yielded shreds of pottery and other remains of Malta's first settlers dating from around 5000 BC, as well as the skeletal remains of prehistoric animals flushed into the cave at the end of the last Ice Age. Before and during the Ice Age, the level of the Mediterranean Sea fluctuated between 30 and 200m lower than today, and intermittently Malta was connected to continental Europe via land bridges. **Prehistoric animals** retreated south to escape the masses of ice and their carcasses drifted down ancient rivers to be deposited in Għar Dalam – where the skeletal remains of two variations of hippopotamus, a giant swan and two species of dwarf elephant, all 125,000 years old, were unearthed. Other skeletons found belonged to **European fauna** – red deer, wolves, foxes and swans – that had migrated to Malta during the same period. When the ice thawed and the sea levels rose, they found themselves marooned in Malta where they had limited territorial space and scarce food, a situation that stunted the animals' growth. The femurs of red deer, for example, are half the size of their European counterparts.

The remains of the animals, and implements fashioned by Neolithic settlers – primitive tools, incised pottery and human skeletal remains – are on display at the small **museum** outside the cave. The labelled exhibits fill up a small hall of glass cabinets organized by chronology and types of relic, enough to keep you absorbed for half an hour. Sadly, though, the most important specimens – four tusks of the dwarf elephant and the skull of a Neolithic child – were stolen from the collection in 1980. Beyond the museum, a flight of stairs leads to the electrically-lit **cave**, which, post-excavations, is virtually bare save for a pillar of the original deposits that was left untouched to illustrate the distinct layers of sediment throughout the last 180,000 years and a handful of beautiful stalactites and stalagmites.

MARSAXLOKK AND AROUND

Sprawled around an inlet on the northern side of the deep scoop of Marsaxlokk Bay, to Malta's extreme southeast, **MARSAXLOKK** (Map 1, M7) is the island's principal **fishing town**, its bay a riot of colourful boats and its promenade swarming with fishermen mending nets and unloading their catches from crates. Bus #27 from Valletta and #427 from Buġibba drop you off at the waterfront, effectively Marsaxlokk's town centre, skirted by a road and a promenade. A small flea market is held along the road here every morning; ignore the uninspired souvenirs in favour of the incredibly fresh **fish**.

Enveloped by the salty, fishy smell of the sea, the small town spreads along the inner mouth of the bay in attractive weathered townhouses. But its former seaside charm has been irreversibly tainted by the recent construction of the Delimara Power Station at the outer left lip of the bay and a freeport on the other side. Although the latter is far from the promenade, the massive cargo ships piling into the bay spoil the ambience, and the prom is pretty dirty and nasty. The best time to visit Marsaxlokk is for **dinner** in one of its handful of excellent fish restaurants (see p.277), when the bustle has died down and the dim light and still water lend a romantic atmosphere.

The only other reason to visit is to **scuba dive** at a World War II wreck in the middle of the bay (see p.311), or to go swimming and snorkelling at Xrobb L-Għaġin, an attractive bay on **Delimara** promontory, which encloses Marsaxlokk Bay to the northeast.

Delimara
Map 1, L7.

Forming the southernmost tip of Malta, the **Delimara** promontory is mostly comprised of agricultural fields and bird-trapping sites among groves of Aleppo pines. Hunters here are renowned for their aggressiveness, though as in other parts, they'll ignore you if you give them a wide berth and don't appear inquisitive (or worse still, disgusted).

Delimara's main draw are its three **beaches** – or, more aptly, bathing holes – gouged into the promontory's southeast flank, which are popular with young Maltese during the summer. Working south to north, **Long Bay** and **Peter's Pool** are little creeks cut into the cliffs, but as the shoreline is jagged and uncomfortable, and there are no ladders to help you get into and out of the water, they're not really worth the effort it takes to find them. The most northerly of Delimara's swimming spots, **Xrobb L-Għaġin** (Island Bay) is far more appealing, a large, horseshoe-shaped cove girdled by chalky cliffs, with a natural arch eroded into the south lip of the bay and no development save for a car park. You can wade around in the bay to get different perspectives of the scenic setting, and the waters offer good snorkelling.

To **get to** Xrobb L-Għaġin by car, you don't have to go into Marsaxlokk proper; as you approach the town (just as you reach the first houses), take the left fork into Triq Axtart, then turn right into Triq Delimara. This winds its potholed way up to Delimara; turn left at the crossroads past the Island's Dog Sanctuary until the road ends at the car park. If you're walking, follow the signs to Delimara and Island's Dog Sanctuary from the Marsaxlokk promenade. Long Bay and Peter's Pool are reachable by veering right at the crossroads near the Island's Dog Sanctuary, a kilometre on.

GOZO

The island of **Gozo** (Għawdex, as the Gozitans and Maltese call it) is roughly one-third the size of Malta (only 14km from end to end at its widest point), and is separated from its neighbour by just 8km of sea, but it's a world apart nonetheless, both topographically and culturally. Gozo is less built-up, with cleaner and less congested roads, and each town is a neat, self-contained unit of houses clustered round a massive parish church. Its people – Gozitans – have a rural, laid-back demeanour, making the island a favoured spot for holiday homes owned by well-to-do Maltese. The **landscape** is characterized by table-top hills and steep valleys, with terraced fields stepping up the slopes, and owing to the fact that the layer of blue clay is thicker and more exposed on the slopes, Gozo's steppe landscape is greener than Malta's. The beaches, and the entire **coastline**, have been left largely untamed and retain a glorious, natural look. The underwater topography is also more dramatic than Malta's, and Gozo offers the best **scuba diving** sites in the Maltese islands (see p.311). The last ten years, however, have seen a **development** rush that has already made intractable inroads on Gozo's charm, and some big projects that will alter the island forever – an international airport, the development of the Ta' Ċenċ plateau – are slated. Until then, Gozo remains unashamedly romantic and alluringly beautiful, but it hangs delicately in the balance.

There are several historically significant sights – most concentrated in Rabat's walled Citadel, as well as the magnificent **Ġgantija Temples**. Otherwise, you'll probably spend your time soaking up Gozo's natural beauty, particularly in evidence at the **beaches**, which range from delicious sandy swaths to winding creeks or rocky plateaux close to the water level. Gozo is a place to linger and unwind, and you need at least a couple of days to slow down to its rhythm and soak up its atmosphere.

There are markedly less tourists on Gozo than in Malta, and as most visit in the summer months, the island is **seasonal**: many restaurants and some bars and clubs close during the winter between November and April. Most people stay in **Marsalforn** or **Xlendi**, where there are minimal nightlife and restaurant scenes, but as Gozo is so small, seeing the island is easy wherever you base yourself. You can **walk** practically anywhere if you have the time and inclination, and buses cover the main routes. Renting a **motorbike** is a favourite option considering the short distances, the low cost, and the relatively empty roads.

Some history

Although Gozo, like Malta, was settled around 5000 BC by Neolithic settlers, who built the first temple in the Maltese islands here, its separation from the mainland has ensured an independent, self-reliant bent. Because the island lacks any deep natural harbours, many of the ancient powers largely ignored it: the Phoenicians called it *Gwl*, meaning "something round", and the Arabs rechristened it *Ghudash* (from which Għawdex is derived). A limited **ferry** service, informally and arbitrarily operated by freelance boat owners, connected the islands at around 1000 AD at the earliest, but Gozo had to wait until 1800 for a more formal, albeit still irregular, service.

The island's first urban settlement, the **Citadel** in Rabat, dates back to the Romans. It's setting, on a ledge in the geographical centre of the island, was chosen as the best vantage point for defence. The Arabs destroyed it when they invaded the islands in 870 AD, and soon after another medieval citadel rose out of the ruins of the original. **Dragut Rais**, the Ottoman corsair, attacked Gozo in 1551, razed the Citadel and dragged virtually the entire population – 5000 out of 5500 – into **slavery**. Even after this event, Gozitans continued to retreat to the Citadel at night, where they enjoyed a measure of protection from the frequent lightning raids carried out by **corsairs** and **pirates**, who also ambushed boats plying the Gozo Channel. The situation improved in the mid-seventeenth century, when the Knights fortified Comino and launched an integrated plan for **Gozo's defence**: they strengthened the Citadel, built a fort to protect Mġarr Harbour, as well as a chain of coastal towers and batteries in strategic locations around the coast.

For more background on Maltese history, see Contexts, p.327.

During the uprising against French rule in 1798, Gozo was the first to slaughter its small French garrison, and for the following two years the island enjoyed **independence** from Malta. Gozo remained self-reliant, its economy based on agriculture and fishing, and in the next major phase of its history, during World War II, the island provided refuge for those fleeing from war-ravaged Grand Harbour, and shared its stockpiles of agricultural produce when the mainland's population was close to starvation.

The **economy** is still partly reliant on agriculture, and Gozo continues to act as Malta's food basket; the main earner, though, is **tourism**. Over the last fifteen years, the tourist infrastructure and the number of arriving visitors have increased steadily, and the 1990s saw a development boom (although nothing on the scale of some of Malta's resorts). The numbers are largely made up of inter-island visitors: the many Maltese who have second homes or who visit for weekend rural retreats. This phenomenon has brought the Maltese and Gozitans closer together. Historically, the Gozitans' simmering **antipathy** towards their neighbours has risen from both the urban–rural dichotomy (Gozitans could be said to be deeply conservative while the Maltese are more culturally liberal), and from the fact that development and infrastructural initiatives in Malta were not paralleled in Gozo. In 1987, responding to Gozitans' complaints, the PN government introduced a **Ministry for Gozo**, which has improved infrastructure and services, expanded work opportunities and presided over rapid economic development. In thirty years, Gozo has become a wealthy place that has more cars per capita than anywhere else in the world. Many Gozitans who emigrated to Australia and North America in the 1960s in search of a better life are now returning to retire, proudly flaunting imported cultural symbols, and today you'll see foreign flags alongside the Maltese standard flying from rooftops during *festas*.

ARRIVAL AND GETTING AROUND

Most people arrive in Gozo by sea on a Gozo Channel Company **ferry** – the cheapest means of getting here and a pleasant journey in itself, taking in the sculpted cliffs of Comino's west coast and the picturesque approach to the island. Ferries shuttle between Ċirkewwa (Map 1, A2), at Malta's northernmost tip, and Mġarr Harbour (Map 8, K6) in Gozo, and **schedules** change several times throughout the year; during the busy summer months, ferries run every half an hour between 6am and 6pm, and about every two hours throughout the night, while in the winter months, services run about every two hours during the day, and not at all between midnight and 6am. You can pick up a copy of the latest schedule from the tourist offices or call the Gozo Channel schedule enquiry service on ☎ 556114, 561622 or 580435. Return **fares** are Lm1.75 for a passenger, Lm0.50 for children, Lm3 for motorbike and rider, and Lm5.75 for a motor vehicle plus rider. The Gozo Channel Company also operate a high-speed **catamaran** service from Valletta, between Sa Maison in Marsamxett Harbour and Gozo's Mġarr Harbour, and tailored towards the needs of Gozitan workers commuting to Malta; schedules change seasonally, but generally, there are three or four trips a day, in the mornings, early and late afternoons; one-way tickets cost Lm5, and journey time is 30min.

A quicker but more costly means of getting to Gozo are the 10min **helicopter flights** run by Malta Aircharter (☎ 22999138 ℱ 663195 ⓦ www.airmalta.com/malta_air_charter.htm) from Luqa Airport (Map 1, J7), near the main International airport in Malta, to Gozo heliport in Għajnsielem (Map 8, I6). **Tickets**, which must be purchased from the Air Malta desk in the International Airport's departure hall, cost Lm25 for a return and Lm17 one-way (student-card holders pay Lm10 and Lm5 respectively). **Flight schedules** change seasonally, but generally speaking there are about twelve trips spread over 24hr during the summer, and six in the winter.

Bus #25 (services are tailored to the ferry schedule) departs from Mġarr Harbour for the bus terminus (Map 9, I7) in Rabat, and calls at the heliport along the way. There are **taxi** stands at Mġarr Harbour and the heliport. Fares are pretty much arbitrary – don't be shy to haggle – but you'll typically pay about Lm5 from either the heliport or the harbour to Rabat.

Getting around

Though the #25 route is reliable, **bus services** around the rest of the island are rather haphazard and finish fairly early (around 8pm), and services (other than the #25 and the #21 to Marsalforn) are drastically reduced on Sundays and public holidays. Schedules change seasonally and some routes are extended in the summer months; up-to-date schedules are available from the tourist offices (see below) or by calling the bus terminus on ☎562040. All bus routes depart and return to the Rabat bus terminus. In addition to the #25, there are eight routes that cover all towns in Gozo.

INFORMATION

There are two **tourist offices** in Gozo. The main one is at the Banca Giuratale on Pjazza Indipendenza, Rabat (Map 9, F4; Mon–Sat 9am–12.30pm & 1–5pm, Sun 9am–12.30pm ☎561419), and another (same hours) at Mġarr Harbour. Both dole out leaflets on the sights, a quarterly calendar of cultural events, and listings of self-catering apartments, villas and converted farmhouses that you can rent direct from the owners.

The best place to get on the net is Internet House, 44 Triq L-Assunta, Rabat (Map 9, D5; June–Aug Mon–Sat 10am–11pm; Sept–May Mon–Sat 10am–7pm ☎558764) where access costs Lm0.75 for 15min, Lm1.00 for 30min, Lm1.50 for 1hr.

Rabat and the Citadel

Smack in the centre of the island, Gozo's capital of **RABAT** (also known as Victoria) is the largest town on the island, with a population of 6000. It's a pleasant place of sunny, tree-splashed squares bustling with hole-in-the-wall cafés, handsome Baroque townhouses and a handful of churches. Its centre is defined by **Triq Ir-Repubblika** (Republic St), which dissects the town along its east–west axis, and holds most of the retail outlets on the island, as well as two theatres, the police headquarters and the main post office. At its western extreme, Triq Ir-Repubblika opens into **Pjazza Indipendenza** – locally known as It-Tokk – a pedestrianized square laid out in front of the attractive Baroque Banca Giuratale, erected in 1733 as the seat of the Gozo Universita and now home to the Rabat local council and tourist office. Just south of here is **St George's Basilica**, the most sumptuously Baroque of Gozo's churches and boasting some lovely paintings. Otherwise, Rabat's **old quarter**, where the maze of alleys are overhung by Baroque townhouses with elaborately carved stone balconies, is good for a wander. Southeast of here, the delightful **Pjazza San Franġisk** (St Francis Square) is the largest plaza in Rabat, a pleasant place to relax under the shade of ficus trees.

However, for Gozo's most significant historical sights you'll need to head for the Gozitan landmark of the **Citadel**, a fortified town built on a ledge and projecting its bulk over Rabat proper. Within its walls is the Gozo **cathedral** (as well as a handful of second-rate museums), and the ramparts of its fortifications offer all-round views of Gozo.

THE CITADEL

Less than 200m long by 200m wide, the **Citadel** stands on a high ledge overlooking Rabat; its amber-hued bulk is visible from most of Gozo, and in its sideways profile it has an uncanny resemblance to an aircraft carrier. After the Roman and medieval citadels were destroyed, Grand Master Martin Garzes commissioned the Italian engineer Giovanni Rinaldini to review Gozo's defences in 1599; he drew up the plans for the Citadel that exists today, whose rebuilding commenced in 1600 and dragged on until the mid-seventeenth century.

Allow about a morning to see the Citadel. If you plan on seeing the government-run sights here – the Museum of Archeology, Folklore Museum and Natural Science Museum – it's worth buying a comprehensive **day ticket** from the Museum of Archeology; this costs Lm1.50 and is valid on the date of purchase to enter all three attractions.

Museum of Archeology

Map 9, G3. Triq Bieb L-Imdina. Mon–Sat 8.30am–4.30pm, Sun 8.30am–3pm; Lm1.

At the top of Triq It-Telġha Tal-Belt, the entrance to the **Citadel** is marked by two gates. The larger arch on the left was created in 1957 by breaching the fortifications; To its right is the **Mdina Gate**, the Citadel's original entrance; passing through this takes you to a two-storey townhouse that houses the **Museum of Archeology**, which showcases well-labelled archeological remains found in Gozo – it's a small and dull collection, though, and can be perused in less than half an hour. Dedicated to the Neolithic era and the Bronze Age, the **ground floor** features a model of the Ġgantija temples (see p.219), some intact clay pots, clumps of red ochre used to paint temple interiors, and the petrified horn of a bull found under the threshold of Ġgantija's South Temple. The Bronze Age remains amount to several primitive tools and pottery. The **first floor** is mostly cluttered by amphorae made by the **Phoenicians** and **Romans**, and there's also a skeleton found in Comino from the Phoenician era, a Roman olive press and two **Arab** tombstones with their ornately engraved epitaphs.

The Cathedral and museum

Map 9, H3. Pjazza Katidral. Daily 9am–4.30pm; Lm0.15.

Opposite the Museum of Archeology, a tunnel cut through the first floor of a townhouse opens into Pjazza Katidral (Cathedral Square), dominated by the **Cathedral** itself. Designed by the celebrated Maltese architect Lorenzo Gafa, it was built between 1697 and 1711. Gafa died when the cathedral was still in the initial stages of building – just as well, because his dome (Gafa's architectural signature) was never completed. The cathedral was originally planned as a simple place of worship, but became the obvious choice for the island's cathedral when Gozo became a separate diocese from Malta in 1864. As a result, it's pretty lame architecturally and artistically; compared to other churches in Gozo, it's not much more than a glorified chapel. Its facade has a panelled compositional unity, erupting towards its pier and ornate with stone scrolls and a niche holding a statue of the Madonna. Its interior, however, is pretty stark, and the only thing worth a look is the spectacular trompe l'oeil painting on the ceiling. When finance ran dry during the cathedral's construction, leaving no money to build the dome, parishioners commissioned the Italian painter Antonio Manuele to execute an illusory dome on the flat ceiling – from the nave, it's difficult to convince yourself that you're not looking at the real thing.

The entrance to the cathedral's small **museum** is on Triq Il-Fosos, the alley that runs parallel to the north side of the cathedral itself. It's a second-rate effort, and the displays of well-labelled vestments, ceremonial silver and gold paraphernalia and a few obscure religious paintings by Giuseppe Hyzler, Michelle Busetti and Tommaso Medion, are hardly gripping stuff.

Folklore Museum

Map 9, H2. Triq Bernardo DeOpuo. Mon–Sat 8.30am–4.30pm, Sun 8.30am–3pm; Lm1.

From the cathedral museum, follow Triq Bernardo DeOpuo, which strikes off Triq Il-Fosos to the north, to get to the **Folklore Museum**, housed in a Siculo-Norman townhouse dating to the medieval era, which displays the characteristic two-light windows. The exhibits of traditional tools range from farming implements and blacksmith's tools to lace-weaving equipment, and a whole room dedicated to hunting paraphernalia. It's a poorly thought out collection, a sort of catch-all for pieces relating to Gozitan traditions that foreign visitors might find mildly charming, but it fails to evoke the spirit of what it displays – or even decide what it wants to show. Besides, the haphazardly arranged collection is poorly illustrated, badly maintained and only worth checking out of you're at a loose end – a far more diverting array is on display at the Folklore Museum in Għarb (see p.212).

Natural Science Museum

Map 9, G2. Triq Il-Kwartier San Martin. Mon–Sat 8.30am–4.30pm, Sun 8.30am–3pm; Lm1.

From the Folklore Museum, turn right onto Triq Bernardo DeOpuo; at the top, take a left onto Triq Iz-

Żenqa, and north again onto Triq Il-Kwartier San Martin to reach the **Natural Science Museum**. This is another small museum whose collections of minerals and stuffed mammals, fish and insects are well-displayed and well-labelled but haphazardly chosen and incomplete. The only sections that are of marginal interest – because they shed some light on the surprising variety of the island's fauna – are those that deal with Gozo's environment, with displays on geological strata, seashells and fish, and moths and butterflies. The cabinet full of stuffed birds, however (mostly protected birds of prey and waterbirds) shows little sensitivity, though, and feels like a celebration of the ravages of Maltese hunters.

The old prisons

Map 9, G3. Triq II-Kwartier San Martin. Mon–Sat 8.30am–1.30pm; free.

A couple of doors down from the Natural Science Museum are the **old prisons**, built in the early seventeenth century and used to incarcerate prisoners until the nineteenth century. The first room, originally holding the prison's reception, has been dedicated to an illustrative permanent exhibition of the Knights' **military architecture** in Gozo, ranging from prints and original designs to pictures of the Citadel, Fort Chambray (now being converted into a tourist village) and Gozo's coastal towers and batteries. Past here, the hive-like, dank and dim prison cells are built along a corridor and a small courtyard. In a recent restoration project, the waterpaint was carefully flaked off the walls to reveal the graffiti engraved by prisoners on the globigerina limestone walls. The two most recurring symbols are the outline of a palm, which prisoners traced as a form of signature, and of a multiple-masted galley – each mast marks a year of sentence served.

THE CITADEL

Around the fortifications

More than the sum of its individual sights, the allure of the Citadel lies in its ambience, its magnificent fortifications and, as one of the highest points in Gozo, the panoramic views it affords. The best way to enjoy all this is by walking round the perimeter walls. Start in front of the old prisons, where a passageway tops the wall over both entrance gates, and walk anticlockwise along the parapet (the railings) of the fortifications. Beyond the Mdina Gate, the passageway opens into **Il-Bastjun ta San Mikiel** (Map 9, G4), a triangular bastion jutting out over Rabat and offering views of the close-knit maze of buildings that make up the town's old quarter. Heading east, the flat wall – framed by the bastions of San Mikiel and Id-Demibastjun ta San Ġwann – conceals an escape **tunnel**, which starts near today's Museum of Archeology and winds down to the foot of this wall; its mouth is hidden behind a thin crust of stone that could be breached with a pickaxe in the event of an evacuation. Pressing past the vaguely triangular **Id-Demibastjun ta San Ġwann** (Map 9, I3), a staircase climbs past **St John's Cavalier** (Map 9, I2), a stout raised gun platform that served as a rearguard gun emplacement. Atop the stairs you step over stone **silos** – you can see their raised lids – hewn underground to store grain and water to feed the defenders in the event of lengthy siege. Peer over the wall here to see the **battery** (Map 9, I2), another simple gun emplacement annexed to the fortifications to compound the defensive positions.

The north ring of the fortifications are characterized by relatively low walls that skirt the edge of the ledge the Citadel is built upon. The view stretches past table-top hills all the way to Marsalforn (see p.215) on the north coast. Inside the walls is the prickly-pear smothered rubble which represents all that's left of the **medieval citadel** destroyed in Dragut Rais' 1551 raid. There are some lovely views over Gozo's hilly northwest, a peaceful scene with the rolling landscape pierced by the spires of Baroque churches. When you reach **Id-Demibastjun ta San Martin** (Map 9, F3), north of the Mdina Gate, you can see the imposing Gelmus Hill across a narrow valley. Its flat plateau is Gozo's highest point, and the Knights were painfully aware that an enemy positioned here could shower the Citadel with cannon fire; their fears, however, were never realized.

THE TOWN

Despite the fact that Rabat proper holds few individual sights, the bustling town centre, between the Citadel and Pjazza San Franġisk, is good for a gentle wander. You can lounge at the outdoor tables of the cafés at **Pjazza Indipendenza** (Map 9, G4–G5), or buy fresh fish from the square's small open-air fish market (Mon–Sat 8am–noon).

St George's Basilica

Map 9, G6. Pjazza San Ġorġ. Daily 7am–7pm; free.

At the southern flank of Pjazza Indipendenza, Triq San Ġorġ opens into Pjazza San Ġorġ, which holds **St George's Basilica**. Built between 1672 and 1778, the church was subsequently extended and tinkered with structurally on several occasions, and today, its ornate Baroque belfries, dome and transepts, all studded with various stone-carved torches and flames, dominate the square. The interior is equally sumptuous, covered in marble, with a bronze and black canopied altar modelled on the version in St Peter's in Rome. Notable features include an attractive set of stained-glass windows in the dome, and a handful of good **works of art**. On the left-hand side of the nave hangs Mattia Preti's *St George*, painted in 1678 in rather lurid tones, with St George brandishing the sword used to sever the dragon's head as he subdues the dragon underfoot. The altarpiece features a stirring portrait of the saint by the Italian painter Stefano Erardi, a technically excellent and somewhat unusual portrayal of a weary St George humbly leading his horse. Francesco Zahra painted the two pieces that flank the altarpiece: one shows St George being tried in court, the other his beheading. Finally, it's worth heading for the side chapel to the right of the altar, which holds a remarkable **statue** of St George, carved by Paolo Azzopardi in 1841 from a single tree trunk.

The old quarter to Pjazza San Franġisk

From the left flank of St George's Basilica, diminutive Triq Il-Karita winds through Rabat's **old quarter**, its ornate Baroque townhouses mostly dating from the seventeenth century. Shaded from the fierce sun by the houses, the pedestrianized winding alleys here are a delight, wafted by fresh breezes carrying the smell of cooking and the sound of voices drifting from open windows. Many of the houses feature small, hollow **niches** next to their doors, holding statuettes of the Madonna or other saints, while life-size statues of St George guard some of the street corners.

Triq Il-Karita gives way to Triq L-Iskola; at the end of this road, turning left along Triq Vajrinġa takes you to **Pjazza San Franġisk** (Map 9, I8). At its centre, the waters of a large Baroque fountain trickle down a series of stone trays, while St Francis Church presents an attractive back-drop. This small church – perhaps more aptly described as a glorified chapel, since it lacks belfries and dome – is part of the Franciscan convent behind the church. Its simple Baroque facade, highlighted by two niches holding statues of St Francis, tapers off to a pediment, and its exterior is an attractive subdued auburn. The square is ringed by ficus trees and benches where you can sit and watch the goings-on, and *Tapie's Bar* is another excellent people-watching spot, serving good *pastizzi*.

Xewkija and the south

Southeast of Rabat, **Xewkija** sprawls along a largely flat plateau and is surrounded by Gozo's best agricultural land. It's a quiet town of empty, shaded streets, and a town core lined with characterful townhouses with lovely Baroque balconies; groups of pensioners while the day away on the pavements while gangs of children play football in the streets. Occasionally, a truck or a tractor thunders through the streets on its way to one of the dairy and sheep farms on the southern fringes of town. Most of the surrounding land is taken up by wheat production, particularly on either side of **Wied Ħanżira**, a mini-gorge eroded through the flat topography, which opens downstream into the scenic fjord at **Mġarr Ix-Xini**. South of the valley, the topography rises gently towards the small towns of Munxar and Sannat, and beyond these towns, the land levels off at the Ta' Ċenċ plateau before falling sharply into the sea at **Ta' Ċenċ Cliffs**, the massive meandering headlands that girdle the coast from Mġarr Ix-Xini to Xlendi Bay. **Xlendi** is a small resort with a ribbon of ugly apartment blocks built around the bay. Nonetheless, it's a pleasant spot for an evening wander.

XEWKIJA

Map 8, H6.

A sprawling town some 2km east of Rabat, **XEWKIJA**'s centre is dominated by the massive dome of its parish church, visible throughout southeast Gozo. From the central old quarter, the town's recent buildings spread out in concentric circles, with the buildings in each progressive layer of development displaying an ever lighter and brighter hue. There's no need to waste time on the newer parts of town, though, as the only sight of any significance is the towering **St John the Baptist Church** (daily 6am–noon & 3–7pm; free) on the central Pjazza San Ġwann Battista. Italian architect Giuseppe Damato's design – a circular floor plan tapering upwards towards the dome and framed by a bell tower detached from the main structure – is modelled on the church of Santa Maria della Salute in Venice. Construction commenced in 1951, but the bell tower that flanks the church was only completed in the early 1990s. Supported by eight internal pillars, its **dome** is the tallest in Malta, and is 6m higher than London's St Paul's Cathedral. Just inside the entrance, a series of pictures depict parishioners carrying building stones on donkey-driven carts, while tracts of texts describe the hardships they suffered during the construction, and you can't help but feel a certain sympathy for them, despite the fact that it was their own delusions of grandeur that led them to decide on such a massive structure. The interior – the internal volume is only marginally smaller than St Peter's Cathedral in Rome – is a sight of awe-inspiring proportions: craning your neck to look upwards, the building is large enough to make your head spin.

Buses #42 and #43 from Rabat's bus terminus drop you off at the Pjazza San Ġwann Battista.

WIED ĦANŻIRA AND MĠARR IX-XINI

South of Xewkija's town square, the signposted road to Mġarr Ix-Xini meanders past farms and skirts the south flank of the dramatic **Wied Ħanżira**, (Map 8, H7–I7) a miniature gorge that snakes through the crust of upper

Valletta skyline

The Armoury Corridor in the Grand Master's Palace, Valletta

Coastal cliffs

Valletta Festival

Gozo's interior from the Citadel

Għarb parish church, Gozo

Għajn Barrani, Gozo

Salt pans, Gozo

coralline limestone formed when the level of the Mediterranean was lower and rivers flushed through Malta, and named "the valley of the sow" for the pigs that were formerly kept in makeshift sties here. The sides of the gorge are pockmarked with caves, and the ledges overlooking the valley are mature stretches of garigue. Wied Ħanżira deepens as it gets closer to the coast, and then disappears under the sea some 3km southeast of Xewkija at **Mġarr Ix-Xini** (Map 8, J7), an attractive little fjord fronted by a small patch of sandy shore, where the transparent water beckons you in for a dip.

Mġarr Ix-Xini translates as "the harbour of the galleys", harking back to the time when it served as a landing place for **corsairs**' frequent raids on Gozo; it was here that Dragut Rais' forces landed in 1551 (see p.193). At the mouth of the bay lie the crumbling remains of a coastal **tower** built by the Knights in 1658. Before it was constructed, the beleaguered local peasants devised an ingenious method to warn them that a galley was attempting a landing. At a high vantage point, they balanced a large rock; when a ship approached, the rock would be banged down on the bedrock, producing a loud booming sound that echoed throughout the valley.

The road to **Mġarr Ix-Xini** is well signposted from Xewkija; if you're not driving, it makes a pleasant half-hour walk (there are no public transport connections). The country road comes to an end at the bottom of the fjord, where there's a small car park.

TA' ĊENĊ CLIFFS

Map 8, H8.

South of Xewkija, a signposted main road snakes towards the nondescript town of **Sannat**; from the central church square here, a signposted minor road, served by buses #50 and #51 fro Rabat, takes you the 2km to the desolate and dramatic **Ta' Ċenċ Cliffs**. At the edge of a large garigue plateau severely degraded by hundreds of trapping sites, the cliffs form a solid wall east along the coast – the sheer 150-metre drop is dizzying. Ta' Ċenċ are at their most picturesque at sunset, when the sea shimmers on the rock and fishing boats throb past far below. You'll see plenty of **rock centuary** clinging to the cliff edges; Malta's national plant, it has small, succulent leaves and fluffy, marble-sized mauve flowers during the summer. The cliffs are also home to several pairs of **blue rock thrushes**, the national bird; the male is dark blue and the female dark brown, and they're usually perched on rocky outcrops, uttering a melodious warble and flicking their tails. The cliffs are more renowned, however, for the 10,000-odd pairs of **Cory's shearwaters** which nest here, comprising one of the largest colonies in the Mediterranean. Duck-sized and sporting dark, smoky plumage, they roost here during the May–August nesting season, returning to their perches after a day's fishing. At twilight, you can see them gathering in flocks out to sea, and when nightfall sets in, you can hear the din of their collective melancholy calls and beating wings as they head home.

XLENDI AND AROUND

Some 3km south of Rabat via the scenic Lunzjata and Xlendi valleys, and connected to the capital by bus #87, **XLENDI** (Map 8, E7) is Gozo's second largest seaside **resort**. Laid around cliff-lined Xlendi Bay, the dense fabric of high-rise hotels and apartment blocks lend a claustrophobic feel and have largely ruined Xlendi's natural beauty. Nonetheless, this stark disposition mellows in the soft evening light, and, with one of the two good **restaurants** (reviewed on p.279), it's a delightful place to have dinner or a late stroll down the promenade that fronts the bay, lined by quiet waterfront cafés. Cory's shearwaters nest in the cliffs in the outer reaches of the bay, and you'll hear their plaintive mewling as they swoop towards the rocks.

The bay proper is not particularly attractive for a dip; opaque with silt and polluted with motorboat fuel, the water sometimes takes on a slimy green hue. For better swimming, head towards the hunchback promontory of **Ras Il-Bajda**, on the southeast reaches of the bay.

Ras Il-Bajda

Map 8, D7.

From Xlendi it's a fifteen-minute walk along the footpath that skirts the southern shore of the bay to the **Ras Il-Bajda** promontory, meaning "the white head" after its beige-coloured crust of clay – it's commonly referred to simply as Tar-Ras. The route passes the **Xlendi Tower** – another of the Knights' coastal defences, it was built in 1658. The view of the cliffs meandering towards the horizon across the bay is reason enough for the walk, but most people come to swim. Beyond the tower, a curiously eroded globigerina-limestone plateau, peppered with scattered salt pans, tilts towards the waterline. The water here is over 20m deep, yet the rockface that slopes sharply underwater offers intriguing rock formations for **snorkelling**; there's a good chance of seeing starfish, sea urchins and octopus. Across the water, at the opposite mouth of Xlendi Bay, you can spot the black gape of a large cave at water level that winds deep into the cliff and emerges on the inner part of the bay; if you want to explore the length of the cave, bear in mind that a three-metre stretch of it is underwater – seasoned swimmers should be able to navigate it fairly easily, however.

The west

Western Gozo is far less built up than the south. The towns are small and the topography more hilly and undulating, comprised largely of cultivated land, and even in the sleepy towns, you'll still encounter the occasional farmer trundling his produce home on a mule-driven cart or herding flocks of sheep and goats through the streets. Nightlife is virtually non existent and there are only two restaurants, but such tranquillity has not gone unnoticed: the villages of Għarb and Għasri are littered with the exclusive holiday homes of the Maltese middle class, alongside clusters of self-catering villas aimed at the tourist market. The few notable sights in this region, though scattered, can all be seen in a day. Although the shrine of **Ta' Pinu Basilica** is connected with somewhat dubious tales of miracles and holy apparitions, it's not strikingly attractive but it's worth a quick peep en route to **Ġordan Hill** to the north, which affords lovely panoramic views over the northwestern coast. One of the oldest settlements on the island, **Għarb** retains a pleasantly traditional farming ambience and holds one of Gozo's most attractive parish churches as well as an absorbing **Folklore Museum**, but the prettiest spot is on the coast at **Dwejra**, where geological movements have created a landscape of outstanding natural beauty.

TA' PINU BASILICA

Map 8, D4.

Daily 7am–12.30pm & 1.30–7pm; free.

An imposing Romanesque church, the **Ta' Pinu Basilica** is located in open countryside at the foot of a hill between the towns of Għasri and Għarb; bus #91 from Rabat stops right outside. A chapel has existed on this site since the medieval era; by 1575, it had fallen into disrepair, and Pope Gregory XII's apostolic delegate Pietro Duzina ordered the building to be demolished. It's alleged that the workman who struck the first blow with the sledge hammer broke his arm – a sign interpreted as divine intervention, thus sparing the chapel. In 1883, the chapel gained notoriety when local peasant Karmela Grima, while working in the neighbouring fields, is said to have heard a disembodied **voice** summoning her to the chapel, where it instructed her to "recite three hail Mary's in honour of the three days my body was confined to the tomb". Grima's story spread like wildfire, and the islanders started making **pilgrimages** to the chapel. The present church was built between 1920 and 1932 to accommodate the ever-increasing number of pilgrims, who still flock here today.

The Romanesque church is designed on the standard Latin cross outline, with a separate bell tower. It's not an impressive building, its bare stone interior walls left unadorned; the still-intact **original chapel** behind the altar of the modern church holds more aesthetic appeal. On the way to the chapel you pass through corridors brimming with the votive offerings made by people allegedly healed by Ta' Pinu's miraculous powers; there's everything from crash helmets, crutches, wheelchairs and prosthetic limbs to rather graphic pictures of wounded people. The small, whitewashed chapel itself is pretty basic, but the devoted prayers of the pilgrims lend a rapt feel, and the simple but moving altarpiece, painted by the Italian artist Amadeo Perugino and depicting eight angels buzzing around and crowning the Madonna in heaven, is a delight.

GORDAN HILL

Map 8, C3.

About 3km north of Ta' Pinu Basilica, a signposted country

road winds through the fringes of Għasri to the table-top summit of Ġordan Hill, girdled by an amber, jagged cliff face and slopes of blue clay, and topped by a lighthouse – both are visible from Ta' Pinu and are impossible to miss. From the top of the hill, you get an excellent panorama over the undulating northwest coast. The Ġordan lighthouse was built in the nineteenth century, and though its revolving beam still shines at night, the building also serves as a meteorological station.

GĦARB

Map 8, C5.

At the centre of Gozo's western tip, and connected to Rabat by bus #91, **GĦARB** is the most traditional and the sleepiest town in the Maltese islands, and has seen relatively little new development. The Baroque parish **Church of the Visitation** in the central square, built between 1699 and 1729, has one of the most attractive exteriors in Gozo – an ornate dome atop a concave facade framed by two twin bell towers, adorned with three female statues that represent Faith (standing above the door), Hope (to the left) and Charity (to the right). Opposite the church, the **Folklore Museum** (Mon–Sat 9am–4pm, Sun 9am–1pm; Lm1.25) is housed in a restored eighteenth-century townhouse. The collection is spread over 28 rooms, and centres on the tools, machinery and manufacturing techniques of small-scale local industries that operated in Gozo before the advent of electricity and motor machinery in the early twentieth century. Each room is dedicated to a different **trade**, and captions describe the exhibits and explain how they were employed. Most of the tools were ingeniously created locally and constructed out of wood. It's an interesting collection, and sheds light onto Gozitan life – some of the tools and traditional methods are still employed today by the older generation, such as the wooden grape presses employed by home wine-makers, and equipment for making *ġbejniet* cheeses.

Otherwise, Għarb offers no specific attractions, but it's well worth roaming around to admire the old townhouses, whose stone balconies are inscribed with intricate Baroque motifs. During your wanderings, keep an eye out for **"houses of character"**, the local term for the immaculate, painstakingly restored luxury dwellings, usually owned by Maltese businesspeople and well-off foreigners. Għarb holds the islands' highest concentration of these imposing dwellings, dripping in rustic charm and boasting expansive vernacular gardens, swimming pools and rooms that smack of an interior designers' touch. Houses of character are highly prized by Malta's elite, a phenomenon that has turned Għarb into a town of a few hundred locals and many more absentee residents.

DWEJRA

Map 8, B6.

Southwest of Għarb via the neighbouring village of San Lawrenz, a road trundles through the countryside to **Dwejra**. An undulating landscape shaped by geological rifts and characterized by bowl-shaped valleys, its coastline pockmarked with bays, the crater-like topography here has a bleak, alien attraction. Offshore, the underwater cliffs, valleys, ledges, massive plateaux and deep caves supporting soft coral offer what many consider the best **scuba diving** to be had in the Mediterranean. However, Dwejra is in an advanced state of degradation: several quarries continue to shred the hillsides to pieces and clog the valleys with rubble, while bird-trapping sites and off-road vehicles are leading to serious erosion.

In front of the car park (where bus #91 from Rabat drops you off) is the **Azure Window**, a natural window over 100m in height and width created by the waves pounding into the cliffs. Standing near the Azure Window, look towards the cliffs rising in the south to spot the outline of a face in profile: a bulging brow, narrowed eyes, crooked nose and pursed lips. To the northwest, a short walk down a road leads you to the **Inland Sea** – a land-locked body of seawater connected to the Mediterranean via a tunnel in the cliffs. Spread along the shores of the Inland Sea are clusters of so-called boathouses that are more usually – and illegally – used as summer houses, one of the blights that smear Dwejra's natural beauty. Southeast of the car park, a path takes you past **Dwejra Tower**, one of the seventeenth-century coastal defences built by the Knights; beyond here is the horse shoe-shaped **Dwejra Bay**. The shallow water here is almost pitch black due to a thick blanket of seaweed on the seabed.

At the mouth of the bay, majestic **Fungus Rock** (Il-Ġebla Tal-Ġeneral) soars seventy metres out of the sea into a stout pinnacle. Its English name derives from an endemic **fungus** which only grows on this rock, and was discovered here by a general of the Knights (hence its Maltese name, "the rock of the general"). The Knights erroneously considered the fungus, which looks like a brown, forearm-sized phallus, to have medicinal properties. and used it in a concoction to cure dysentery and as a dressing for wounds. To preserve it for the Knights' use only, Grand Master Pinto put the rock under 24-hour guard and decreed it out of bounds in 1746; any trespassing was punishable by three years in the galleys. Today, Fungus Rock is a **nature reserve** and, to protect the fungus, its still out of bounds to the public.

The North

Most visitors to Gozo spend most of their time in the **northern** portion of the island. Although it's Gozo's busiest region, a gentle feel remains: the wide, quiet streets bask in the sunshine, and even at the height of the summer, the volume of tourists only amounts to a trickle of stragglers at **Marsalforn**. This is Gozo's largest resort, its low-rise apartment blocks and hotels spread around an open bay where children splash in the sea and local youths play water polo. The cafés and restaurants that skirt the water only get busy on summer evenings, when strollers – tourists and Gozitans alike – throng the promenade; in winters, Marsalforn is battered by waves and largely deserted. West of Marsalforn, you can take pleasant afternoon strolls to the **Salt Pans**, hundreds of man-made depressions used for the traditional production of sea salt, while further on along the coast, **Wied Il-Għasri** is a bleakly attractive creek. Up the hill southeast of Marsalforn, and northeast of Rabat, **Xagħra** is one of Gozo's largest towns. After touring the sights – which include **Ġgantija Temples**, Gozo's major attraction – you can observe town life from the cafés that line the attractive square. To its northeast, Xagħra leads to some excellent rural and coastal milieus, including the legendary **Calypso's Cave** and **Ramla Bay**, the most scenic sandy bay in the Maltese islands.

MARSALFORN

Map 8, G3.

More or less in the middle of the north coast, and connected to Rabat via a main road, **MARSALFORN** is Gozo's largest seaside resort, comprised of a ribbon of high-rise apartment blocks and hotels spreading around

Marsalforn Bay. While the apartment blocks all have the same bland architecture, their low density lends an airy and gentle feel to the town. The wide streets remain quiet even in the height of the summer, and the main activity revolves around the handful of supermarkets and the beaches. Few Maltese live in Marsalforn all year round, and up to seventy percent of the dwellings are vacant in winter, when Marsalforn wears the desolate demeanour of a resort in the off-season and most restaurants shut down.

On the waterfront, across the road from the promenade that rings the whole of Marsalforn Bay, a clutch of **restaurants** and **cafés** rub shoulders; most are fairly bland, tourist-oriented operations, though there are a few notable exceptions (reviewed on pp.264 and 279). There's a small sandy **beach** adjacent to the centre of town, but it's exposed to passers-by and the water is relatively silty. Locals swim off the rocks that trace the waterline along the west side of the bay, where the promenade gives way to the rocky shoreline, and there are ladders to get in and out of the water. There's more good swimming to be had west of town, however, at **Għar Qawqla** (see opposite). **Il-Menqa**, the small breakwater-enclosed harbour on the east flank of the bay, is the docking station of several brightly painted *luzzu* fishing boats. During the *lampuki* season (late Aug to Oct), the area jostles with locals waiting for the fishermen to return and unload their catches, which are sold on the spot – it's a vivid scene, with sales pitches wafting through the air alongside the smell of freshly caught fish.

Marsalforn is served by **bus** #21, which stops on the promenade at the centre of town. There is no public transport west of town towards the Salt Pans and Wied Il-Għasri.

Għar Qawqla

Map 8, G2.

Five-minutes' walk around the bay east of Marsalforn proper, immediately beyond the last apartment blocks, the globigerina-limestone and clay plateau of **Għar Qawqla** perches above the coast. Though dusty and battered by heavy seas during windy conditions, it attracts hordes of swimmers during calm weather. Bathers jump into the deep waters straight from the rocks, while local youngsters perform somersault dives from the rock that rises out of the water several metres offshore. Towards Għar Qawqla's eastern extreme, the sea has carved out a natural, small, shallow pool where children can splash about.

QBAJJAR AND XWEJNI

Map 8, F2.

Around 1km along the coast road west of Marsalforn, **Qbajjar** is a relatively large bay, where the clear seas offer good snorkelling; the beach, though, is a small strip of uncomfortable pebbles. A few minutes stroll west, **Xwejni** is another stretch of pebbly shoreline that's better for its views than its swimming: it's picturesquely framed by Il-Qolla Il-Bajda, a mound of clay that has been eroded into the shape of a mushroom.

THE SALT PANS

Map 8, E2.

Just west of Xwejni, Gozo's **salt pans** – hundreds of depressions gouged into the soft globigerina limestone for the production of natural salt – take up a fairly sizeable stretch of coastline, some 2km long by 50m wide. During the winter, heavy waves splatter seawater over the rocks to fill the pans; this evaporates during the calm of the summer, leaving a beige crust of salt over the bottom. If you visit in August, you'll see gangs of workers shovelling the salt into bags; the uncrushed crystals are sold in most local supermarkets. Despite the commercial slant, the pans are quite beautiful to look at: a lip of warm, auburn-coloured rock separates each pan, creating an intriguing web of abstract patterns, and during the winter the saltwater reflects the sky and the area takes on the look of a field of mirrors. The concave waves of the eroded globigerina limestone behind the salt pans adds to the effect.

WIED IL-GĦASRI

Map 8, D3.

A further 2km west of the salt pans and overlooked by the Gordan Lighthouse (see p.211), the coast road swerves inland and forks: the left fork climbs up to the nondescript town of Zebbug, while the right fork is a dirt road that leads down to **Wied Il-Għasri**, a deep, snaking gorge about 500m long with a creek at the bottom. The only human intervention here are the flight of stairs pickaxed into the cliffside to provide access to the inner mouth of the creek, where a tiny pebbly beach gives way to the narrow body of green-blue water. This is an excellent spot for **snorkelling**; look out for stingrays, and some curious underwater topography towards the outer reaches of the creek.

XAGĦRA

Map 8, H4.

XAGĦRA, 3km northeast of Rabat and connected by buses #64 and #65, is one of Gozo's largest towns, sprawling over a series of ridges and bluffs. It's a comparatively busy place, and boasts one of the island's liveliest, most attractive town squares, **Pjazza Vittorja**. Graced by an imposing parish church and ringed by oleander trees, the square holds a handful of traditional winebars that pay tribute to colonial rule – the *Diamond Jubilee* and *Olympic* bars are particularly good – as well as the renowned local restaurant *Oleander*, which has become a focal point for local youth who hang out outside. Xagħra's proud parishioners also celebrate one of the largest *festas* in the Maltese islands each September 8, a public holiday which holds special significance for Gozitans, as it commemorates the Great Siege of 1565 (see p.336).

Xagħra also holds some of Gozo's most delightful sights. **Ġgantija Temples**, the oldest of Malta's Neolithic temples, are an absolute must-see, and there are several less monumental attractions within the town that are worth checking out too, including the stalactite- and stalagmite-filled **Xerri's Grotto**, and the cache of antique and modern toys at the **Pomskizillious Museum**. At the northeastern reaches of the town, **Calypso's Cave** was, according to Homer's *Odyssey*, home to the nymph Ogygia, and though it's a claustrophobic cavern, the panorama from its mouth is mesmerizing.

Ġgantija Temples

Map 8, H5. Mon–Sat 8.30am–4.30pm, Sun 8.30am–3pm; Lm1.
Five-minutes' walk southeast of Pjazza Vittorja, down Vjal It-Tmienja Ta' Settembru, stand the colossal **Ġgantija Temples**; if you're travelling from Rabat by bus, you will reach the temples before the Pjazza Vittorja. Of all of the Neolithic temples in the Maltese islands, the two at Ġgantija are the most impressive – and the oldest: constructed around 3600 BC, they are the oldest human-built structures in the world. The site was originally excavated in

1827, and work between 1987 and 1994 unearthed the **Xagħra Stone Circle**, an underground burial shrine located 300m east of the temples proper, which yielded thousands of Neolithic skeletons that deepened archeologists' understanding of Neolithic culture. The entrance to the stone circle faced the temples, a deliberate configuration that symbolized the Neolithic peoples' worldview that death was a reflective continuity of life. The circle is closed to the public, however.

Sadly, like all other Neolithic sites in Malta, Ġgantija complex is suffering from neglect, its walls teetering dangerously close to collapse, and there's little information on the structures themselves. Nonetheless, Ġgantija remains fairly intact, its massive walls projecting high above the bluff on which they're situated. The circular complex is comprised of the North and South temples, which share one perimeter wall, and save for its altars and passageway megaliths Ġgantija is built entirely from upper coralline limestone; its largest megalith, weighing 55 tonnes, is as large as a pick-up truck. The inner shrines of the five-apsed **North Temple** holds the crumbling remains of its simple altars: a flat slab of rock resting on two upright stones. The **South Temple** is markedly larger, its arrangement more sophisticated and its five apses more protracted. You first step on the large stone slab that served as the **threshold** (symbolically marking the transition from the physical life to the divine), while a series of **bowls** cut into the rocks immediately behind it suggest some sort of purification ritual before entry into the temple. Dramatically pitted upright megaliths frame the passageways, and in the first apse on the right are several slabs of stone arranged in a spatial configuration that probably had some divine or ceremonial significance; if you look closely, you can still detect the eroding **spiral motifs**. Also lining the passageways are the **libation holes** that are thought to have been used to drain blood from sacrificed animals offered to the earth for its providence. In the second chamber, the three altars of the apse have survived virtually intact. Some believe that the South Temple is enveloped by some kind of uncanny **energy**, and exponents of the theory claim to have been overwhelmed by hallucinations or a sense of some kind of sacred aura after entering. Though this may well be simply a projection of believers' imagination, archeologists have long reported that dowsing sticks are particularly active here.

Ta' Kola Windmill Museum

Map 8, H4. Triq Il-Mithna. Mon–Sat 8.30am–4.30pm, Sun 8.30am–3pm; Lm1.

From Ġgantija Temples, head northeast along Triq L-Imqades, and take the second left into Triq Il-Mithna, which takes you to the **Ta' Kola Windmill Museum**. Recently restored as a tourist attraction having ceased commercial wheat-grinding at the beginning of the twentieth century, the windmill dates from 1725, and is an attraction in its own right. The square two-storey main building, built out of yellow-coloured stone, gives way to a round turret and sails. **Inside**, the ground floor holds a rather dull exhibition on traditional trades (mainly carpentry, as well as a blacksmith's workshop) which are best bypassed in favour of the second floor, where you can peruse re-created millers' living quarters, including the kitchen with its traditional *kenur* (stone cooking hearth), as well as the dining room, living room and two bedrooms, all with period furnishings. The apparatus for grinding wheat in the turret has been left in place, and you can go up the spiral staircase to get a close look at the workings, an intriguing piece of engineering with its huge cogwheels fashioned out of timber.

Xerri's Grotto

Map 8, H4. Triq L-Għar Ta' Xerri. Daily 10am–5pm; Lm0.50.

Head down the alley in front of the Ta' Kola Windmill Museum, then left into Triq It-Tigrija, which takes you to Pjazza Vittorja. Situated in a private house (but accessed via a separate corridor) **Xerri's Grotto** was discovered in 1923 when the owner was digging a well and stumbled on this small cavern bursting with intricate formations. To enter the cave, you go down a spiral staircase – the shaft of the unfinished well – into fantasyland: yellowish stalactites and stalagmites have formed into curious shapes, ranging from flat plates that resemble elephant's ears to the tumour-like growths that cover most of the walls. You are accompanied by a guide, who struggles to explain things in broken English.

To get to the cave from Pjazza Vittorja, take Triq Il-Knisja across the square, turn right into Triq Il-Bullara at the end of the road, then left from here onto Triq L-Għar Ta' Xerri.

Pomskizillious Museum of Toys

Map 8, H4. 10 Triq Ġnien Xibla. May to mid-Oct Mon–Sat 10am–noon & 3–6pm; mid-Oct to April Mon–Sat 10am–1pm; Lm0.90.

Five-minutes' walk east of Pjazza Vittorja, via Triq It-Tiġrija (turn off to the right at Triq Ġnien Xibla), the **Pomskizillious Museum of Toys** borrows its tongue-twisting name from the imagination of the eccentric British poet **Edward Lear**, who visited Gozo in 1865–66 and described the coastal scenery as "pomskizillious and gromphiberrous…there being no other words to describe its magnificence".

In addition to a section dedicated to Lear, where a life-sized model of the man himself scribbles at a desk, alongside some of the poems he wrote about Gozo, the museum's glass cases brim with toys from Western Europe and North America, dating from the nineteenth to the twentieth centuries. If you want more detail on the pieces, you can ask for an informal tour, which provides a contextual background on the eras in which they were made. Highlights include British dolls' houses from the Victorian era, suitably decked out with period furnishings; British model railways made in 1930s Britain, spooky Pelham puppets from the 1950s, with their jester-like garb and Pinocchio noses, and heaps of nineteenth-century German and French dolls made from wood, bisque, cloth or rubber.

Calypso's Cave

Map 8, I3.

From the Pomskizillious Museum, backtrack into Triq It-Tiġrija, from where you can follow signs to **Calypso's Cave**, about fifteen-minutes' walk away. Perched on a bluff above the sea, this is said to be the legendary cave inhabited by the nymph Ogygia in Homer's *Odyssey*, where she kept Odysseus captive of her love for seven years. The claustrophobic cavern, in which you can hardly stand upright, is formed by fissures in the rocky bluff; if you crawl along, you can get to the end of its 20m depth. For a tip, touts hand out candles and matches to enable you to see the interior, and will point out the flight of stairs fashioned down a crack on the rock's surface to provide access to the damp interior. Though the cave itself isn't particularly impressive, the **view** here is well worth the walk: a clay slope tumbles to Ramla Bay where the orange sand meets the clear, blue Med, while inland is the rolling Ramla Valley. About 20m offshore, you can spot a black thread crossing the bay underwater: this is a **defensive wall** built by the Knights to prevent boats landing in the bay. East of the wall you can pick out the **fougasse** holes in the rockface that were packed with gunpowder and stones that were fired on boats attempting to breach the wall and land.

RAMLA BAY

Map 8, I3.

Three kilometres north of Xagħra, **Ramla Bay**, enclosed between two headlands, is among the most stunning sandy beaches in the Mediterranean, and gets understandably crowded as a result. Its lurid, orange-crimson sand covers a 500m stretch of shoreline, giving way to undulating sand dunes at the back. Along its sides, the bay steps up in terraced fields interspersed by thick meadows of bamboo whipped into elegant ripples by the sea breezes; further up the slopes, the cliffs are mottled with amber streaks and pockmarked with caves. When the breeze is down, the silvery body of water laps the shore, while in windy conditions it rolls ashore in long, tufted waves that are, however, too shallow for surfing. Ramla Bay's beauty is very fragile, though, and the **sand dunes** at the back of the bay, bound by tamarisk trees and characterized by sparse vegetation, represent the last surviving stretch in the Maltese islands and have been afforded official protection by the authorities. They harbour a handful of rare plants and insects, some of which are endemic and easily destroyed: avoid lying on the sand dunes, let alone camping or having a barbecue. There are a couple of kiosks where the main road from Xagħra peters out, serving drinks and fast-food snacks, and renting out umbrellas and deckchairs. East of the bay a path winds along the coast to **Blata L-Bajda**, a deserted, scenic clay plateau at the mouth of the bay that's a popular gay cruising zone. West of the bay, another path leads to a small sandy cove about 100m away from the main beach, which is usually quieter than its neighbour and is backed by bulging clay slopes.

The **road to Ramla Bay** is well signposted from Xagħra's Pjazza Vittorja; alternatively you can scramble down the path from Calypso's Cave. In the summer, there are a couple of daily buses to and from Rabat to Ramla Bay.

GĦAJN BARRANI

Map 8, H3.

The scenic cove of **Għajn Barrani** is along a plateau of hard-packed clay and large rocky boulders, but because it's hard to find and access is poor, it's mostly deserted. Legend has it that Muslim corsairs used to shelter here and collect water from the spring that trickles down the beach, hence the name Għajn Barrani or "foreigner's spring". The water is clear and inviting, and favoured by nude bathers – as stories of flashers are common here, it's wise to visit in a group. To **get to Għajn Barrani**, take the road that runs between Xagħra and Marsalforn; from here, around 2km northwest of Xagħra, a farmer's dirt road branches off to the east near a roundabout with a well in its centre. Follow this dirt road until it peters out, after which you'll have to park and walk the final ten-minute stretch down to the sea.

The southeast

Gozo's **southeast tip**, while not home to any historical sights, does have several beaches and creeks that are well worth exploring. North of Nadur, the area's sizeable but eminently missable main town, **San Blas** and **Daħlet**

Qorrot are two dramatic bays cut into bluffs and backed by valleys. East of Nadur, the smaller settlement of Qala serves as the gateway to **Ħondoq Ir-Rummien**, a small beach that gets hideously packed in summer, and to **Il-Ġebla Tal-Ħalfa**, one of Gozo's loveliest and loneliest bathing holes, a great place for some snorkelling.

Buses #42 and #43 from Rabat run to Nadur's church square and on through Qala's church square before doubling back to the capital.

SAN BLAS

Map 8, K3.

A small, sandy beach with bright-orange sand, **San Blas** is cut among bluffs of rocky cliffs. The slopes backing the beach step up in terraced groves of citrus trees that thrive in the sandy soil, and are screened from wind and sea spray by bamboo hedges. San Blas is a relatively quiet spot, with inviting water, and has been left in its pristine natural state – there are no facilities, and it's a great spot for a day of solitude by the sea.

To **get to San Blas** by car, follow the signs from Nadur's church square; otherwise, you'll have to manage the 4km journey on foot, as the beach isn't served by public transport. The route is marked all the way, and the final leg, past where the houses end, is via a farmer's road that heads down a steep slope.

DAĦLET QORROT

Map 8, L3.

A kilometre or so east of San Blas, the inlet of **Daħlet Qorrot** is reachable via another 4km-long signposted road from Nadur, which ends at a car park by the beach. There are no facilities here, and the only developments are the scattering of illegally erected boathouses around the edge of the bay, used by fishermen who moor their boats here. Dahlet Qorrot is backed by a wide, undulating valley that rises towards the coast into dramatic, bulging headlands. The patch of dull beige sand is pretty small, and gives way on either side to rocky plateaux. You can jump off the rocks into the water and then climb back via fixed ladders. East of the bay, the topography of rock and garigue slopes gently towards the waterline, and you should head this way if you're looking for deserted spots to spend a day by the sea. Along this stretch, the water is an inky blue, deep but delightful, and there are plenty of nooks and crannies to explore with a snorkel and mask.

ĦONDOQ IR-RUMMIEN AND ĠEBLA TAL-ĦALFA

Well-signposted **Ħondoq Ir-Rummien** (Map 8, M5) about 3km east of Qala's town square, is a small sandy creek that gets packed with locals in the summer, despite the fact that of all the beaches in Gozo, it's one of the least attractive. Part of the shoreline has been given an unsightly covering of concrete, and an ugly water-desalination plant is tucked behind the bay. The crowds here can get pretty raucous, so it's not the place to be if you want some peace. A couple of kiosks serve refreshments.

Nearby **Ġebla Tal-Ħalfa** (Map 8, N5) is a much better place to swim. It's reachable via the road to Ħondoq Ir-Rummien from Qala, just outside the town, you pass a chapel; take the second left past this, a farmer's road that veers east and winds downhill until it peters out near the coast, where you can park in a disused field. From here, take the path that heads towards the sea; Ġebla Tal-Ħalfa is not the first creek you pass, but is a further ten-minutes' walk round the coast to the northeast, recognizable by the 50m rock towering majestically out of the water at the mouth of the bay. A beautiful inlet untouched by development, Ġebla Tal-Ħalfa's soft globigerina plateau gives way to a pebbly beach backed by a steep slope of clay that's crisscrossed by mini-gullies. To the west, the shoreline steps up the coast in a profile of jagged rocks. The blue-green water is inviting, and if you've a **snorkel**, swim towards the rock at the mouth of the bay to explore the bright red and yellow tube fishes attached to cracks in the rock face, and the clouds of small fish darting through the water.

Comino

From the sea, **Comino** (Kemmuna) looks like little more than barren rock with patches of stunted shrubs, but its garigue plateaux harbour a surprising variety of flora and fauna, including some endemic species. The charming islet – now a protected **nature reserve** – is midway between Malta and Gozo and is only 2km long by 1.7km wide, traversed by dirt roads that serve a handful of motor vehicles. Its largely unspoilt attractions include the largest patch of undissected garigue in Malta, superb beaches, breathtaking clifftop scenery, and some excellent **snorkelling** and **scuba diving**.

Throughout spring and summer, Comino sees its fair share of campers, day-trippers and beach bums, but for the rest of the year, things are very much quieter. The best time to visit is in the spring, when the sun is pleasantly warm and the garigue blooms into a mosaic of flowers. A day of lazy **walking** – with the essential accoutrements of a hat and some drinking water – is the finest way to get acquainted with the island.

For more on the garigue, one of Malta's
most important natural habitats.

Some history

There's scant evidence of Comino's history before the thirteenth century, when the island became a parish centred on the chapel of Our Lady's Return from Egypt, which is still standing. The most illustrious figure in Comino's past, the self-proclaimed prophet **Abraham ben Samuel Abulafia**, fled to the island in 1285 after offending the Catholic sensibilities of the Maltese. His insults were harmless enough – a vision for a new religion uniting Christianity, Judaism and Islam – but when Pope Nicholas III had a heart attack after meeting him in the Vatican, Abulafia had to escape or face execution. Abulafia lived out his days on Comino, expounding his philosophy in the *Book of the Sign*, which included his controversial proposal that Palestine be merged, physically and religiously, into a larger Jewish state.

For centuries after, Comino was a hideout for **pirates**, who lay low in sheltered inlets, rushing out to ambush boats crossing between the islands. It was the **Knights** who swept them away in the sixteenth and seventeenth centuries, fortifying the isle with St Mary's Tower, St Mary's Battery and an outpost at Santa Marija Bay, and designating Comino their private game reserve.

Progressive administrations since have tried to populate Comino, with varying degrees of success. The island's agricultural prosperity reached its peak in 1926 when it was leased to Captain **Arthur Zammit Cutajar**. Cutajar employed 65 peasants, who created fields enclosed by rubble walls and exported vegetables and cash crops such as honey and cumin (from which the island had got its name in previous centuries). By World War II, Cutajar's agricultural estate was facing financial hardship, and as Cutajar cut back his operations, the population dwindled.

In 1960, in a drive to develop the tourist industry, the government ended Cutajar's lease and handed Comino to a private company, which built the **Comino Hotel** and a cluster of resort bungalows. Yet, in a dramatic turnaround in 1975, Prime Minister Dom Mintoff discovered a small-print breach of the contract and snatched everything outside the hotel grounds back into government hands.

Modern Comino

Today, four people live on Comino – two brothers, their aunt and a cousin, all descendants of Cutajar's farming community. Their home is now a **nature reserve**, overrun by wild rabbits, rats and snakes, home to endemic species of snails, beetles and ants, and at least four pairs of the blue rock thrush, Malta's national bird.

Over the past decade, environmentalists have successfully blocked various development proposals, including a golf course and agrotourism centre. The organization Birdlife Malta is keen to exploit the island's potential: poised between Malta and Gozo, Comino funnels migratory birds from one to the other. In 1991, they launched an ongoing study across Comino, in collaboration with fourteen other Mediterranean islands, trapping and ringing birds to learn more about their migratory behaviour, and are also keen to turn Comino's most fertile valley, **Wied L-Aħmar**, into a bird observatory. Yet they are facing stoic resistance from one of the residents, who continues to defy the law by hunting on Comino and bullying visiting birders off the island.

Arrival and orientation

Comino Hotels (☏529821 ⓦwww.cominohotels.com) operate **ferries** to Comino; the trip from either Ċirkewwa on Malta or **Mġarr harbour** on Gozo takes about twenty minutes, and costs Lm2 return. This service, however, is matched to the hotel's needs: in summer, boats run about every two hours (6am–10pm), with reduced service in

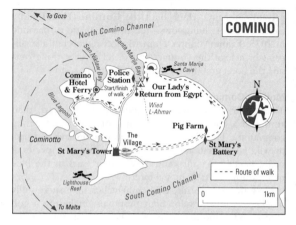

spring and autumn, and no service at all when the hotel is shut in winter (Nov–March). During winter, you might be able to find a fisherman at Mġarr harbour willing to make the crossing (agree a price in advance – Lm5 is a generous offer); otherwise track down the parish priest who goes to Comino every weekend. An alternative is to take a Captain Morgan day-trip, which departs from the **Sliema Ferries** daily at 9.15am direct to the Blue Lagoon, heading back at 3pm (Lm8.95, including lunch; ☏343373).

The Comino Hotels ferry drops off in front of the hotel at San Niklaw Bay, a short walk from the famous beach of the **Blue Lagoon**. Comino's other star beach is the glorious **Santa Marija Bay**, which features, in addition, good snorkelling and scuba diving. To take in the few sights, and the dramatic seacliffs pockmarked by caves, the best walking route runs anticlockwise around the coast, a 9km loop that would take, at a stroll and allowing for stops, about half a day.

THE BLUE LAGOON AND AROUND

From **San Niklaw Bay**, take the dirt road beyond the hotel and take the left turn at a crossroads. On the crest of a hillock to your left, you'll spot a grey, weathered wall that encloses the old cemetery, its graves now collapsing from neglect.

This road leads to the **Blue Lagoon**, a fittingly evocative name for this sweep of turquoise water ringed by sandy beaches, sandwiched between Comino and its sister islet of Kemmunett. Take a dip as early as possible: from mid-morning until late afternoon, boats packed with day-tripping bathers drop off here, and you can taste the petrol in the water.

Heading south on the coastal walk, skirt the cliff-edge towards Comino's landmark **St Mary's Tower**, built in 1618 by Grand Master Alof de Wignacourt and perched at the edge of 150m cliffs. In 1645, the tower was the focus of the Knights' deployment of cannons and troops to protect the Malta–Gozo channel, while in 1800, after the British succeeded in driving away the French, some two thousand prisoners-of-war, including 53 Maltese suspected of spying, were corralled into the tower (and the Village; see below). It's still in military hands today, as an army outpost.

From the cliff-edge, you can enjoy a peaceful and lonely view over the water, broken by Gozo Channel ferries chugging past. Crevices in the cliffs hereabouts are the home of Malta's national bird, the blackbird-sized **blue rock thrush**; the male is dark blue, the female brownish-grey. Their distinctive melodious warble gives them away, as does the way they perch on outcrops and flick their tails like robins.

THE VILLAGE AND AROUND

Backtracking past St Mary's Tower, head east to the **Village**, a horseshoe-shaped two-storey building, with loggias overlooking a courtyard. Erected in 1912, it served as an isolation hospital for plague and cholera victims before becoming the living quarters of Cutajar's farming community. Now it's abandoned, the sea-spray eroding its limestone walls.

Keep walking east along the dirt road that runs parallel to Comino's south coast until you stumble on a pig farm, built here to raise disease-free animals after foot-and-mouth disease decimated Malta's pig stock in the 1980s. Behind it, at the edge of a cliff, is **St Mary's Battery**, built by the Knights in 1714 and recently restored from its advanced state of collapse. This is the best-preserved example of the dozens of batteries erected by the Knights in their seventeenth-century drive to reinforce Malta's coastal defences. Like its counterparts, St Mary's Battery is a semicircular gun platform overlooking the sea, and in its heyday eight cannons poked out of its saw-toothed parapet. The defenders ate and slept in rooms in the basement under the parapet. The door to the battery is usually open, and you can go in or else climb over the low wall.

WIED L-AĦMAR

Pressing east along the cliff-edge, the land climbs towards Comino's highest point as you round the coast. The view east takes in Comino's rolling profile, and the trough that is **Wied L-Aħmar**, the island's most fertile valley, with its carpet of bright yellow flowers of cape sorrel in spring, its carobs, olives, Aleppo pines and acacias. Here, the garigue is at its thickest, with a huge diversity of plant life, including musty-scented wild thyme, the bulbous onion-like seaside squill, and St John's wort with its pea-sized yellow flowers. If you're lucky, you might stumble on the rare **giant orchid**, with its single stem bursting into pink flowers clustered in a bushel.

SANTA MARIJA BAY AND AROUND

Follow the cliff-edge downhill until you arrive at the outermost tip of the eastern side of **Santa Marija Bay**, another excellent beach and an ideal spot for picnics and swimming in the glittering turquoise water. If you explore among the rocky boulders on this eastern side of the bay, you'll find the mouth of a **tunnel**, which winds its way on until it opens out in a cave at sea level at the foot of the cliff. Venture into the tranquil cave, lit by reflected sunlight dancing on the roof, and you'll find that it opens out to form an inlet, dubbed **Santa Marija Cave**, enclosed by soaring cliffs. This is the only way to access this inlet, which is renowned for its good **snorkelling** and scuba diving; if you're there to explore below the surface, keep close to the cliff-face where most marine life searches for food.

Crossing Santa Marija Bay brings you to a cream-coloured building on the water's edge. This is another outpost built by the Knights in 1743, these days serving as Comino's **police station**.

Behind the police station at Santa Marija Bay
is Comino's only **campsite**. It's free to stay, to use
the two toilets and to fill your bottles.

Across the road from the police station are the stepped bungalows of the *Club Nautico* resort, an annexe of the island's hotel. Some 50m behind the police station, an oleander-lined road leads to Comino's little thirteenth-century chapel, mysteriously dubbed **Our Lady's Return from Egypt** (open for weekend services only), shaded by cypresses and a palm tree. Its simplicity of design, typical of medieval Malta's vernacular architecture, makes the building striking, with its three bells dangling inside hoops of stone, snout-like rainwater spouts, and timber doors and windows.

Continuing along the road beyond the chapel, turning right at the first crossroads, then right again, will bring you back to San Niklaw Bay for the return ferry.

LISTINGS

Accommodation

Though most people visiting Malta book their **accommodation** as part of a package holiday, the islands are awash with options for independent travellers, ranging from self-catering apartments and villas to hostels and all grades of guesthouse and hotel. In the summer high season, when tour operators' block-bookings account for the majority of beds in the islands, it's essential to book your room as far in advance as possible.

The cheapest places to stay are Malta's two **hostels**, where you can get a bed in a dorm for Lm2, or share a room for a little more. **Guesthouses** – small, basic places, often family run – are the next step up; they usually have shared bathroom facilities, ceiling fans in the rooms, and an on-site restaurant or bar; rates are between Lm5–10. The Maltese government is keen to encourage upmarket tourists, and this has resulted in plenty of high-end **hotels** with the full range of facilities: en-suite bathrooms, TVs, phones, safe and fridge, and swimming pools and a variety of restaurants and bars on the property; rooms cost Lm30–45. Bear in mind that almost all types of accommodation option charge you more for a room with a balcony that affords a sea view, usually about Lm3. If you're travelling in a party of two or more, renting a **self-catering** apartment is an inexpensive option; most of these are not officially registered, and are promoted by adverts in bars and shops, or by touts who approach you in the resorts. Most properties are fine, but you should always have a look before committing yourself. One reliable operator, offering a variety of basic or luxury apartments scattered in Sliema and St Julian's, ranging from two to three bedrooms, and costing Lm5–8 per person per night for a double room, is Simon's Holiday Apartments (☎317008 or 09471623 ✉simonsapt@vol.net.mt). In Gozo, Maria's Farm (☎560554 ℻560554 ✉pgrima@maltanet.net) rent out farmhouses at a bargain rate of Lm5 per person per night for a double room, and also offer other self-catering options, including lodging with a young host family for Lm10 for a double bedroom. Tourist information offices can also provide lists of registered self-catering options on request. It's worth bearing in mind that many hotels, guesthouses and self-catering properties **slash their prices** by as much as half in the December to March low season. A smaller number of places rack their prices in three cycles – summer, winter and the "shoulder" months during autumn and spring – while some even scale their prices in six cycles a year.

Camping is illegal, and there are no officially designated campsites; however some visitors do put up their tents on abandoned land, and if you're discreet and environmentally aware, you're unlikely to be asked to pack up. Popular beaches are policed, however, and you shouldn't even think of camping on the delicate sand dunes at Ramla Bay in Gozo.

Most accommodation options are located in northern Malta, with a concentration in Sliema, St Julian's and Buġibba; in Gozo, accommodation is centred in the seaside resorts of Marsalforn and Xlendi. Since public transport in both islands is relatively slow and inefficient, and taxis a rip-off, you should think carefully about where you base yourself if your budget won't stretch to a rental car or bike.

ACCOMMODATION PRICE CODES

Accommodation listed in this guide has been graded on a scale of ❶ to ❾. These categories show the cost per night of the **cheapest** double room in the high season; where more than one category is shown (e.g. rooms ❻, apartments ❾), the establishment has a selection of accommodation classes. Unless otherwise specified, rates for all the properties listed in this section include breakfast. Most hotels and guesthouses include the mandatory ten percent VAT in their rates, and all the places reviewed in this guide take VAT into account.

❶ under Lm5	❹ Lm15–20	❼ Lm45–60
❷ Lm5–10	❺ Lm20–30	❽ Lm60–80
❸ Lm10–15	❻ Lm30–45	❾ Lm80–100

If you're looking for regular doses of nightlife, the best options are St Julian's or Sliema, which are close to the concentration of clubs in Paceville; Valetta is great if you want historical character, and if you want a beach holiday, head for the St Paul's Bay area in northwest Malta. The best place for rural tranquillity – and some great beaches – is Gozo.

VALLETTA

British Hotel
Map 2, J7. Triq Sant Ursula
☎ 224730 ℻ 239711
🌐 www.britishhotel.com
One of Malta's oldest hotels, founded in the nineteenth century, though with a bland exterior and dull interior. Boasting pine furnishings and beautiful geometric-patterned tiles, rooms have en-suite bathrooms and phones; it's worth paying an extra Lm2 per night for a room with a balcony overlooking the Grand Harbour. ❹.

Castille Hotel
Map 2, H7. Pjazza Kastilja
☎ 220173 ℻ 243679

Ⓔ castillehotel@vol.net.mt

Sumptuous Baroque place across the street from Auberge de Castille, offering large and basic rooms connected by wide, attractive staircases and corridors. *La Cave*, A pizzeria in the barrel-vaulted cellar, dishes good, crusty pizzas. ❺.

Grand Harbour Hotel
Map 2, J7. Triq Sant Ursula
Ⓣ 246003 Ⓕ 242219
Ⓦ www.grandharbourhotel.com
Small hotel with cramped spaces, corridors and staircases, and dull double rooms with en-suite bathroom; nonetheless, it's ideal as a budget base from which to explore Valletta. Try to get one of the rooms that afford an excellent panorama of the Grand Harbour from the balcony. ❸.

Osborne
Map 2, G5. Triq Nofs In-Nhar
Ⓣ 247293 Ⓕ 243656
Recently refurbished but

retaining its old-world charm, this is an intimate and friendly place, and the large but worn out 59 rooms have a/c, phone, TV and private bathroom. Ask for a room on the rear upper floors, as these afford a lovely view over Valletta and Marsamxett Harbour. ❺.

YMCA Hostel
Map 2, K5. 178 Triq Il-Merkanti
Ⓣ & Ⓕ 240680
Ⓔ ymcavalletta@ymcamail.com
Malta's cheapest and most welcoming hostel, geared toward budget-minded independent travellers. Rooms have four/six bunk beds (costing Lm2 per night) some wardrobe space and racks for storing rucksacks, while communal facilities include self-service kitchen, lounge with TV sets, card telephone, a small library of secondhand books, and internet connection at the nearby. *Internet Café*. Breakfast optional for an additional Lm1.50.

SLIEMA AND ST JULIAN'S

Carlton Hotel
Map 2, F4. Tower Rd, Sliema
ⓣ 315764 ⓕ 316736
ⓔ carlton@digigate.net
Lean tower block overlooking Peace Promenade on the outskirts of Sliema, with small, cosy rooms, equipped with a/c and hairdryer, overlooking the St Julian's bays. The better rooms at the front, with en-suite bathrooms and balconies, cost a little more. ❷.

Dean Hamlet
Map 1, I4. Upper Ross St, St Julian's
ⓣ 314838 ⓕ 374144
This complex of one- to three-bedroom apartments and studios in the heart of St Julian's is an ideal base for Paceville. Although pretty tasteless, all units are equipped with fans and full kitchen, and there's a good gym and games room in the basement. The studios are priced at Lm20 in the high season. Studios ❹, apartments ❺.

Fortina
Map 1, K4. Tigne Seafront, Sliema
ⓣ 343380 ⓕ 339388
ⓦ www.hotelfortina.com
Large, whitewashed place five-minutes' walk from the Sliema Ferries that affords stunning views of Valletta across Marsamxett Harbour. Rooms are cosy, with mini-kitchen and TV sets, and as part of its bid to attain five-star status, the *Fortina* offers free bonus attractions, such as boat trips to Comino and scuba diving lessons; concentrated seawater healing techniques are also available in its Thalassa Therapy Spa. ❻.

Galaxy Hotel
Map 4, E5. Triq Depiro, Sliema
ⓣ 344205 ⓕ 344241
ⓔ galaxy@waldonet.net.mt
Massive block set in expansive grounds in the centre of Sliema, where the rooms offer warm colours and privacy; self-catering apartments are comfortable, but decorated in rustic kitsch style. There are

three pools on site and a restaurant and bar. Rooms ❹, apartments ❻.

Hibernia House

Map 4, E6. Triq Depiro, Sliema
Ⓣ 244983 or 246628 (office hours only)
Ⓔ hiberniahouse@yahoo.com
Located in central Sliema, this is Malta's largest hostel. The male and female dorms have twenty bunk beds, which cost Lm2.50 per night. Modern, attractive and comfortable apartments, ranging from studios of three single beds to larger units of six single beds, can also be rented privately. Studios ❹, apartments ❺.

Hilton

Map 1, J4. Portomaso, St Julian's
Ⓣ 336201 Ⓕ 341539
Ⓦ www.hilton.com
Large, exclusive and set in its own grounds on the coast. The 294 tasteful, luxurious and spacious pastel-coloured rooms come equipped with TV, mini-kitchen, phone and internet access. Berthing facilities for yachts are available in a small marina. ❾.

Imperial

Map 4, I6. Rudolph St, Sliema
Ⓣ 344093 Ⓕ 336471
Ⓔ imperial@waldonet.net.mt
The pleasant, tidy and spacious rooms here are a bargain, given the excellent location in the heart of Sliema. The building – a sizeable Baroque townhouse with classy touches such as ceiling murals and an elegant garden framed by stone arches – retains its early twentieth-century charm, and the interior is quiet and cool. ❹.

Lapsi Waterside Hotel

Map 4, C4. Main St Balluta Bay, St Julian's
Ⓣ 378800 Ⓕ 373227
New tower block overlooking Balluta Bay, where the 140 attractive rooms have a/c, hairdryer, TV, radio, minibar, phone and safe. The furnishings are cheerfully rustic with brass touches, and there's a good but expensive French restaurant on the ground floor. ❻.

Pebbles Aparthotel

Map 4, I8. 88–89 The Strand, Sliema

ⓣ 311889 ⓕ 316907

ⓔ pebbles@keyworld.net

Bland multistorey apartment block, centrally located on the seafront near the Sliema Ferries. The 25 studios are somewhat dull, but are well-equipped with kitchenette, TV, fans, and can sleep three for a little extra. You can pay a supplementary Lm4 per night for a room with a view of Marsamxett Harbour and Manoel Island. ➍.

Radisson SAS Bay Point Resort

Map 1, I3. St George's Bay, St Julian's

ⓣ 374894 ⓕ 374895

ⓦ www.islandhotels.com

The last of the string of upmarket hotels slung around the St Julian's coast, this is a cream-painted boomerang-shaped building with a grand lobby, numerous restaurants and pools, a large gym and a row of shops. The large, open-plan rooms have all mod cons as well as a sea view, and are sumptuously decorated with bright colours and potted plants. ➒.

Rokna Hotel

Map 1, J4. Church St, St Julian's

ⓣ 330595 ⓕ 343240

This corner building at the edge of Paceville is rather tasteless, and the 21 rooms are comfortable but characterless, with a/c and TV. There's a quiet piano bar and an inexpensive pizzeria, popular with groups of Maltese, on site. ➍.

Sprachcaffe Club Village

Map 1, I3. Pembroke, St Julian's

ⓣ 373574 ⓕ 373577

ⓔ sprachcaffe@maltanet.net

Large two-storey complex set in the former barracks of the British services, about a kilometre north of Paceville, which incorporates an English language school and a boisterous bar. There are a variety of accommodation options based on a minimum stay of one week, ranging from rooms with a ceiling fan and shared kitchen and bathroom, to studios for one

SLIEMA AND ST JULIAN'S

or two persons. Rooms ❸, studios ❺.

The Victoria

Map 4, I6. Triq Ġorġ Borġ Olivier, Sliema
☏ 334711 ⓕ 334771
ⓦ www.victoriahotel.com
Situated in the heart of Sliema ten-minutes' walk inland from the seafront, this is a lean tower block with a rustic finish. The modern and elegant rooms, with wrought-iron balconies, are decorated in warm colours and have all mod cons including a/c and en-suite bathroom, but common facilities are limited to a restaurant, cramped pool and sun deck. ❼.

Villa Rosa Hotel

Map 1, I3. St George's Bay, St Julian's
☏ 342707 ⓕ 316531
Tucked back from St George's Bay, the expansive grounds are an oasis of tranquillity in a densely built-up area, with palms, oleander trees, roses and cypresses spread over the crest of a slope dominated by a nineteenth-century Neoclassical building (now serving as an English language school as well as a hotel). At the bottom of the slope, the 105 rooms are large and comfortable with en-suite bathroom and phone, and there's a good range of facilities including mini-golf, a whirlpool, and watersports such as boat rentals and windsurfing. ❹.

The Waterfront

Map 1, J4. The Strand, Gzira
☏ 333434 ⓕ 333535
ⓔ info@water.mizzi.com.mt
For a modern, functional and comfortable four-star hotel with good service and conveniently situated on the fringes of Sliema, the rates here are a bargain. The en-suite rooms are tasteful and have a/c, phone and TV; you pay an extra Lm5 for a sea view. ❻.

Westin Dragonara Resort

Map 1, I3. Dragonara Rd, St Julian's
☏ 381000 ⓕ 378877
ⓦ www.westinmalta.com
Situated on the coast at the

outskirts of Paceville, this Neoclassical hotel is central but secluded, nestled in its own manicured gardens, and has an impressive range of facilities, including two small, private rock beaches and a casino. Virtually all of the exceptionally large rooms have sea views. **9**.

White House Hotel
Map 1, I3. Paceville Ave, St Julian's
Ⓣ 378016 Ⓕ 378032
Ⓦ www.whitehousehotel.com
Small, funky, family-run hotel on the fringes of Paceville, with deep-blue decor and abstract paintings on the corridor walls. The 22 rooms are spacious and warmly decorated, with a/c, and the ground floor holds the excellent *Misfits* DJ bar and one of the island's best French restaurants (see pp.293 and 271). **4**.

Windsor Hotel
Map 4, I3. Windsor Terrace, Sliema
Ⓣ 346053 Ⓕ 334301
Situated in a densely built-up part of central Sliema, a block away from the seafront, this offers no-frills, pine-furnished en-suite rooms with safe and hairdryer. **4**.

MDINA, RABAT AND CÉNTRAL MALTA

Buskett Forest Aparthotel
Map 1, F8. Buskett, Rabat
Ⓣ 454266 Ⓕ 455949
A rural location on the outskirts of Rabat, fronted by Buskett Gardens and backed by Dingli Cliffs, where private transport is crucial. There are three basic double rooms with fan and shared bathroom, and thirteen stark but spacious one-bedroom apartments with kitchen. Rooms **2**, apartments **3**.

Corinthia Palace Hotel
Map 1, H5. De Paule Ave, Balzan
Ⓣ 440301 Ⓕ 465713
Ⓦ www.corinthia.com

Slap in the centre of Malta, in manicured suburbs across the street from San Anton Gardens, this offers respite from the chaos of the resorts. Top-notch service, charming rooms, a renowned South Asian restaurant and The Athenaeum, probably Malta's best spa, offering fifty kinds of therapies and tailor-made regeneration programmes. ❾.

Point De Vue Guesthouse

Map 5, H7. 5 Pjazza Saqqajja, Rabat

ⓣ 454117

Townhouse outside the walls of Mdina, where the fourteen cosy rooms have single beds and an en-suite shower – toilets are communal. You can get a bed for Lm6.50 if you're willing to share a room with another traveller. ❷.

University Residence

Map 1, H5. Robert Mifsud Bonniċi St, Lija

ⓣ 436168 ⓕ 434963 ⓔ info @university-residence.com.mt

University halls of residence offering accommodation to visitors all year round (though availability is greater in the summer). Rooms are all in comfortable but basic three-bedroom shared apartments (the kitchen and bathroom are communal), and you'll pay a reduced rate of Lm5.50 if you share a bedroom with a stranger. For the range of facilities on offer – swimming pool, tennis courts, Internet access – this place is a bargain, but note that there is a ban on visitors after 11pm, and that the location isn't convenient for nightlife. ❷.

Xara Palace

Map 5, H4. Triq San Pawl, Mdina

ⓣ 450560 ⓕ 452612

ⓦ www.xarapalace.com.mt

In a class above the rest, this is Malta's best hotel, set in a beautifully restored eighteenth-century palace. Atmospheric, intimate, private and impossibly romantic, rooms are decorated with antique furniture and portraits, and have all mod cons; some afford excellent views and have en-suite jacuzzis. Breakfast costs an extra Lm5.50. ❽.

THE NORTHWEST

The Buccaneers

Map 6, 6A. Triq Ġulju, Buġibba

Ⓣ & Ⓕ 571671

Situated in the built-up core of Buġibba, five-minutes' walk from the seafront and the centre, this guesthouse offers thirty large but stark and basic bedrooms with communal bathrooms. Sharing a room with another traveller is cheaper than a regular double. ❷.

Cape Inch Hotel

Map 6, D5. Il-Merluzz, Buġibba

Ⓣ 572025 Ⓕ 570351

Ⓦ www.capeinchhotel.com

Round the corner from the bus terminus and five-minutes' walk from the seafront, this small, recently refurbished place is a bargain: guesthouse rates for the standards of a two-star hotel, plus friendly service. The en-suite rooms are furnished with neat wardrobes, mirror cabinets, TV sets, bedside tables and attractive double beds. ❷.

Coastline Hotel

Map 1, F3. Salina Bay, Salina

Ⓣ 573781 Ⓕ 581104

Ⓦ www.islandhotels.com

Large imposing hotel on the outskirts of Buġibba, its stepped, pyramidal profile set back from the main road on the coast and bordered by rugged garigue landscape. The grounds are spacious, and the massive lobby and long corridors lead to large, comfortable, pastel-coloured en-suite rooms with a/c and phone. You pay an extra Lm4.50 per night for a room with sea view. ❺.

Corinthia Mistra Village

Map 7, B2. St Paul's Bay

Ⓣ 580481 Ⓕ 582941

Ⓦ www.corinthia.com

Exclusive cluster of one- or two-bedroom semi-detached apartments, designed and decorated with rustic charm, and set around a large freeform pool with lush landscaping; all have a/c, phone, TV, kitchen and balcony. Ideal for families –

the full range of facilities includes a free Kid's Club and theatre performances in an amphitheatre. ❻.

Gillieru Harbour Hotel
Map 7, I4. Triq Il-Knisja, St Paul's Bay
ⓣ 572720 ⓕ 572745
ⓔ gillieru@vol.net.mt
Attractive place with circular balconies and wrought-iron balustrades, situated in between St Paul's Bay and Buġibba and overlooking St Paul's Islands and a small creek dotted with fishing boats. The cream-coloured rooms are cheerful, with a/c, phone and TV, but you pay an extra Lm2.50 a night for a sea view. The restaurant cooks up good seafood. ❺.

Ħal Ferħ Holiday Village
Map 1, C5. Għajn Tuffieħa
ⓣ 573882 ⓕ 573888
Set in landscaped, spacious grounds and surrounded by some spectacular countryside, this sprawling former British military barracks is functional without frills, but private transport is essential. The 154 rooms have fans and shared

bathrooms, and the 74 apartments have double bedroom and kitchen. Rooms ❷, apartments ❸.

Mellieħa Holiday Village
Map 1, B3. Mellieħa Bay, Mellieħa
ⓣ 571727 ⓕ 575452
ⓔ dff@vol.net.mt
Scattered around neatly landscaped grounds of tamarisk trees and palms, these 150 bungalows are tastefully decorated, with a/c, kitchen and a terrace fronting the gardens; most consist of one double bedroom, but there's a handful of studio apartments too. The Danish restaurant is reliable, and there's a supermarket and folk music and weekend live jazz at the bar. Though it's virtually booked out by Danish tour operators in the summer, vacancies are guaranteed between November and April. ❺.

Mercure Selmun Palace
Map 1, D3. Selmun, Mellieħa
ⓣ 521040 ⓕ 521159
Situated on the outskirts of Mellieħa in the midst of

craggy fields and garigue plains, with good views of the sea and the northeast coast, this old-fashioned property has uninspiring en-suite rooms with a/c. The suites are located in the Selmun Palace built by the Knights in the seventeenth century. There is a courtesy bus service to the main sights and beaches. ❺.

New Dolmen Hotel
Map 6, D4. Dawret Il-Qawra, Buġibba
ⓣ 581510 ⓕ 581081
ⓦ www.dolmen.com.mt
On the coast overlooking St Paul's Bay, this is one of Buġibba's largest hotels. An imposing, tasteless exterior leads to a garish interior, but there are a huge range of facilities, including two swimming pools, casino, nightclub, a private lido and watersports. Rooms have all mod cons, and you pay Lm4 extra for one with a sea view. ❺.

Porto Azzurro
Map 7, A5. Triq Ridott, St Paul's Bay
ⓣ 585171 ⓕ 585170

New, attractive, mauve-painted hotel off the coast road in St Paul's Bay, and backed by a ridge of garigue. It's modern and functional, offering 25 en-suite rooms with a/c, as well as studio apartments which have kitchen, bathroom and ceiling fan, and can sleep four. Rooms ❹, studios ❺.

Porto Del Sol Apartments
Map 7, A5. Triq It Telgħa Tax-Xemxija, St Paul's Bay
ⓣ & ⓕ 523804
Apartment block on the coast, where the one-bedroom studios have a shower, kitchenette and shared bathroom. En-suite two-bedroom units, with kitchen, lounge and balcony, are more expensive. ❸.

Sea View
Map 6, C5. Triq L-Imsell, Buġibba
ⓣ 573105 ⓕ 581788
Small, family-run property near the coast in the centre of Buġibba that's ideal as a cheap base. The rooms are basic, with shared bathroom and fan. ❷.

THE NORTHWEST

THE SOUTHEAST

Golden Sun Aparthotel
Map 1, N7. Triq Il-Kajjik, Marsaxlokk

ⓣ 651762 ⓕ 681133

Situated on a side road just back from the seafront, the rooms and apartments here are clustered around a pool and courtyard with a large mural of a pond splashed across one of the walls. Rooms have ceiling fan, phone, TV and shared bathrooms, while the basic and functional one- or two-bedroom apartments have kitchen, phone and iron. Rooms ❷, apartments ❸.

GOZO

Atlantis
Map 8, F3. Qolla St, Marsalforn ⓣ 554685 ⓕ 555661
ⓔ atlantis@digigate.nt

Clean and bright rooms, with a/c, phone and TV, in a family-run hotel just up the coast from the main Marsalforn seafront. Facilities include sauna, gym, squash courts and internet access. ❷.

Cornucopia
Map 8, G4. Triq Ġnien Imrik, Xagħra
ⓣ 556486 ⓕ 552910
ⓔ vjbgozo@maltanet.net

Large, comfortable and tastefully decorated hotel on the fringes of Xagħra, spread around a central courtyard with three pools. Rooms have en-suite bathrooms and a/c; if possible opt for one on the north wing for a panoramic view of Marsalforn Valley and its table-top hills. ❺.

Electra
Map 8, G3. Valley Rd, Marsalforn
ⓣ 556196 ⓕ 555666

Cheap and basic family-run property in Marsalforn's centre. The fifteen dully decorated doubles have en-suite bathrooms: the single rooms, with showers and shared toilets, are a better deal, with a balcony that overlooks the bay. ❷.

Grand Hotel
Map 8, K6. Mġarr, Gozo
☎ 556183 ⓕ 599744
Imposing property overlooking Mġarr Harbour, where the pleasant, spacious en-suite rooms are decorated in a Baroque-cum-Neoclassical theme and have a/c and phone. ❺.

L-Imġarr
Map 8, K6. Għajnsielem, Gozo
☎ 560455 ⓕ 557589
Baroque, mauve-painted property at the edge of a cliff overlooking Mġarr Harbour, offering romantic views of the fishing boats in the harbour and the Gozo Channel beyond. Intimate, fully equipped and comfortable rooms, and facilities include a courtesy bus that shuttles you to the sights or beaches. ❼.

Lantern Guesthouse
Map 8, G3. Triq Il-Mungbell, Marsalforn
☎ 556285 ⓕ 562365
One of Gozo's cheapest options, this friendly, family-run converted townhouse is conveniently situated just off the waterfront in Marsalforn. The en-suite double rooms are large if stark, with ceiling fans; opt for one at the back to avoid the rumble of trucks in the mornings. Discounts on stays of over three days. ❷.

San Lawrenz
Map 8, C5. Triq Ir-Rokon, San Lawrenz
☎ 558639 ⓕ 562977
ⓦ www.sanlawrenz.com
Baroque-style with timber-coffered ceilings, loggia-framed balconies and plenty of paintings, this newly built, upmarket place in western Gozo, just up the coast from Dwejra, is surrounded by hills and agricultural land. The 87 suites are airy, comfortable and have all mod cons, and hotel facilities include hammams and holistic health treatments in the spa. The service, however, falls short of the pomp and prices. ❽.

Ta' Ċenċ
Map 8, H7. Sannat
☎ 556819 ⓕ 558199

GOZO

ⓔ vjbgozo@maltanet.net
Eighty-three semi-detached rooms set amongst sprawling gardens; though the property is showing its age, it still merits its excellent reputation. Rooms have en-suite bathroom, a/c, TV, phone, fridge and an outdoor terrace. If you can afford the Lm60 rate, go for the cosy igloo-shaped bungalows. ❼.

Tal-Fanal Village
Map 8, D4. 11 Capuchin's St, Rabat
ⓣ 563520 ⓕ 558397
ⓦ www.gozovillageholidays.com
On the outskirts of Għasri, near the Ġordan Hill in northwestern Gozo (you'll need private transport), these rustic-style semi-detached apartments are set around a swimming pool and courtyard. The luxurious units have a/c and kitchen. ❻.

Xagħra Lodge
Map 8, H4. Triq Dun Ġorġ Preca, Xagħra
ⓣ & ⓕ 562362
ⓔ xagħralodge@waldonet.net.mt
Run by a British expat couple, this B&B, secreted away from the tourist honeypots in the residential heart of Xagħra, is grandly decorated with mahogany furniture, electric chandeliers and elaborate curtains. The lush rooms – two doubles, family room, a large honeymoon room with an attractive poster bed and some rooms with single beds – have en-suite bathrooms and ceiling fans. Communal facilities include a small pool and restaurant. ❸.

COMINO

Comino Hotels
St Nicholas Bay
ⓣ 529821 ⓕ 529826
ⓦ www.cominohotels.com
The only accommodation option on largely uninhabited Comino, this is set on St Nicholas Bay and makes an ideal retreat. The en-suite rooms are spacious and have

a/c, TV, phone and balcony, and there are also more-exclusive semi-detached bungalows clustered along the flank of St Mary's Bay. Watersports facilities are excellent, and there are ten tennis courts, and two restaurant/bars. The boat shuttle to both Malta and Gozo is free for residents. Open between April and October only. **5**.

COMINO

Eating and drinking

With over eight hundred eateries, from cheap take-away joints and cosy cafés to expensive upscale restaurants, you're spoilt for choice when it comes to **eating out** in Malta and Gozo (Comino's only restaurant is an uninspired Italian place within the sole hotel). The restaurant scene is somewhat experimental, though: new places open and fold frequently, but quality and value-for-money are on the up and up.

At the cheap end of the market are the hole-in-the-wall **takeaways** and eateries which churn out dishes that combine Maltese and British home cooking. You'll see fish and chips or pies as well as favourite local snacks such as *ħobż biż-żejt*, *ftira* and *pastizzi* (see p.257). Due to Malta's proximity and historical ties with Italy, **restaurants** are predominantly Italian, but there are many other types of cuisine on the menus, from Asian or Russian to African and Argentinian, as well as "international" and Maltese cuisine, which many middle-bracket places combine with pastas and pizzas. Many of the upscale restaurants offer crosses of Italian and French cuisines, and virtually all restaurants feature fish dishes – a Maltese culinary highlight.

If you're vegetarian, choices are limited. There are a few restaurants (noted in the reviews that follow) that offer side menus of vegetarian dishes, but in most instances you'll have to make do with a pizza or pasta with veggie sauce.

MALTESE CUISINE

Maltese cuisine, which is heavy on meats and fish, takes influence and ingredients from its Mediterranean neighbours as well as from the long list of colonizers, from the Arabs to the British. The favourite springtime soup, *kusksu*, is derived from North African couscous dishes, but the Maltese substituted couscous with beads of pasta, added soft sheep's cheese and fresh broad beans, and changed the dish into a soup. British-style Sunday **roasts** – cuts of lamb, pork or chicken cooked in gravy and served with vegetables and potatoes – are also extremely popular. Another adaptation in the kitchen, spurred by the shortage of firewood, is in the **cooking process**. Dishes were traditionally prepared on a stone hearth called a *kenur*, which needed the minimum of firewood and constant fanning and attention, leading to slow simmering becoming the classic Maltese cooking method – simmered stews are still widespread. Maltese cooking developed and survived in the home, and only in the past ten years have restaurants adopted Maltese dishes, with a handful now specializing in local fare. Most of them, however, still repeat the common flaws of Maltese cuisine – everything is overcooked, from side vegetables to meat or pasta. Main dishes are normally heavy in bulk and density, with meat drenched in gravy and pasta submerged in sauce, but soups are fabulous and combine unusual rustic ingredients.

SNACKS AND BREAD

Cheapest of all foodstuffs are the **pastizzi** – pockets of puff pastry filled with ricotta or mashed peas, sold by specialized kiosks on city streets and in cafés. Cheap, tasty and filling, they're great if you're on a budget. Bear in mind, though,

GOZITAN FTAJJAR

Dense rustic pizzas made on crusty bread-dough and topped with local delicacies, Gozitan **ftajjar** (singular *ftira*, though a different dish to the Maltese snack of the same name), make a filling meal, and at Lm1 each, an inexpensive one to boot. They come in two types: the *ftira tas-sardin*, with anchovies, capers, tomatoes, potato slices, fresh herbs and olive oil; and the *ftira tal-ġobon*, a closed pizza stuffed with *ġobon frisk* (fresh sheep's cheese) mashed with beaten eggs and herbs. You can substitute one ingredient with another – say anchovies with tuna – or choose your own ingredients.

Not long ago Gozitan families used to have family reunions that centred on a feast of *ftajjar*; now the microwave and a faster pace of life has killed this tradition. The two surviving bakeries that make *ftajjar*, both in Nadur, Gozo (Map 8, K5), are listed below.

Maxokk Bakery
21 Triq San Ġakbu
☎ 564746.
Daily 8am–8pm.
Gozo's best *ftajjar*, baked in a wood-fired oven which adds a warm, smoky country flavour. Call or drop in three hours in advance to order.

Mekren's Bakery
Triq Hanaq
☎ 552342.
Mon–Fri 9.30am-7.30pm
Made with a finer and softer dough than that used at *Maxokk*, and more choices of ingredients, *ftajjar* must be ordered a day in advance; excellent, crunchy *pastizzi* are also worth sampling.

that as the pastry is glazed with fat, you're likely to end up with heartburn if you overindulge. Dense and crusty, local **bread** is excellent and avidly consumed by Maltese. Bakeries are extremely numerous, and you can buy cheap, oven-hot fresh bread almost anywhere on the islands. Bulky and cheap

MALTESE CUISINE

bread-based **snacks** include the popular *ħobz biż-żejt*, a roll filled with capers, olives, basil, mint, tomatoes and tuna or anchovies and drizzled with vegetable oil; and *ftira*, a roll of flat bread, usually grilled and filled with a variety of ingredients of your choice (go for Maltese sausage – a mildly spicy pork and beef mix – and local peppered sheep's cheese). Other snacks – though many cheap eateries serve them as full meals – are the *timpana* and *ross bil-forn*. Baked macaroni and baked rice respectively, both are laden with bolognese sauce, chopped boiled eggs and grated cheese – the baking process can make these dishes too dry for some tastes.

Maltese **specialities** include **ġbejniet** – sheeps' milk mini-cheeses, which are dried and pickled in pepper, vinegar and salt as *ġbejniet bil-bżar*, or eaten soft as *ġbejniet friski*. The best place to eat these is on Gozo, where they originated. Other toothsome morsels include **zalzett**, a pungently salty and spicy pork and beef sausage seasoned with herbs and served grilled, and **bigilla**, a dip made from dried broad beans, garlic, chilli peppers and herbs.

MAIN MEALS

Though there's no official national dish, most Maltese would nominate the hugely popular **fenkata**, which some restaurants make as their specialty. More of a feast than a meal, *fenkata* is rabbit and potatoes stewed in wine and tomato sauce, served in two courses: the stewing sauce is poured over the spaghetti, and the meat and potatoes served as the second course. Another popular dish is **braġioli** (inappropriately called beef olives in English-version menus): thin sheets of beef wrapped around mincemeat, beaten eggs and breadcrumbs, and served on a bed of potatoes and gravy. Cuts of chicken and pork, as well as marrows, peppers and aubergines, are filled with the same stuffing; marrows are particularly good. *Pulpetti* – deep-fried

MALTESE CUISINE

meatballs – are also widespread, served as a main course with baked potatoes and boiled vegetables.

Soups are a staple dish in Maltese homes, though few restaurants serve them, a sad fact given their healthiness and unique blends. If you have the opportunity try *kusksu*, *soppa tal-armla*, *soppa tal-qarabagħli* or *minestra*, all vegetable soups flavoured with the addition of fresh sheep's cheese. *Soppa tal-armla* (widow's soup) is made from chunks of cauliflower, potatoes and courgettes, while *soppa tal-qarabagħli* is a tasty marrow soup.

FISH AND SEAFOOD

With fresh fish readily available (over eighty species are consumed, many of them netted seasonally), and plenty of specialist restaurants, you really can't go wrong with seafood in Malta.

The two most popular seafood options are *lampuki* (dorado) and octopus. A white fish caught throughout autumn as it migrates through the central Mediterranean, **lampuki** is usually marinated in garlic, herbs, vinegar and olive oil, then baked or grilled and served with sautéed potatoes and vegetables. It's also made into the *torta tal-lampuki*, a pie stuffed with lampuki, tomatoes, cauliflower, spinach, olives, onions, sultanas and walnuts. **Octopus** is stuffed with rice, pine nuts and herbs, served on a salad, or more popularly stewed in red wine, herbs and pulped tomatoes, and served either as a main course with stewed potatoes or on a bed of spaghetti as a starter. **Amberjack**, caught all year round, is also very popular and eaten as a more delicate alternative to *lampuki*, while red mullet is also commonly seen, as are tuna, in steaks or whole when caught young, and swordfish. In recent years, sea urchins, with their exquisite deep-sea and rock taste, are appearing on menus as part of pasta dishes. Another Maltese speciality is **aljotta**, a soup based on fish stock, with marjoram, tomatoes, onions, garlic, lemon juice and vinegar.

DESSERTS AND PASTRIES

The most popular **sweet** is *imqaret*, a deep-fried pastry pocket of dates, sold from stands and kiosks. During Easter you'll find the *karammelli tal-ħaruf*, deep-fried sweet pastries stuffed with *ġulepp* – a light jam extracted from the pods of carob trees. Summer *festas* are the time to look for stalls selling *qubbajt*, a brown, nutty nougat which can be over-sweet and harder than old bread to bite into. A teatime favourite, *kannoli* are deep-fried pockets of pastry filled with ricotta, slivers of chocolate and candied fruits.

DRINKING

With around one million barrels consumed annually, the Maltese are avid **wine** drinkers, accompanying most meals with a glass or two, and concocting home-made brews as well. Restaurants usually have a fair selection of international wines, but it's worth looking out for the locally produced stuff. The three main **local winemakers** – Emmanuel Delicata, Marsovin and Meridiana – use the local *ghirgentina* and *gellewza* grape varieties topped up with imported Italian fruit to make everything from Chardonnay to Pinot Grigio. Delicata and Marsovin wines are on a par with their Italian counterparts, while Meridiana produce more upmarket wines that compete with fine international brands. Cheap and potent, **home-made wine** is generally produced from local grapes, but as its amateur brewers are unlicensed, quality and hygiene cannot be guaranteed. Most home-made wines are decidedly rustic, and taste varies from one producer to the next: some are delicious, others are little more than jumped-up vinegar. If you want

DRINKING

to sample it for yourself, it's sold from the vans of vegetable hawkers and farms where it's produced, as well as cheaper restaurants and some bars.

Restaurants and bars serve all other drinks, including beers, soft drinks and spirits, such as the Maltese concoction anisette, similar to sambuca or Turkish raki, with the addition of bitter almonds. Farsons brew two brands of Maltese **beer**: the most popular is Cisk, a pleasant and relatively mild lager, and there's also the milder, sweeter Hopleaf. Locally-brewed Lowenbrau is also available, but has yet to catch up with Farsons' brews.

Farsons also produce **kinnie**, a fizzy, rust-coloured, bittersweet soft drink. It's popular, though not as heavily consumed as lemonades and colas, and is one of those tastes that you either like or hate.

CAFÉS

Malta's seaside resorts and urban centres hold plenty of **cafés**, serving anything from coffees, teas and cakes to snacks and alcoholic drinks. Many of these are pretty bland, with neon or brass decor, plastic chairs and tables scattered on the pavement: the listings below concentrate on the more original and engaging places, excellent for people-watching, an afternoon over a coffee and a book, or a quiet evening drink and snack.

VALLETTA

Café Jubilee
Map 2, I5. 125 Triq Santa Lucia.
Daily 8am–1am.
Cosy place that serves great coffee and snacks, and attracts a hip and friendly clientele. The interior walls are a kaleidoscope of curio prints and the tasteful music ranges from world to ambient techno.

CAFÉS

Internet Café
Map 2, K5. 178 Triq Il-Merkanti.
Mon–Sat 10am–10pm.
With artwork and leftist ideology notices on the walls, books to browse through, all the local and international newspapers as well as internet access at Lm0.75 per thirty minutes, this funky place is the natural home of New Age types and loners.

Labyrinth
Map 2, I5. 44 Triq Il-Dejqa.
Mon–Sat 9am–1am, Sun 10am–3pm & 6pm–1am.
Set in a delicately converted townhouse full of nooks and crannies – hence the name – and with a basement dedicated to rotating exhibitions by both established and new local artists; there's also an antique shop and bookshop on site. Patronized by cultured, artistic types, many of whom come for an informal meal in the "supper club" – the concept is to bring like-minded people together. Otherwise, coffees, teas, cakes, alcohol and snacks are available, and there's a live jazz pianist on Wednesday and Friday evenings.

SLIEMA

Café Giorgio
Map 4, K8. 17 Triq Ix-Xatt
Ta' Tigne.
Daily 9am–midnight.
Decorated in brass and wood, this is an elegant corner café in the centre of Sliema with outside seating; serves good coffee and tea, as well as spirits, cakes and some snacks. Great for people-watching alongside the area's middle-classes, who watch the world go by from behind dark glasses.

Stella's Coffee Shop
Map 4, K8. Level 3, Plaza Shopping Complex, Tower Rd.
Mon–Sat 9am–7pm.
Cosy café that offers an array of cakes as well as snacks: sandwiches, lasagne and baked macaroni. Friendly and cool, it's packed by office

CAFÉS

workers during lunch, but relatively quiet at other times, when you can browse the day's local newspapers.

Waves

Map 4, K4. 139 Tower Rd.
Daily 4pm–1am.
Cocktails, coffee, beers, spirits, pool and internet connection in a seafront bar in Sliema that doubles as the hangout for local English-speaking teenagers.

MDINA

Ciappetti Tea Gardens

Map 5, F1. 5 Il-Wesgħa Ta' Sant' Agatha.
Daily 10am–6pm.
Set in the courtyard and terrace of a townhouse, the romantic atmosphere is complemented by oleander trees and a canopy of climbing vines. Good coffees and teas, plus cakes, snacks and pizzas.

Fontanella Tea Gardens

Map 5, G1. 1 Bastion St.
Daily: May–Oct 10am–11pm; Nov–April 10am–6pm.

Sip a coffee or tea, sample an excellent cake, and sit at tables spread out on the parapet of the Mdina fortifications enjoying a dreamy vista over central Malta and the east coast, which is even better at night, when the beautifully lit bastions make this an impressive spot for a drink.

THE NORTHWEST

Joseph Bar

Map 1, B3. *Mellieħa Holiday Centre*, Mellieħa Bay.
Daily 10am–2am.
The poolside café of this holiday resort is comfortable, and expansive, with indoor sofas and tables near the pool. Good coffees, teas and cakes are served (as is alcohol), and weekend evenings feature live blues, jazz or folk music.

GOZO

Bellusa

Map 9, G5. 34 Pjazza Indipendenza, Rabat.
Daily 7am–10pm.

CAFÉS

Good coffee, *pastizzi* and other snacks served outdoors in the atmospheric Pjazza Indipendenza. The owners are attentive and chatty proprietors, and in the mornings it's the perfect place to observe the goings-on at the fish market.

Café Jubilee
Map 9, G4. Pjazza Indipendenza, Rabat.
Daily 8am–1am.
Gozo's best café, attracting a crop of hip regulars and loners, and serving teas, coffees and snacks as well as alcohol. The crowd here are more laid-back than in the Valletta sister-branch (see p.262), and this is the place to go in the evenings to meet the more urbane locals.

Ritz Café
Map 8, G3. Valley Rd,

Marsalforn.
Daily 10am–1am.
Long-established bar and café with outdoor seating on the waterfront. As young people seek newer places, it's starting to show its age and in winter it's virtually deserted, but it remains friendly and full of idiosyncrasies, with an eccentric owner/barman who's part of the allure. This is *the* place in Gozo to buy tobacco and related accessories.

St Patrick's
Map 8, E7. Xlendi.
Daily: June–Sept 7am–2am; Oct–May 7am–11pm.
Right on the Xlendi promenade, and part of *St Patrick's Hotel*, with chairs you can snuggle into and tables splayed along the water's edge. Good coffees, teas and cakes, as well as alcohol.

RESTAURANTS

In the reviews that follow, restaurants have been graded in four price categories: **inexpensive** (under Lm6 a head for a three-course meal without drinks), **moderate** (Lm6–12), **expensive** (Lm12–18) and **very expensive** (over Lm18). On weekends and any day during the high season (mid-June to mid-Sept), it's wise to **reserve a table** at any restaurant graded higher than inexpensive. The closing times in the reviews are the last-order times.

VALLETTA

The Carriage
Map 2, G6. Valletta Buildings, Triq Nofs In-Nhar
☎ 247828.
Mon–Fri noon–3.30pm, Fri & Sat also 7.30–11.00pm.
Moderate–Expensive.
One of Malta's best restaurants, this attracts a crop of upscale regulars who come for the creative French cuisine and professional service. Asparagus Benedictine, drizzled with tarragon vinaigrette and served with truffles, or tortellini with prawns, leeks and saffron, are great starters, while main courses include the excellent pear and Roquefort salad with mixed greens. Tables are spaciously arranged for privacy and the terrace offers romantic views of Marsamxett Harbour and Valletta's medieval maze of streets.

Cocopazzo
Map 2, G6. Valletta Buildings, Triq Nofs In-Nhar
☎ 235706.
Mon–Sat 9am–3pm & 6.30–10pm. Moderate.
Patronized by a discerning crowd of business lunchers, *Cocopazzo* offers consistently good Italian food, with attention to detail even in the side dishes. Look out for *Al Cartoccio*, pasta with deep-fried courgette and aubergines, or fried swordfish fillet served with tomatoes, olives, capers, courgette and anchovies. This is not the place for long social dinners, though, as tables are packed together with little elbow space.

Deli Café
Map 2, K5. 141 Messina Palace, St Christopher's St
☎ 244863.
Mon–Fri 11.30am–10pm. Inexpensive.
Informal eatery in a stark covered courtyard, popular

with office workers. Eating is a one-plate affair – large and tasty portions of pasta are served from a daily changing menu, and desserts – particularly the well-flavoured chocolate cake – are reliable. Service is instant, and prices a bargain.

Giannini

Map 2, F5. 23 Triq Il-Mithna
☎237121.

Mon–Sat noon–2.30pm & 7–11pm. Moderate–Expensive.
Upmarket place patronized by the business classes and boasting a dreamy panorama over Manoel Island and Marsamxett Harbour. Service is good, the Italian cuisine is excellent and the atmosphere is elegant.

The Lantern

Map 2, F5. 20 Triq Sappers
☎237521.

Mon–Fri 11am–3pm, plus Fri & Sat 7–11pm. Inexpensive.
Pink tablecloths, pale sunrise walls and electric chandeliers set a calm mood, and though the decor is a bit overdone, the tables are well spaced and comfortable. The Italian menu is basic but satisfying,

and the set lunch of starter, main course and drink is a bargain at Lm3.

Malata

Map 2, J5. Misrah San Ġorġ
☎233967.

Mon–Sat noon–3pm & 7–11pm. Moderate.
Cheerful place in a stone-walled cellar, serving up a standard Italian menu: antipasti, soups, pasta and rice dishes, meats and fish – look out for the swordfish marinated in lemon and olive oil starter, and the mixed grilled fish drizzled with deep-flavoured marinade for a main course.

Da Pippo

Map 2, H6. 136 Triq Melita
☎248029.

Mon–Sat noon–3.30pm. Inexpensive–Moderate.
Small informal place that's good for quick lunches. Daily specials and Maltese staples such as marrows stuffed with *bragioli*, as well as hybrid Italian and Maltese dishes, including grilled fish with salad and roasted potatoes. The handsome antipasto is

RESTAURANTS

free and includes *ġbejniet*.

Rubino

Map 2, H5. 53 Triq Il-Fran

ⓣ 224656.

Mon–Fri 12.15–2.30pm, Tues
and Fri also 7.45–10.30pm.
Moderate.

Eating at this informal, rustic
nineteenth-century
townhouse, with framed
pictures of Valletta
streetscapes on the
whitewashed walls, is a
culinary and cultural
experience. Proprietor Julian
Sammut has lifted Maltese
cuisine to professional levels,
unearthing forgotten dishes,
and changing the menu
every few days, which has
ensured a loyal following
amongst Valletta's business
elite. A recurrent favourite is
pasta beads with minced
pork, white wine and bay
leaves, but you're best off
going by Sammut's
recommendations. Book a
table well in advance.

Sicilia Bar and Restaurant

Map 2, J7. 1A Triq San Ġwann

ⓣ 240569.

Mon–Sat noon–2.30pm.
Inexpensive.

Popular lunch spot serving
generous portions of Sicilian-
style pasta, and main meat or
fish dishes, plus a selection of
Maltese snacks including *ftira*.
Try the pasta *al vongole*,
drenched in an inky sauce
with clams. Seating is on an
outdoor terrace with narrow
views of the Grand Harbour;
watch out for the cats, dogs
and pigeons vying for your
food.

SLIEMA AND ST JULIAN'S

The Avenue

Map 1, I3. Gort St, Paceville,
St Julian's

ⓣ 311753.

Mon–Sat noon–2.30pm &
6–11.30pm, Sun 6–11.30pm.
Inexpensive.

Cheerful place with funky
decor and industrious service
which manages to keep up
with groups of young Maltese
who grab a quick dinner en
route to Paceville. The eclectic
menu of mostly Sicilian dishes
– from pasta and pizzas to

grilled meats and fish – also includes English breakfasts, burgers and omelettes; portions are generous.

Barracuda

Map 4, D4. 195 Main St, Sliema
☎ 331817.
Daily 7–10.30pm.
Moderate–Expensive.
Popular with the business classes, with suitably formal decor and service, and an extensive wine list. The Italian food is subtle, and the fish dishes adventurous and creative yet perfectly cooked; the fish of the day is prepared to your taste.

The Big Blue

Map 4, N8. *Crowne Plaza Hotel*, Tigne, Sliema
☎ 34911536.
Daily noon–midnight. Moderate.
Mediterranean cuisine, from Moroccan to Turkish and French as well as Maltese: you can have fun with textured tastes by mixing different cuisines in one meal. Look out for specialities such as Maltese aubergine cannelloni filled with goat's cheese, and French pork medallions for a main course. The atmosphere is thematically Mediterranean – mosaics above the arched doorways, wooden tables with coloured chairs and paintings of regional scenes.

Bon Pain

Map 1, J4. 181 The Strand, Gzira
☎ 330755.
Mon–Sat noon–3pm, Fri also 7–10.30pm. Moderate.
Based heavily on French cuisine, the food here is consistently good. The endlessly creative, daily changing menu of salads are the speciality, and are the best in the islands. There's anything from rocket and bacon to avocado and orange with mixed greens, and all can be taken as a starter or main course.

Bouzouki

Map 4, B1. 135 Spinola Rd, St Julian's
☎ 317127.
Mon–Sat 6.30–11pm.
Inexpensive–Moderate.
Popular and cheerful Greek place decorated on a classical theme and overlooking the

RESTAURANTS

romantic *luzzus* and lights shimmering across Spinola Bay. The dip platter, served with crusty Maltese bread, makes an excellent starter, and the moussaka is usually good, too.

Christopher's

Map 1, J4. Ta Xbiex Marina, Ta Xbiex

☎ 337101.

Tues–Fri 12.30–2pm & 8–10.30pm, Mon & Sat 8–11.30pm. Very expensive. Decorated in pastel colours, with an oak floor and furniture, *Christopher's* consistently lives up to its reputation as Malta's top restaurant. Service is impeccable, the wine list impressive, and the artistically presented French cuisine is subtle yet pervasive. The menu is changed seasonally; main courses include smoked duck, wild boar and pheasant or grilled fish fillets in a tomato and chicken-stock sauce – even sautéed in duck fat, are unusual.

La Dolce Vita

Map 4, A1. St George's Rd, St Julian's

☎ 337036 or 337086.

Daily 6.30–10pm. Moderate.

A delicious smell of cooked fish envelops the air of this Italian restaurant overlooking *luzzu*-dotted Spinola Bay, and the seafood lives up to the promising aroma – stick to fish, as it's a speciality. The funky tempo and emphasis on the good life (hence the name) draws in crowds of chattering Italians.

The Haven

Map 4, K6. Alborada Apartments, High St, Sliema

☎ 311019.

Daily noon–2pm, plus Mon–Sat 6.30–9.30pm. Inexpensive. Worn out Formica tables and chairs and the kind of food you'll find in Maltese homes; great for filling up if you're on a budget. You can choose from a dozen staple soups, pastas, fried fillets of chicken and beef, and fried fish in season, all served with chips and salad, and usually slightly overcooked.

King's Head

Map 4, J8. 4 Annunciation St, Sliema

☎ 335714.

Mon–Tues & Thurs–Sat

10am–2pm & 6–10pm, Sun 10am–2pm. Inexpensive. Popular with locals and bus and taxi drivers, the cheap, poster-covered wall panelling and fixed Formica tables may look uninviting; but the food is good: a no-nonsense, anglicized take on Maltese home cooking, with most things fried and drizzled in gravy. The soups – particularly beef – are tasty, as are Maltese specialities such as *bragioli* or *pulpetti*.

Krishna
Map 4, H9. 97 The Strand, Sliema
℡346291.
Daily 7–11pm. Moderate.
One of Malta's best Indian restaurants, this small place, decorated in pastel shades, serves all the standard dishes. Curries are generally mild and creamy, and fish curries are particularly good. The naan bread, especially the keema naan, is excellent.

Il-Merill
Map 4, J8. St Vincent St, Sliema
℡332172.

Mon–Sat 6–10pm. Inexpensive. All rustic wooden beams, chipped walls and traditional collectibles such as gas lamps, this family-run restaurant is popular with Germans, but the Maltese home-style cooking is somewhat flawed: most things are overcooked, meats are universally drenched in gravy and pasta submerged in sauce. Nonetheless, service is attentive, the plates are heaped, and it's good value for money overall, if not the place to sample local food at its best.

Misfits
Map 1, I3. *White House Hotel*, Paceville Ave, St Julian's
℡378016.
Daily noon–3pm & 6.30pm till late. Moderate.
Situated on the fringes of Paceville, this funky place rates among Malta's better eateries, with abstract paintings, murals on the counter, world music and a crackling fireplace in winter. French cuisine at its best, plus professional service and presentation.

RESTAURANTS

271

Peppino's

Map 4, A1. St George's Rd, St Julian's

☎ 373200.

Mon–Sat noon–3pm & 7–10pm. Moderate.

A hive for the snobbish high society, *Peppino's* is always busy, with a menu of fine-tasting continental dishes, especially French and Italian; try the rich, French-style fillet steak with pepper sauce. Tables are set on two floors – downstairs doubles as a raucous and smoky wine bar, while upstairs is more elegant, with black tables draped with white and pink tablecloths.

Piccola Padre

Map 4, D4. 195 Main St, St Julian's

☎ 344875.

Daily 6.30–11pm. Inexpensive. Industrious and informal Italian pizza and pasta house on the edge of Balluta Bay, serving agreeable Sicilian dishes such as the pasta with sautéed aubergines, courgettes and olives. The large, crusty pizzas, including the Maltese-style favourite

topped with *ġbejniet*, *zalzett*, mozzarella and tomatoes, are among the best you'll find in the islands.

The Plough and Anchor

Map 4, E4. 1 Main St, St Julian's

☎ 334725.

Tues–Sun noon–2pm & 6.30–10.30pm. Moderate. Warm and cosy setting, brimming over with nautical paraphernalia, with racks of wine hanging from the ceiling. Inspired by French cuisine, the pasta, fish, meat and poultry are rich in cream and cheeses. Try the pork wrapped in spinach and drizzled with an asparagus sauce; the chocolate fondue makes a memorable dessert.

Terrazza

Map 4, C1. Spinola Bay, St Julian's

☎ 384939.

June–Sept daily 7pm–1am; Oct–May Tues–Sun noon–3pm. Moderate.

North African-style decor of earth-coloured sponged walls, and with tables spilling onto a terrace overlooking Spinola

RESTAURANTS

Bay. The dishes are grouped under country of origin – Greece, Turkey, Lebanon, Spain, France, Morocco and Malta – and the daily specialities include a vegetarian choice. Dips are excellent.

XII
Map 4, A1. St George's Rd, St Julian's
℡ 324361.
Mon–Sat 12.30–3pm & 7–10.30pm. Moderate.
Offbeat restaurant in a funky café-club setting, with purplish lights, blue and yellow tablecloths and piped world music. The fusion fare of Mediterranean dishes spiked with Far Eastern spices is excellent, with cooking taken to artistic levels: the "duck Karl's style" is marinated in lemon grass and ginger oil and served with a teriyaki and orange-scented honey sauce. Ask the cook or proprietor for recommendations, or order your own tailor-made meal (even sushi) a day in advance.

MDINA, RABAT AND CENTRAL MALTA

Bacchus
Map 5, G4. Triq Inguanez, Mdina
℡ 454981.
Daily noon–3pm & 6–11pm. Moderate–Expensive.
Set in an atmospheric fifteenth-century ammunition store built by the Knights, this is a romantic hideaway offering good food and service. The adventurous and innovative French dishes include ricotta and smoked chicken samosas, and braised duck breast served with chartreuse and shallots.

The Baron
Map 5, E9. 3 Triq Ir-Repubblika, Rabat
℡ 455561.
Mon 6.30–11.30pm, Wed–Sun 10am–2.30pm & 6.30–11.30pm. Inexpensive.
Friendly and informal place dishing out local cuisine, and renowned amongst the Maltese for its *fenkata*, and for its horse steak marinated in brandy, grilled, then stewed

RESTAURANTS

273

with vegetables and potatoes (you have to order this one day in advance). Portions are massive.

Bobbyland

Map 1, E8. Dingli Cliffs, Dingli ☎452895.

Tues–Fri 10.30am–2.30pm & 6.30–10.30pm, Sat 6.30–11pm, Sun 11am–3pm. Inexpensive.

Housed in a former RAF signal station, this large, no-nonsense place attracts a regular crop of Maltese and British expats for its three specialities: roast duck, rabbit Maltese style and roast fillet of lamb, all served with chips and soggy boiled vegetables. The unrefined, cheap and strong house wine fuels the merry atmosphere.

Cuckoo's Nest

Map 5, D7. Triq San Pawl, Rabat ☎455946.

Daily 11.30am–9pm. Inexpensive.

Eccentric, basic place – the name is inspired by the film starring Jack Nicholson – that serves an assortment of fried food such as steak and chips,

as well as octopus and beef stews, and the Maltese lunchtime favourite *balbuljata*, sautéed vegetables scrambled into beaten eggs and served with chips.

The Medina

Map 5, F3. Triq Is-Salib Imqaddes, Mdina ☎454004.

Mon–Sat 7–10.30pm. Moderate.

Set in an atmospheric, sensitively restored farmhouse, with tables spilling into a courtyard canopied by climbing vines, and serving good French-style dishes. Duck and ostrich are particularly tasty, and for a starter, try the deep-fried *ġbejniet* or the duck liver and orange terrine. The service is more professional and attentive than the prices would suggest.

Il-Veduta

Map 5, H6. Saqqajja Pjazza, Rabat ☎454666.

Daily noon–3pm & 6–11pm. Inexpensive.

A large, characterless place just outside the Mdina walls,

this is brilliant for families – kids are distracted with crayons and drawing paper, and there are high-chairs and nappy-changing facilities. The extensive menu of filling, palatable dishes includes everything from omelettes to pizzas, burgers, pasta, grills and local fare.

Żmerċ
Map 1, H5. Triq Birbal, Balzan
☏ 444576.
Daily 9.30am–2.30pm & 6.30pm–2am. Inexpensive.
Popular with young Maltese, and relatively undiscovered by tourists thanks to its out-of-town location, this lively place is primarily a bar, with blaring pop music and a large TV screen which airs sports events. You need to order a meal a couple of days in advance (the place is always packed in any case) and the huge portions of Maltese food – rabbit, horsemeat, chicken, fish and steaks – come with chips and gravy, and are nothing special, but you're here for the atmosphere rather than the food.

THE NORTHWEST

The Arches
Map 1, 3C. Triq Il-Kbira, Mellieħa
☏ 573436.
Mon–Sat 6.30–10.30pm. Expensive.
The classical, formal milieu here complements the French-inspired menu, which changes every couple of weeks. The dishes are imaginative – guinea fowl breast with vegetables wrapped in filo pastry, or roasted guinea fowl legs coated in seeds – and are particularly good. *The Arches* boasts the finest and the largest selection of wines in Malta; some are aged in the in-house cellar, where you can browse around and make your selection.

Bis-Tit African
Map 6, B5. 69 Triq Sant' Antnin, Buġibba
☏ 585820.
Jan & Feb Fri–Sun 6–11pm; March–Dec daily 6–11pm. Inexpensive–Moderate.
Small, colourful place just off

RESTAURANTS

Bay Square, with an extensive menu of African dishes, all subtly spicy and aromatic. Specialities, such as the mixed grill combining five meats, or the chicken with yam, sweet potatoes and mushrooms, are excellent, and there's a small selection of vegetarian dishes. The set menu of three courses plus a glass of wine is a bargain at Lm4.50.

Giuseppi's
Map 1, C3. Triq Borġ Olivier, Mellieħa
☎ 574882.
Tues–Sat 7.30–10.30pm.
Moderate–Expensive.
North Mediterranean cuisine meets old world charm in this converted wine bar set in a townhouse. The menu changes every two or three weeks, and there are a handful of daily fish-based specialities such as spaghetti with sea urchins, subtly spiced with chilli and pesto. Some of the dishes are minimal and fluffy, others are heavy in sauces and textured in tastes, but all are excellent. Try the rabbit stewed in tomato sauce and chocolate.

The Grapevine
Map 6, B7. Pioneer Rd, Buġibba
☎ 572973.
Mon & Wed–Sun 7–11pm.
Moderate.
A funky place with riotous abstract paintings on the bright yellow walls, and an open-plan kitchen. The extensive menu, which has a small vegetarian section and a daily selection of specialities, consists of largely Italian dishes with spicy hints. Look out for the *filetto blu*, fillet steak cooked in stilton, brandy, cream and walnuts.

Mange Tout
Map 7, C6. 356 Triq Zan Paul, St Paul's Bay
☎ 572121.
Mon–Sat 7.30–10.30pm.
Moderate–Expensive.
One of Malta's top restaurants, this is a small, intimate place serving adventurous French food. The creative menu changes regularly and the chef is continually mixing and concocting new dishes such as cannelloni-filled salmon and crab, or rabbit with

capers, wild mushrooms and rosemary. Service is excellent, and the wine list extensive.

Da Michele
Map 6, D5. Triq It-Turisti, Buġibba
ⓣ 582131.
Daily 7–11pm.
Moderate–Expensive.
Fine French cuisine at Buġibba's best restaurant, with tables set around a warm-coloured interior with some excellent modern art paintings on the walls. The open kitchen allows you to observe the chef concocting delicious dishes such as stuffed mushrooms with snails, ravioli of wood pigeon, or stuffed rabbit leg. There is a small selection of good vegetarian dishes.

Out West Argentinean Steakhouse
Map 6, B7. Pioneer Rd, Buġibba
ⓣ 580666.
Daily 6.30–11.30pm. Moderate.
With sumptuous leopard-patterned sofas and dull-red walls punctuated with Wild West motifs and a stuffed

bulls' head, the decor reflects the meat-heavy menu: several types of steaks, chicken breast, burgers and kangaroo fillets, accompanied either by salad or potato side dishes and free bruschetta.

Porto del Sol
Map 7, A5. 13 Triq It-Telgħa Tax-Xemxija,
St Paul's Bay
ⓣ 573970.
Mon–Sat noon–2.30pm & 6.30–10.30pm. Moderate.
Bright and elegant setting overlooking St Paul's Bay, and food that's inspired equally from Italian and French cuisine; soups and pastas as well as a small selection of vegetarian dishes; go for the grilled swordfish or roast duckling with orange sauce.

THE SOUTH

Al Fresco
Map 1, M8. St George's Bay, Birżebbuġa
ⓣ 653422.
Daily 11am–2.30pm & 6.30–11.30pm. Inexpensive.
A large eatery down the road

RESTAURANTS

from Għar Dalam Cave, with mismatched decor, and a vista over Marsaxlokk Bay that's tempered by the cranes of the Freeport on the horizon. Starters, and main courses of fish, meat and poultry, served with salad and chips, are uninspiring; steaks and the wide range of massive, crusty-based pizzas are the menu highlights.

Grabiel

Map 1, N5. Pjazza Mifsud Bonnici, Marsascala
⊕ 634194.

Mon 7–10pm, Tues–Sat noon–2pm & 7–10pm. Moderate.

Celebrated among an upmarket clientele for its consistently high-quality cooking and seafood-dominated menu, which changes daily to accommodate a wide selection of specials. The *fritto mesto* – a seafood feast of octopus, squid, prawns, clams, king prawns, calamari rings and baby calamari, some deep fried and others steamed in wine, garlic and brandy – is particularly delicious.

Kingfisher

Map 1, I9. Wied Iz-Żurrieq
⊕ 647908.

June–Sept Tues–Sun 11am–3pm, plus daily 7–10pm; Oct–May Tues–Sun 11am–3pm, plus Fri & Sat 7–10pm. Inexpensive.

Basic and clean but stark place doling out Maltese home cooking – overdone pasta and meats – but the best and cheapest option in Wied Iz-Żurrieq nonetheless. Stick to burgers or fish and you're less likely to be disappointed.

Pisces

Map 1, M7. 49 Xatt Is-Sajjieda, Marsaxlokk
⊕ 654956.

Mon–Tues & Thurs–Sun noon–3pm & 6.30–10.30pm. Inexpensive–Moderate.

Popular with families, this is a bland, aluminium-fronted but friendly place on the Marsaxlokk seafront, a location which ensures extremely fresh seafood; fish is a menu highlight, and the *aljotta* is excellent. The local fare, such as *fenkata*, meat and poultry dishes, is palatable too.

Il Re del Pesce

Map 1, N5. Triq Id-Daħla ta San Tumas, Marsascala ☏ 636353.

May–Oct Mon–Sat 7–11pm; Nov–April Mon–Sat noon–2.30pm & 7–11pm, Sun noon–2.30pm. Moderate. Informal and friendly, this large eatery offers a selection of good seafood dishes, including octopus in garlic and fish-stuffed ravioli, as well as the ubiquitous "fish of the day"; some specimens are scooped out of the large aquarium and cooked there and then.

GOZO

Brookies

Map 8, F5. 1–2 Triq Wied Sara, Rabat ☏ 559524.

Mon & Tues–Sun 6.30–10.30pm. Moderate. Romantic and tranquil setting in a converted farmhouse with a bougainvillea-bedecked outdoor terrace, and the Citadel towering overhead. Service is swift and professional – ideal for a one-to-one intimate dinner – and the fish is the best thing on the solid Italian menu; keep an eye out for the salmon-stuffed ravioli starter.

Gesther

Map 8, H4. Triq Tmienja Ta' Settembru, Xagħra ☏ 556621.

Mon–Sat noon–2.30pm. Inexpensive. Small, unassuming eatery round the corner from Pjazza Vittorja, churning out large portions of excellent Maltese staples. Soups are especially good – look out for the *kusksu bil-ful* (marrow soup) – as is the *bragioli* for a main course. The setting – fixed Formica tables, leather-padded benches, cramped legroom and garish wall panelling – is less inspiring than the food, however.

Iċ-Ċima

Map 8, E7. St Simon St, Xlendi ☏ 558407.

Daily noon–2pm & 6–10.30pm. Inexpensive. A standard, agreeable selection of Italian recipes

RESTAURANTS

enhanced by creative twists – risotto with strawberries, or chicken in a rich black olive sauce – from a menu that changes weekly. Pleasant rustic atmosphere, relaxing music and friendly service.

Ta Frenċ

Map 8, 4G. Triq Għajn Damma, Xagħra
℡ 553888.
Daily noon–2pm & 6.30–10.30pm. Expensive.

Impressive setting in a restored farmhouse, with summer seating in a courtyard amid lush palms, bougainvillea and oleander trees. The extensive menu of French dishes (which includes some vegetarian choices), is heavy on creams and cheeses; try the excellent baked avocado stuffed with seafood. The wine list is pretty comprehensive, and the service aims for infallibility but feels awkward at times.

Il-Kartell

Map 8, 3G. Triq Marina, Marsalforn
℡ 556918.
March–Oct Mon–Tues &

Thurs–Sun noon–3.30pm & 6.30–11pm. Moderate.

With tables set at the water's edge, this is one of the best restaurants in Marsalforn, specializing in seasonal fish – look out for the tender amberjack grilled in salt and served with sautéed potatoes and vegetables, and for the pre-starter speciality, pickled tuna. The servings are generous and the friendly staff pay attention to detail.

Il-Kċina Tal-Barrakka

Map 8, K6. 28 Triq Manoel de Vilhena, Mġarr Harbour
℡ 556543.
May–Oct Tues–Sun 7–11pm. Moderate.

One of Gozo's best fish places, in an uncluttered, stone-walled converted boathouse on Mġarr Harbour. The fish of the day is excellent, usually grilled or poached, and octopus stewed in red wine is equally good.

Namaste

Map 8, G5. Triq Fortunato Mizzi, Rabat
℡ 561619.
Mon–Tues & Thurs–Sun

6.45–11pm. Moderate.

Top-notch Indian restaurant with elaborate vernacular decor, wailing music and overly theatrical barefooted waitresses wearing sarongs. The classic dishes, such as chicken tikka, are topped with various creative specialities such as romali roti; lobster masala is a delicious choice.

Oleander

Map 8, H4. 10 Pjazza Vittorja, Xagħra

T 557230.

Tues–Sun 11.30am–3pm & 7–10pm. Moderate.

A romantic setting in the Pjazza Vittorja, and favoured by a crowd of loyal regulars, this place has a solid reputation for local specialities: purse-sized ravioli stuffed with goat's cheese, beaten eggs and olive oil are wonderful, as is the the spaghetti with rabbit sauce.

Il-Panzier

Map 9, G7. Triq Il-Karita, Rabat

T 559979.

Jan–Oct noon–2.30pm &

7–11pm. Moderate.

Reliable Sicilian fare accompanied by good wine, and served in the courtyard of a converted farmhouse in Rabat's old quarter, amid palm and yucca trees. Dishes change seasonally, but one staple favourite is the excellent *saltimbocca* – rolls of beef stuffed with cheeses and ham. Attentive and personal hospitality in a romantic setting.

Park Lin

Map 8, K6. Triq Manoel de Vilhena, Mġarr

T 561967.

April–Oct Mon 6–10pm, Tues–Sat 12.30–2pm & 6–10pm, Sun 12.30–2pm. Moderate.

Delightful and friendly family run place, set in a former garage restored with stone arches and pine furniture, with an outdoor terrace overlooking a boatyard of *luzzus*. The creative dishes are influenced by French and Italian cuisine and are creative; ask for the day's specialities such as chicken stuffed with blue cheese.

RESTAURANTS

Pulena

Map 8, G3. Marina St, Marsalforn

ⓣ 551237.

March–May Fri–Sun noon–3pm & 6.30–11.30pm; June–Dec daily same hours; Jan–Feb Sun same hours. Moderate.

Highly creative Mediterranean cuisine at what is indisputedly the best restaurant in Gozo, with attention paid to every little detail. The pizzas, home-made pasta, meats and poultry are all good, but for something different, opt for one of the numerous and excellent daily specialities: aubergines stuffed with *gbejniet*, *gbejniet* ravioli topped with a tomato and basil sauce, cream and parmesan, or strawberries sautéed in butter and flameburned in balsamic vinegar.

Rexy

Map 8, K6. 100 Mġarr Rd, Għajnsielem

ⓣ 560873.

Daily 11am–2pm & 6–11pm. Inexpensive.

A limited menu incorporating pastas, meats, poultry and fish dishes, plus some starters, served in a bland setting. Service is fast, the portions are generous, and the food filling but unremarkable; the low prices attract lots of Gozitan families.

It-Tmun

Map 8, E7. 3 Triq Mount Carmel, Xlendi

ⓣ 551571.

March–Oct Mon & Wed–Sun noon–2pm & 6–10pm; Nov–Feb Fri–Sun same hours. Moderate.

Friendly yet professional, this is one of Gozo's best. The extensive menu marries Maltese and Italian cuisines; look out for starters of fried aubergines, or deep-fried goat's cheese bruschetta; for main courses, try the excellent catch of the day, either grilled, poached or baked, while the seafood platter for two is a bargain at Lm5.25. A small selection of vegetarian dishes are available if ordered a day in advance.

RESTAURANTS

Nightlife and entertainment

Largely laid-back and mainstream, **nightlife** in the Maltese islands is best experienced during summer weekends, when thousands of youngish revellers descend on the Paceville area. Here, a couple of crisscrossing streets hold a glut of **bars** and a few **clubs** – most of the latter are a cross between regular dance dens and clubbars, with no cover charge. Elsewhere, you'll find a few bars and discos in Buġibba that seem stuck in the tacky sun'n'sea mentality of the 1980s, while the handful of quieter drinking dens in Valletta attract a more sophisticated local crowd fleeing the commerciality of Paceville. In Gozo, bars fill up with the same faces night after night, the music is mundane, and after 1am you'll only find two or three places open.

If you're after some more sedate evening entertainment, you can head to one of the **theatres** or **cinemas** located in both Malta and Gozo, which put on operas and ballets as well as dramas and musicals, and there are also a few **casinos** if you fancy a flutter.

BARS

Although Maltese **bars** only really fill up on weekends (from around 10pm onwards), they can be pretty raucous, playing loud music and often opening until the wee hours. Most bars attract a core group of regulars, and many have at least one TV, used to air English and European sports events to eager, beery crowds. In both Malta and Gozo, bars start filling up at around 10pm, and the crowds move to clubs and club-bars (see p.289) at around 1am.

SLIEMA, ST JULIAN'S AND PACEVILLE

Black Gold
Map 4, H9. The Strand, Sliema.
Daily 9am–1am.
The regular watering hole for British sailors and other yacht-hands based at Marsamxett Harbour. With smoky wooden decor and lots of mirrors, it's boisterous and beer driven, with a playlist of singalong rock classics and TV screens airing sporting events, often football.

City of London
Map 4, C3. 193 Main St, St Julian's.
Daily 10am–1am.
Jukebox bar on Balluta Bay that attracts a mixed clientele, ranging from intellectual types and British expats to lesbian women and young crowds of snobbish middle-class students. Weekends see a rather poor, conversation-suppressing selection of loud music.

Ghall Kafe
Map 1, I3. 118 Triq San Ġorġ, Paceville.
Daily 11am–7am.
Expansive place, with maroon carpets, pink walls and lots of mirrors, that opens all night and doubles as a restaurant, serving barely palatable pizzas and pastas to a trickle of punters who stop here for coffee or some grub on the way home from a night out.

Also offers Malta's cheapest internet connection (Lm1 for 75min).

Hacienda
Map 1, I3. Level 3, Bay Street Complex, St George's Bay, St Julian's.
Daily 9pm–4am.
Popular place, where you can hardly move and talk on weekends, with loud commercial garage for alcohol-fuelled dancing. A large screen airs music videos and programmes on other fringe-clubby pursuits such as skateboarding.

Henry J. Bean's
Map 1, I3. *Corinthia Beach Resort*, St George's Bay, St Julian's.
Mon–Thurs 6pm–1am, Fri–Sun noon–1.30am.
Spacious bar that smacks of Americana, with roadway signs plastered across its walls. Pop music and commercial house dominate the playlist, and the middle-class, post-adolescent clientele quaff an extensive range of cocktails and half-decent grilled foods such as nachos, burgers or barbecue chicken with chips.

Muddy Waters
Map 4, C4. 56 Main St, St Julian's.
Daily noon–1am.
A boisterous rock and blues bar in Balluta Bay; concerts featuring local bands, some good, some cranky, are staged every Thursday, when packs of university students mean you have to fight your way to the bar.

O'Casey's
Map 1, I3. St George's Bay, St Julian's.
Daily 11.30am–3.30pm & 5.30pm–4am.
Irish pub that plays loud pop tunes, attracts a mixed clientele of stragglers and only gets really packed and inebriated on weekends.

Peppino's Wine Bar
Map 4, A1. 31 Triq San Ġorġ, St Julian's.
Daily 6pm–1am.
Friendly, smoky and loud wine bar that caters for Malta's self-styled high society, both the twenty-something's and the middle-aged.

BARS

Ryan's Irish Pub
Map 4, A2. Spinola Bay,
St Julian's.
Mon–Fri 4pm–2am & Sat–Sun
11am–2am.
Standard, pleasant Irish pub
that attracts groups of beer-
swigging English lads
mingling with Maltese young
people. Always merry and
busy, dishing out popular
Irish tunes and occasionally
serving as a concert venue for
live Irish acts.

The Scotsman Pub
Map 1, I4. Triq San Ġorġ,
St Julian's.
Daily 9am–4am.
The closest Malta comes to
an English pub, attracting
mostly British tourists and
young Maltese. You can
exhibit your singing prowess
at the popular, funny and
inebriated karaoke nights
(Tues, Thurs, Sat & Sun).

Simon's Pub
Map 4, E6. 115–116 Triq
Depiro, Sliema.
Tues–Sun 11am–2pm &
8pm–1am.
Appealing, friendly and
relatively cheap place bristling
with delightful bric-a-brac
and football memorabilia.
Located in a residential area
of inland Sliema, it attracts a
regular clientele who demand
rock music. The cocktails are
a grand affair – the best you'll
find in Malta.

Snoopy's
Map 4, E4. 265 Tower Rd,
Sliema.
Daily noon–2.30pm &
6pm–1am.
A small, dim bar on the
seafront in Sliema that
attracts a drop-in crowd and
is particularly popular with
English language students.
Music policy is rock and
pop.

White Arrow
Map 1, J5. 74 Quarries St,
Msida.
Daily noon–1am.
Tucked in the centre of
Msida, south of the yacht
marina, this is the hangout of
teenage students from the
Junior College up the road. It
gets crowded, loud, and
functions as something of a
chat-up joint.

BARS

CENTRAL MALTA

Żmerċ

Map 1, H5. Triq Birbal, Balzan.
Daily 9.30am–2.30pm &
6.30pm–2am.
Well away from the tourist
circuits, and attracting mostly
young, boisterous Maltese
and international students
who live at the nearby
university residence. Pop and
rock blare loudly from the
stereo, there's a large TV
screen to air sports events,
and the free finger food –
tortellini, chips, chicken
wings, stewed snails, Maltese
sausage, *ġbejniet* and so on – is
plentiful.

THE NORTHWEST

Corner Pocket

Map 6, C6. Triq Il-Kavetta,
Buġibba. Daily 6pm–4am.
Loud and raucous pulling
joint popular with a young
inebriated crowd, who join
in the karaoke or totter about
to the commercial house
music. In the basement,
Browsers internet café (daily

10am–1.30am) also has a
games room with pool tables
and video games.

Grapevine

Map 6, B7. Triq Il-Korp
Tal-Pijunieri, Buġibba.
Daily 4pm–4am.
Appealing Irish pub with a
laid-back atmosphere and a
music policy of Irish and pop
tunes, where groups of
middle-class young people
mingle with mostly British
holiday-makers.

Miracles Pub

Map 6, B5. Bay Square,
Buġibba.
Daily: June–Sept 10am–3am;
Oct–May 10am–6pm.
Small corner bar with marble
and neon decor. Seating is
outside on the pedestrianized
square and the thumping,
commercial dance music
plays for a young crowd of
Maltese who stop here en
route to Paceville, as well as
British tourists staying in
Buġibba.

Tal-Baħri

Map 6, C6. Triq It-Turisti,
Buġibba.

BARS

●

Daily noon–2am.

Small corner café with cosy wooden decor, and a pop and rock music policy. The friendly, chatty atmosphere attracts mixed ages, and it's good for a nightcap or to meet people in a largely sober and amicable setting.

Wise Guys

Map 6, C5. Triq Mazzola, Buġibba.

Daily 8pm–4am.

Large, dimly lit and pretty characterless place with a relaxed attitude, playing loud commercial dance tunes, this is a sort of catch-all place for late-night stragglers.

GOZO

Dive Bar

Map 8, G3. Triq Il-Port, Marsalforn.

Daily 8.30pm–4am.

Opens later than most places in Gozo, with an interior that mimics that of a submersible: prints of marine life serve as the "portholes". The music ranges from pop to garage to hard-house, and there's internet access in the basement for Lm1 per hour.

Id-Dverna Tal-Mewta

Map 9, F6. Triq San Ġorġ, Rabat.

June–Sept daily 7pm–1am; Oct–May Tues & Fri–Sun 7pm–1am.

Wine bar in a restored nineteenth-century building behind St George's Basilica, attracting a mixed clientele. Groups of young teenagers swig cheap, home-made wine alongside an older, more sophisticated crowd lured by the old-world setting. Poetry performances on Tuesdays by a dedicated group of British expats.

Gleneagles

Map 8, K6. 10 Victory St, Mġarr Harbour.

Daily noon–1am.

Opened in 1885, this former fishermen's watering hole, decorated on a nautical theme, caters for middle-class regulars and British expats as well as fishermen. Effortlessly hip and friendly, with a music policy of pop and house.

La Taverna Del Ponte

Map 8, E7. Xlendi Rd, Xlendi.
June–Sept Thurs–Sun
8.30pm–3am; Oct–May Fri–Sun
8.30pm–3am.
Charming wine bar in a
converted farmhouse halfway
between Rabat and Xlendi,
with an outdoor terrace
overlooking Xlendi Valley. Its
popularity ebbs and rises
intermittently, and its regulars
are young Gozitan middle-
class whose musical tastes –
pop, garage and rock classics
– dictate the music policy.

CLUBS AND CLUB-BARS

The Maltese **club** scene, which is largely fuelled by alcohol
rather than drugs, is pretty uncreative, with trends lagging
behind Western Europe by a decade and most places dishing out a jaded mix of the big tunes of yesteryear to non-
discerning crowds. There are few true clubs: most of the
places featured here only have DJs on weekends and select-
ed weeknights, particularly Wednesdays or Thursdays, and
would be more aptly called **club-bars**, with designer decor
and music only slightly less loud than fully-fledged club
sound systems.

For a more interesting clubbing experience, seek out the
one-off weekend events in small venues such as *Pushka* in St
Paul's Bay and the *Liquid Club* on the outskirts of St Julian's,
which open only for one-off club nights with local DJs.
These are publicized via posters and flyers left in venues
such as *Places* and *Misfits* (p.293). In summer, there are regular one-off **rave parties**, large events that feature a line-up
of international DJs backed up by local guys – for more on
these, see the box overleaf.

Following hysteria at the growth of ecstasy use amongst
clubbers in Malta, combined with a widespread sense of
moral objection to their hedonism, the government
imposed a nightlife **curfew** in 1999, which runs from

THE RAVE SCENE

Maltese nightlife is at its most vibrant and adventurous within the **rave scene**, the night out of choice for many of the islands' young people, who want something more exciting than the crop of club-bars that dominate here. In summers, huge rave parties are held every other weekend, usually in open-air spaces or under tents in far-flung corners of the islands. They attract crowds of 4000-strong, sometimes larger, and they invariably feature an impressive line-up of top DJs hailing from all over Europe (particularly London) and North America.

The **music** is varied, although the mainstay genres are house, trance and techno. The **entry charge** for parties is around Lm10, and if you don't buy your ticket in advance, you'll be charged Lm15 on the door, probably after queuing for some time. To find out about upcoming parties, and about advance ticket hotlines advertised, look for **flyers** in Paceville bars such as *Places* and *Misfits* (see p.293), or **posters** slapped up in strategic locations. Although **ecstasy** is widespread, it is consumed under a mantle of paranoia given the Maltese authorities' strict stance on drug-taking. Occasionally, the police set up roadblocks along the junctions leading to parties to search vehicles for drugs, and you may also be frisked on the door.

4am to 9am; most bars are only licensed until 1am as a result. Having said this, enforcement of these laws is often lax, and many places get away with opening throughout the night, while others simply close the doors after 4am and operate a dancing "lock-in".

Unless otherwise specified, none of the
places below attract a cover charge.

ROCK

The Alley

Map 1, I3. Triq Wilġa, Paceville

☎ 372246.

Daily 9pm–4am.

Malta's most popular rock club, this gets impossibly packed on weekends, when a DJ is in attendance and the small dance floor throbs. Popular rock is the usual soundtrack, and local bands play live occasionally.

Coconut Grove

Map 1, I3. Triq Wilġa, Paceville

☎ 333385.

Daily 7.30pm–4am.

Classic and commercial rock songs played for a cool crowd of Maltese teenagers. There are DJs only on weekends, when things are at their busiest. Upstairs is *Remedy* (June–Sept Wed–Sun 9pm–4am; Oct–May Fri & Sat 9pm–4am), a no-nonsense club-bar that plays loud house to an audience of half-hearted clubbers.

Rock Café

Map 1, I3. Triq San Ġorġ, Paceville.

June–Sept daily 9pm–4am; Oct–May Fri–Sun 9pm–4am.

Hard rock for a core group of bikers and the few punks who roam Paceville. Occasional concerts from local hard rock and punk bands.

LATIN

El Barrio Latino

Map 1, I3. 7 Triq Wilġa, Paceville

☎ 378373.

May–Oct daily 8.30pm–4am; Nov–April Wed–Sun 8.30pm–4am.

Dancey salsa and Latin for a sweaty crowd who take their dancing seriously. Tequila fuels the attitude, and there's a small bar downstairs where you can sample excellent tortillas (Lm0.75), caipirinhas and mescal accompanied by a mellower samba sound.

Fuego

Map 1, I3. St George's Bay, St Julian's

☎ 386746.

Daily 10.30pm–4am.

The most popular Latin club

in Malta, with themed decor, plenty of tequila and South American cocktails, and commercial Latin music mixed with pop. One of the few places that gets busy virtually every night throughout the year, the atmosphere here is inebriated and hormone-driven.

JAZZ

BJ's Nightclub and Piano Bar
Map 1, I3. Ball St, Paceville
ⓣ337642.
Daily 9.30pm–4am.
The only true jazz club in Malta, hosting frequent live acts (and the occasional pianist), and attracting an older crowd than most other places in Paceville. Thursdays to Saturdays are the only nights worth going, but even then it's pretty laid-back.

DANCE MUSIC

Bar Code
Map 1, I3. Triq San Ġorġ, Paceville.

June–Sept daily 9pm–4am;
Oct–May Fri & Sat 9pm–4am;
Lm1.50.
Commercial hard-house and techno trance for a crowd of hardcore clubbers. The action peaks at around 2am, when it's packed, sweaty, and the dancing is furious.

Caesar's
Map 6, B5. Bay Square, Buġibba
ⓣ571034.
Daily 9pm–3am.
Small, disco-style club that dishes out commercial dance music, garage particularly, and popular pop songs to an alcohol-fuelled crowd of British holiday-makers and Maltese on the pull.

La Grotta
Map 8, E7. Xlendi Rd, Xlendi, Gozo
ⓣ551149.
May–Oct Wed & Fri–Sun 9pm–4am; Lm2.
Large open-air complex, attractively located on the side of Xlendi Valley, that serves as Gozo's only club in the summer when it's packed to its 3000 capacity most

CLUBS AND CLUB-BARS

weekends. The decor and attitude hark back to the disco days, as does the music, a mix of pop, commercial house, rock and reggae classics, badly mixed and always played the same in the same order. *Paradiso* (daily 9pm–4am; free) is a small indoor club within the complex that serves as a place to dance during the week.

Havana

Map 1, I3. Triq San Ġorġ, Paceville.

Daily 9pm–4am.

Malta's only rap club, catering for a regular crowd of hip-hop followers and young tourists, particularly British and English-language students. It's sweaty and always full, though the commercial playlist shows little experimentation and originality.

Misfits

Map 1, I3. *White House Hotel*, Paceville Ave, Paceville
ⓣ378725.

Daily 9pm–4am.

The only true club-bar in Malta, this arty, comfortable place is decorated in warm, bright hues, and frequented by New Age types, mostly students. The music policy changes nightly; on weeknights it's chilled ambient and world sounds, but on weekends, people get up to dance to the full-on house. Free art-house films are screened every Tuesday at 8.30pm.

Places

Map 1, I3. Ball St, Paceville.

June–Sept daily 9pm–4am; Oct–May Fri–Sun 9pm–4am.

A good place to scope out the latest trends in the local clubbing scene, this spacious club-bar caters for hardcore dancers at the weekends, when there's a DJ, but is a lot more chilled during the week. The music is mostly house, sometimes hard-house, and unless there are no large rave parties going on (in which case it's packed), the lively crowd tend to use it as a warm-up venue before heading elsewhere.

Tattinger's

Map 5, H7. Triq Is-Saqqajja, Rabat

CLUBS AND CLUB-BARS

Ⓣ 451104.

Sat 10pm–6am; Lm2.

Clubby nights crackling with good house for a packed crowd of sweaty, neon-clad, glowstick-waving young revellers. Away from the heavily policed Paceville, it's able to open until 6am, and is something of a pick-up joint.

XS

Map 9, K6. Aurora Complex, Triq Ir-Repubblika, Rabat, Gozo Ⓣ 560113.

Oct–May Fri–Sun 9.30pm–4am.

Gozo's best club and one of the largest in the Maltese islands. Set in a large arena which fills up with some two thousand revellers, the boisterous atmosphere is fuelled by alcohol. A good sound system and minimal decor ensure the dance floor is packed all night, and the playlist of mostly commercial house tunes is tempered with pop. Summers see occasional one-off club nights with international DJ line-ups that are widely advertised in both Malta and Gozo.

THEATRE

There are four theatres in the Maltese islands: two in Valletta, and two in Rabat, Gozo. The theatre **season** runs between October and May only, with occasional one-off plays in the summer. Check the quarterly cultural calendar of events, available from tourist offices in Malta and Gozo respectively, for details of upcoming productions; it's also worth keeping an eye out for posters, and checking listings in local newspapers.

Productions fall into types: mainstream shows touring the Med, often musicals – *Cats* caused quite a sensation when it made its debut in Malta a few years ago – as well as plays put on by Maltese companies (some in English, some in Maltese). These are usually pretty entertaining and worth taking in, with plenty of satirical comment on local life and

THEATRE

culture. Theatres also stage a handful of excellent **operas** every season, as well as the occasional **ballet** or **dance** production; flamenco is particularly popular.

Astra Theatre
Map 9, H4. 9 Triq Ir-Repubblika, Rabat, Gozo
☎ 556256.
The largest Baroque theatre in Malta, staging everything from operas to drama and ballet.

Aurora Opera Theatre
Map 9, K5. Triq Ir-Repubblika, Rabat, Gozo
☎ 562974.
Large Baroque theatre renowned for excellent operas; it's also used to stage drama and other events such as ballet.

Manoel Theatre
Map 2, I5. Triq It-Teatru L-Antik, Valletta

☎ 246389.
Built by the Knights in the eighteenth century, Malta's 600-seater National Theatre boasts perfect acoustics. Mesmerizing drama and concerts are staged on occasional weekends.

Theatre in the Round
Map 2, G7. St James Cavalier Centre for Creativity, Triq Papa Piju V, Valletta
☎ 223200.
A small theatre with sixty seats arranged around the central stage. Productions from classical concerts to experimental plays by fringe theatre groups.

CINEMA

The Maltese are big moviegoers, and there are several **cinemas** dotted around the islands. The cinemas listed overleaf feature the latest commercial releases, particularly Hollywood films, in modern theatres with Dolby surround-sound and air conditioning. Releases are behind the US by a few months and behind the UK by a few weeks. **Tickets** cost between Lm1.75 to Lm2.50, and many cinemas offer discounts on Mondays.

CINEMA

Art-house films are also increasing in popularity, and there are two dedicated cinemas; tickets cost Lm1–Lm1.50. *Misfits* (see p.293), shows art-house films for free every Tuesday at 8.30pm.

MAINSTREAM CINEMAS

Citadel Theatre
Map 9, G4. Pjazza Indipendenza, Rabat, Gozo
☎ 559955.
Two screens.

Eden Century Cinemas
Map 1, I3. Triq Santu Wistin, St George's Bay, St Julian's
☎ 376401.
Sixteen screens.

Eden Imax
Map 1, I3. St George's Bay, St Julian's
☎ 341191.
Two screens.

Embassy
Map 2, I5. Triq Santa Lucia, Valletta
☎ 227436.
Four screens.

Empire Cinema Complex
Map 6, B7. Triq Il-Korp

Tal-Pijunieri, Buġibba
☎ 581787.
Four screens.

Sun City Cine Palais
Map 1, N6. Triq Tal-Gardiel, Marsascala
☎ 632858.
Four screens.

ART-HOUSE CINEMAS

St James Cavalier Centre for Arts Creativity
Map 2, G7. Triq Papa Piju V, Valletta
☎ 223200.
Various art-house films featured every weekend in this small, attractive theatre.

University Film Club
Map 1, I5. University of Malta, Msida
☎ 333903.
One art-house film screened every Saturday evening in the university's film theatre.

CASINOS

To visit either of Malta's **casinos**, both hotel-based and used predominantly by tourists (most Maltese regard gambling as somewhat shady), you'll have to show some sort of identification to prove you're over 18; dress code is smart casual.

Dragonara

Map 1, I3. *Westin Dragonara Hotel*, Paceville.
Mon–Fri 10am–6am, Sat & Sun open 24hr; free.
Situated in the Dragonara Palace, a beautiful nineteenth-century Neoclassical building in the hotel grounds, this offers rows of slot machines and other mainstays such as roulette, blackjack, punto banco and stud poker.

Oracle Casino

Map 6, D4. *New Dolmen Hotel*, Triq Dolmen, Buġibba
℡ 581510.
Daily noon–6am; free.
Large casino with slot machines and the full complement of table games.

Festivals and events

The highlight of the Maltese festival calendar are the **festas** that take place during the summer to commemorate each town's patron saint. For many Maltese, their town's *festa* is the cultural event of the year – a grand, three-day affair of brass bands, fireworks and general merriment, when everyone puts on their best clothes, lets their hair down and guzzles whisky, beer and local snacks such as *pastizzi*.

Aside from *festas*, there are a few annual **music events**, best of which is the Malta Jazz Festival in July, as well as **sports events** throughout the summer, which culminate in the Middle Sea Yacht Race, an international yachting contest which takes place in October. The off-season is quieter, but not without its highlights: Carnival in March, and the Good Friday re-enactments in April, are both worth checking out. The tourist board also stage regular **historical festivals** for visitors; the largest and best is the week-long Valletta Festival, also in April.

The tourist board publish a yearly **calendar of events** that lists everything from sports meets and concerts to exhibitions or re-enactments: you can pick up a copy at any tourist information office, or view the listings online at Ⓦ www.visitmalta.com/events.

FESTAS

If you're in Malta between June and September, you simply can't escape the annual round of **festas**, and even if you make a concerted effort to steer clear of the celebrations, chances are that the petards – rocket-type fireworks that let off a mighty bang – will shatter your morning bliss, or you'll get trapped in the traffic jams that inevitably build up where events are held. Every town celebrates at least one *festa* every year, making a total of 82 annually; only a handful take place in winter. Borrowed from the similar tradition in Sicily, Maltese *festas* were first celebrated in the eighteenth century – modest affairs of bonfires, petards and Mass. They evolved into their present form during the nineteenth century, when parishioners, perhaps out of parochial pride, began to invest more time and money, while the associated pyrotechnics became a professional industry worth thousands of liri. *Festas* show no sign of losing popularity; in fact, they're more popular today than ever before.

Festas bring out the boisterous pomp of Maltese culture. Weeks of preparation climax in three days of street celebrations, from Friday to Sunday. Streets are decorated by strings of multicoloured lights, pennants, banners and statues of saints, while the church exteriors are lit by hundreds of lightbulbs, and the interiors transformed into treasure-troves of ceremonial silverware and red damask, dusted down and brought out of storage for the occasion. Church-based celebrations include pontifical High Masses, accompanied by incense burning and organ music, in the mornings (9.15am) and evenings (7pm) of the nine days preceding the final Sunday of the *festa*. On the Friday and Saturday of each *festa*, **street celebrations** take place in the evenings, focused around brass band processions led by a statue of the patron saint and followed by thousands of pilgrims. On the Saturday, from midnight onwards, there are airborne

fireworks, mostly a series of ten-minute long ear-splitting petard displays, as well as colourful, noiseless displays at street level. Sundays see the celebrations commencing at 11am with more petards and brass band parades followed by processions of inebriated young people dancing wildly. Horse races are held in the afternoon, while the evenings see a formal and sober procession headed by the statue of the patron saint; after this has been taken into the church, drinking and dancing to the brass bands resumes.

Festas are driven and rooted in rivalry. Towns often split into two factions, with each supporting one particular brass band and patron saint; while countrywide, towns compete to stage the wildest celebrations and the largest fireworks displays. The result are the petards – each town tries to outdo the next one in the level of noise it generates, typically blowing up some Lm10,000 worth of pyrotechnics per *festa*. The rivalry has been known to erupt into running bottle-wielding battles, or by sabotaging the rivals' *festa* by, say, spreading nails on streets to ground motorists or wrecking the street decor. Thanks to the firm intervention of the police and parish priests, however, such incidents are rare, and *festas* are normally trouble-free affairs.

Leaflets giving the dates of each *festa* are available from tourist information offices; some dates change annually. The largest three *festas* fall on public holidays and are held in a couple of separate towns throughout the islands: **L-Imnarja**, as its called in Maltese, is on June 29 to commemorate St Peter and St Paul; **Santa Marija** on August 15 is the *festa* of the Assumption; and **Il-Vitorja** on September 8 celebrates the birth of the Virgin Mary. Lija, whose *festa* is on the Sunday closest to August 6, puts on the most impressive and largest fireworks displays, while Hamrun, which celebrates its *festa* of *San Gejtanu* on the first weekend after August 7, throws the wildest street parties (if street scuffles do occur, they tend to happen here).

FESTAS

ANNUAL EVENTS

Below are a selection of the most interesting annual events, but there are many more one-off celebrations or sporting fixtures listed in the tourist board's calendar (see p.291).

FEBRUARY

- -

Held during early February at Ta Qali, Malta's national stadium, the week-long **Rothmans Football International Tournament** is played by small European teams, and offers the chance to see some good international football for under Lm10 per game. For dates and more info, contact the Malta Football Association ☏ 222697 ⓦ www.mfa.com.mt.

The **International Snooker Tournament** takes place in the last week of February, attracting top worldwide players, including Malta's Tony Drago, who has a cult following here. For more info, check the website ⓦ www.visitmalta.com/events.

Late February also sees the **Flora Malta Marathon**, which lures several top athletes. For more info, contact the Organizing Committee ☏ 432402 ⓦ www.maltamarathon.com.mt.

MARCH

- -

In early March, the week-long **carnival** celebrations, organized by the Department of Culture (☏ 248006), consist of colourful evening parades of decorated floats, as well as competitions amongst professional dance troupes. Celebrations are more spontaneous at **Nadur** in **Gozo**, where carnival harks back to its inversive origins as a mock revolution: an unruly romp that allowed peasants to vent their sense of injustice at the ruling classes and the Church. Held over the three days preceding Lent, today's wine- and whisky-soaked carnival still serves as a period of abandonment and mischief before the fasting, and it's quite a sight, attracting more observers than participants. It features concerts by cranky local rock acts, while one or two bars play host to traditional bands that use accordions, bongos, tambourines and a wood-and-sheepskin instrument that lets out a rhythmic humph to create excellent tribal-type rhythms for posses of drunken, whooping dancers. Outside, participants stream through the streets in mock-revolutionary style, dressed in boiler-suits and home-made masks, and brandishing sickles. The event's deliberate, flagrant political incorrectness, barbarism and downright grossness – someone trundling a pushchair filled with animal intestines; or live chickens crucified to crosses or soiled women's knickers slung on a long stick – has provoked an endless debate over whether Nadur's carnival should be banned, or tolerated because it's a tradition that should be preserved.

APRIL

On **Good Friday**, many towns organize impressive and sober biblical re-enactments, starting at dusk – biblical characters parade through the streets and Jesus Christ is herded by Roman soldiers towards his crucifixion. Hooded participants, dressed in white robes and hoods, follow the procession dragging bundles of metal chains from their ankles in penitence and holy self-mortification. On **Easter Sunday** towns erupt in celebrations, including sprinting with the statue of the Risen Christ to symbolize Christ's resurrection.

In April (dates change annually), the capital hosts the colourful, week-long **Valletta Festival**, organized by the tourism authority to celebrate the Knights of Malta, and is the best time to enjoy Valletta. Hundreds of participants in period costumes and pomp re-create life during the Knights' era, while the streets are decorated in banners emblazoned with Maltese crosses and triumphal motifs. Pages parade through town all day playing tambourines and trumpets, the town crier announces decrees and public events, and the re-enactments climax a historical ceremony presided over by the Grand Master and an entourage of Knights. Other events during the week include art exhibitions, cooking displays on the streets, brass band concerts in the squares and so on. For specific dates and an events programme, visit the tourist offices or the MTA website ⓦ www.visitmalta.com.

JULY

A Friday to Sunday affair held at Valletta's waterfront on the third weekend of July, the **Malta Jazz Festival** features top jazz musicians from around the world performing at the three-day festival.

The last weekend in July sees the **Farsons International Food and Beer Festival**, three days of concerts by local rock bands and lots of cheap beer. For more info on this and the Jazz Festival, check the MTA website (see above).

SEPTEMBER

The excellent and exciting **Malta International Airshow** in late September features plenty of airborne acrobatics, including colourful performances by the famed Red Devils. Harriers of the Royal Air Force show their prowess, and American F-16s cleave through the air. For more info, contact the Malta Aviation Society on ⓣ 448745, or visit the website ⓦ www .geocities.com/CapeCanaveral/6152/INDEX.HTM.

OCTOBER

Held in late October, the three-day **Middle Sea Yacht Race** starts and finishes in Marsamxett Harbour in Sliema and loops round Sicily, and attracts top international contenders. For more info, contact the Royal Malta Yacht Club ⓣ 333109 or 318417 ⓦ www.rawsilk.com/rmyc.

ANNUAL EVENTS

Gay Malta

The **gay scene** in the Maltese islands is pretty small, and hinged around various clubs and bars (mostly in the nightlife district of Paceville; see p.117) that attract a mixed gay and straight clientele, as well as a few beaches. Discrimination is rare, and gay-bashing is virtually unheard of; in the urban centres of Valletta, Sliema and St Julian's, you'll feel comfortable displaying affection wherever you go. However, it's worth bearing in mind that in small towns and rural areas, attitudes remain fairly conservative, and you might want to be more discreet.

The age of consent is eighteen for all, and although there are still some **legal** inequalities, political parties show a willingness to give gay men and women the same rights enjoyed by heterosexuals; the latest piece of legislation mooted by the government will give cohabiting gay couples some legal rights and obligations, although gay marriage – let alone child adoption – is still well off the agenda. There are no **gay groups** in Malta, other than the Gay Support Group, a one-man show that, at the time of writing, was constructing what may be a useful website ⓦwww.gaymalta.com.

GAY BARS AND CLUBS

City of London
Map 4, C3. 193 Main St,
St Julian's
☎ 331706.
Daily 9.30am–1am.
Clubby bar where the clientele is largely composed of loud, in-your-face lesbian regulars as well as some gay men. It's best visited at the weekends, when the drinking area mutates into a dance floor and techno blares from the jukebox.

Didies Bar
Map 6, C6. Triq It-Turisti,
Buġibba
☎ 476266.
Daily 7pm–1am.
Quiet lesbian bar away from the hectic, central Bay Square. You can actually have a chat if you choose to, even on weekends, but the music is a monotonous menu of popular pop songs.

Lady Godiva
Map I, I3. Triq Wilġa, Paceville.
Daily 9pm–4am.
Club-bar that functions as a rough-and-tumble pulling joint and is usually heaving with a young gay and straight crowd, who come for the frequent drag shows as well as to get sweaty on the dance floor; music ranges from Madonna to house.

Nix Bar
Map 4, D5. 186 Manwel
Dimech St, St Julian's
☎ 340353.
Daily 6.30pm–1am.
On the Balutta Bay outskirts of bustling St Julian's and Paceville, this small place is Malta's only dedicated lesbian bar (though everyone's welcome); there's a jukebox and the regulars kill time playing video games. Quiet and laid-back, this isn't really the place to go on the pull.

Saints Bar
Map 1, I5. New St (off Nobility St), Mrieħel
☎ 486079 or 09445672.
Daily 9pm–4am.

GAY BARS AND CLUBS

Very camp bar that doubles as a drag club, this is a bit hard to find, holed in an industrial estate that is deserted at night which makes a perfect setting for the hedonistic antics. Can be quiet on weekdays even if the music is pumping, but on Fridays it's packed for the free drag shows.

Taverna Del Ponte
Map 8, E7. Triq Ix-Xlendi, Xlendi, Gozo
T 555934.
Daily 9pm–4am.
Classy bar, set in a converted farmhouse, with terraces of bougainvillea overlooking a gorge. Not strictly a gay bar – there are none in Gozo – but it is gay-friendly and attracts a handful of local gays. Music ranges from house and pop tunes to rock.

Tom's Bar
Map 2, G9. 1 Crucifix St, Floriana
T 250780.
Daily 11.30am–2.30pm & 8.30pm–1am.
Malta's only official gay bar, with a motto of "straight-acting, now and sexy", this is a slickly-designed place spread over two floors: downstairs is a pumping dance floor where you'll hear mostly house, while upstairs serves as the venue for plays and launch parties. Although it's patronized by all ages, *Tom's* is distinctly more mature than the hedonistic, youthful places in Paceville. Occasional lock-ins after the doors close at 1am.

GAY BEACHES

Blata Il-Bajda
Map 8, I3. A remote clay plateau off Ramla Bay in Gozo, mostly used by local men on the pull. To get there, follow the path that winds along the coastline at the south end of Ramla Bay, a fifteen-minute walk.

Ferro Bay
Map 4, L4.
This section of Sliema's rocky main beach, just beyond *TGI*

Friday's on Tower Road, is a popular mixed/gay hangout for the image-conscious.

Ġnejna
Map 1, C5.

The beach proper – the sandy section – is dominated by families, but some 500m north of here, gay men and women congregate on a pear-shaped flat rock. It's set underneath stunning clay slopes and limestone cliffs, and surrounded by inviting sea which affords lots of privacy and means you can swim and sunbathe nude. The watersports operator at the main section of the beach will transport you to the rock and back for Lm2.

Tigne Point
Map 1, K4.

Daytime swimming and cruising spot beyond the deserted army barracks and the water desalination plant.

Beaches, watersports and outdoor pursuits

There are plenty of ways to enjoy the outdoor life in the Maltese islands, and the chief playground is the **sea**. In summer, **watersports** operators set up on all the main beaches, and you can get out onto the water by renting a speedboat or even chartering a yacht. Malta is also one of the best places in the Mediterranean to go **scuba diving**, and there are plenty of dive shops offering tuition as well as dives for those with certification. Snorkelling is another great way to explore life under the sea.

History and Adventure (Victoria Place, High St, Sliema ℡ 347757 ⓦ www.h-adventure.com) organize tailor-made outdoor activities for groups – rock climbing, scuba diving, mountain-bike tours, hiking and so on. Malta Outdoors (Mirob, Triq Il-Ħġejjeġ, Buġibba ℡ 09425439 ⓦ www .maltaoutdoors.com) offer similar activities, including a brilliant four-day trek round Gozo's coast.

Land-based activities include tennis, squash and rock-climbing, while birdwatching is particularly rewarding during the spring and autumn migration periods.

BEACHES

As the Maltese define a **beach** as any stretch of coast from which it's possible to slip or jump into the sea (and many of the most popular "beaches" are simply rocky shorelines equipped with ladders into the water), you'll be disappointed if you arrive expecting mile upon mile of shimmering sands on your hotel doorstep. The upside of this, however,

BEACH GUIDE

The **best overall beach** in the islands is Ramla Bay (see p.224) in Gozo, with glorious orange-red sand leading to a swath of crystal-clear water. Also in Gozo, undeveloped San Blas (see p.226) is a smaller version of the same, and is ideal for a tranquil afternoon by the sea.

Throughout Malta, some beaches have been informally taken over by particular social groups. **Young people** flock to Għajn Tuffieħa and Golden Bay (see p.169), two sandy swaths on the northwest coast, with a merry, flirtatious atmosphere, jet-ski show-offs and nonchalant topless bathing. The rocky strips of Exiles Bay and Ferro Bay (see p.115) in Sliema attract hundreds of young European English-language students. **Families** will find Mellieħa Bay (see p.164) the most agreeable place to swim: it's Malta's largest sandy beach, with watersports facilities, lifeguards and shallow waters. Għejna Bay (see p.173) beyond Mġarr, is popular with families for similar reasons, but has no lifeguard.

Nude beaches include the cove within Għajn Tuffieħa (see p.169), as well as deserted spots such as pebbly **Fomm Ir-Riħ** (see p.145) in northwest Malta.

BEACHES

309

is that, given Malta's small size, you're never further than a ten-minute drive from the nearest swimming spot. In addition to these, however, there are some lovely sandy beaches, and though the best and most accessible are hopelessly crowded at the height of summer, Gozo in particular boasts clean, virgin swaths of sand, as well as stretches of rocky coast and creeks from which to swim.

The Maltese don't tend to make a huge effort to find a great beach, which is a blessing if you are prepared to get off the beaten track to find your own special seashore. There are plenty of lovely lesser-visited spots within a fifteen- or twenty-minute walk from the main beaches; you may have to plod down a clay slope or scramble over a few rocks, but all the routes described in the *Guide* are pretty unchallenging and should be walkable by all.

The waters surrounding Malta, Gozo and Comino generally offer safe swimming, though when the seas are choppy, beware strong **undercurrents** at beaches such as Għajn Tuffieħa in northwest Malta, which can drag you towards the rocks or out to sea; this and other potentially risky spots are denoted by multilingual signs. As operators of speedboats and jet-skis often seem to perceive the open sea as racing ground, it's also sensible to keep a watchful eye out and give them a wide berth when swimming.

Though **topless** and **nude** swimming and sunbathing are illegal in Malta, the police largely turn a blind eye, and unless you strip off in the middle of a family beach (when you may well be told to cover up), you're unlikely to encounter any resistance in your quest for an all-over tan. Some beaches have come to be regarded as unofficial nude beaches, and you can of course use your discretion at out-of-the-way spots, but bear in mind that as peeping Toms and even flashers are fairly common, it's probably best to only get your kit off when accompanied by others.

Gay beaches are listed on pp.306–307.

WATERSPORTS

With clear, warm seas and temperate weather, Malta is an excellent place for **watersports**. From May to September watersports centres set up on virtually all the main beaches, offering anything from **waterskiing** and **wake-boarding** (both around Lm7 per 15min), **parasailing** and **jet-skiing** (both around Lm15 per 15min) to **kayaking** (from Lm2 per hour).

SCUBA DIVING

Malta is generally considered to be the best **scuba diving** destination in the Mediterranean, and some 50,000 enthusiasts dive in the surrounding waters annually. Aside from stunning seascapes (from boulder meadows, gullies, chimneys and ledges to sheer cliff drops) and rich marine life, underwater visibility is excellent – 20m in spring and autumn during plankton build-up, and up to 45m between November and March – while mild weather allows year-round diving (water temperature rises to a peak average of 27°C in summer, down to an average of 15°C in winter). Of the three islands, Gozo offers the most spectacular **dive sites**, especially off Dwejra in Gozo's western tip, but the basic rule of thumb in both islands is the further north you go, the better the diving. Malta has some good wreck dives, but visibility can be poor, especially around the Grand Harbour. There's no space in this guide to detail all the islands' diving (and snorkelling) sites, but Lawson and Leslie Wood's *Dive Sites of Malta, Comino and Gozo* (New Holland Publishers,

WATERSPORTS

DIVING SCHOOLS

Malta

Dive Systems, Qui-Si-Sana, Sliema ☎ 319123.
Maltaqua, Mosta Rd, St Paul's Bay ☎ 571873.
Meldives, *Sea Bank Hotel*, Triq Il-Marfa, Mellieħa ☎ 573116.
Northeast Dive Services, Pebbles Lido, Qui-Si-Sana, Sliema, ☎ 340506.
Sub-Way, Ramon Perellos St, St Paul's Bay ☎ 580611.

Gozo

Calypso Aquatic Sports Club, Marina St, Marsalforn ☎ 310743.
Gozo Aqua Sports, Rabat Rd, Marsalforn ☎ 563037.
Moby Dives, Triq Il-Gostra, Xlendi ☎ 551616.
St Andrews, 1–2 St Simon St, Xlendi ☎ 551301.

UK), contains detailed information: almost all of the sites are graded and described in detail.

You need a **permit** to dive in Malta. These cost Lm2, and the easiest way to get hold of one is via your dive school, which will provide an application form and arrange for a medical certificate. Once you're certified fit, and have handed in your application as well as proof of certification and two passport photos, your permit should arrive in two days. If you're learning to dive in Malta, you don't need a permit until you've qualified. It's cheaper to get a medical certificate in Malta, where it costs Lm2; you'll pay Lm5 in Gozo owing to one doctor's monopoly in issuing certificates on the island.

There are 33 **diving schools** in Malta. Most are professional operators affiliated with the major international schools of instruction – PADI, CMAS and BSAC, as well as the lesser known FUAM and APDS. Diving schools offer all the standard courses plus specialized programmes such as night- or cave-diving. Five-day open-water courses cost about Lm130, and three-day advanced open-water courses around Lm80. Most schools also offer "taster dives" for the uninitiated a one-off dive that costs Lm15. Some diving schools have provisions for divers with **disabilities**; for the most recent list of these, contact the National Commission for Persons with Disabilities, Triq Il-Kbira San Ġużepp, Santa Venera ☏245952.

SNORKELLING

If you don't fancy diving, **snorkelling** is an easy-access means of getting a look at undersea Malta. The best under-water scenery and the largest concentration of marine life are found along **rocky shores**, in the nooks and crannies amid boulders. On **sandy shores** and seabeds, there's little to see, but keep a sharp eye out for small fish such as gobies and flying gurnards; they're very well camouflaged, and you'll probably only notice them when they move. Rocky shores offer richer pickings: clusters of sea urchins, the inquisitive common octopus, and the beautiful red starfish. Finger-sized fish such as blennies, grey triggerfish and Connemara suckerfish float in shallow rocky pools or waters, darting away just as you get close enough to enjoy their variegated colours. Large shoals of bream, mullet, sil-verfish, sand smelt, chromi and wrasse are also seen near the shores. On rocky surfaces and clefts created by boulder heaps, you can explore some colourful growths of soft or false **coral**. For more on marine life, see p.361.

WINDSURFING

Malta isn't exactly a **windsurfing** hot spot (the wind often dies down for days on end), but when the breezes are blow-ing, the best place to indulge is just off **Għallis Point**,

WATERSPORTS

halfway along the coast road between Buġibba and St Andrews. You can **rent** windsurfing equipment for about Lm4 per hour from beaches that have watersports facilities. The best **courses**, tailored to individual needs, are run from the watersports centre (☎522141) of the *Mellieħa Bay Hotel* in Mellieħa Bay (see p.164), and cost Lm10 per hour.

YACHT CHARTERS AND BOAT RENTALS

The coastline of the Maltese islands – especially southwest Gozo – is far more beautiful from the sea than from any terrestrial perspective, and **chartering a yacht** allows some fabulous views as well as access to many coves and creeks that are only reachable from the sea (and hence are uncrowded). But it doesn't come cheap, of course: for a yacht plus skipper, food and drink, and snorkelling gear, expect to fork out about Lm130 per day; most vessels take up to ten people, so it's worth getting a group together. Yacht charters are available from the following centres: S & D Yachts, 57 Gzira Rd, Gzira ☎339908; Nautica Ltd, 21 Msida Rd, Gzira ☎338253; Trader Marine, 37 Ta Xbiex Sea Front, Ta Xbiex ☎313089. For more on yachting, visit the website of the Malta Yachting Federation at Ⓦwww.digigate.net/myf.

You can rent **boats** – either speedboats at Lm12 per hour or tiny sailing boats (suitable for harbours only) at Lm5 per hour – from any of the watersports centres located at the main beaches. The best equipped are Oki-Ko-Ki at Spinola Bay, St Julian's (☎339831), and the watersports centre at the *Mellieħa Bay Hotel* (☎522141).

FISHING

More prevalent even than hunting, **fishing** is a way of life in Malta – in the late afternoons, anglers line virtually every section of accessible coast. It's free to fish, but don't expect impressive catches. You'll often land members of the bream family, including the saddled bream, a palm-sized silver specimen with lots of bones; the gilthead bream has more delicate white flesh. Red mullet and the thick-lipped grey mullet are common in bays and harbours, and mackerel are pretty much everywhere, as are predatory species such as sea bass and amberjack – the latter grows to over 30cm long and is considered a tastier alternative to the deep-sea *lampuka* (see p.260). Silverfish, particularly sardines, are also found in large numbers in bays. You can buy fishing **equipment and tackle** at the following shops: Handyware, 149 The Strand, Sliema ☎314509; Pirotta Fishing Centre, 139 Manoel St, Gzira ☎331279; Ernest's Marina Centre, 61B Zejtun Rd, Marsaxlokk ☎685549.

BIRDWATCHING

Though Malta's birdlife is constantly threatened by hunters (see p.365), the islands nonetheless offer fairly good **birdwatching**, particularly during the spring and autumn months when Eurasian migratory birds cross the Mediterranean. Some **320 species** (including some thirteen resident birds) have been recorded here, and the most spectacular are the **birds of prey**, mainly harriers, kestrels and honey buzzards, which visit throughout September and October. The best place to watch migratory birds of prey is at Buskett Gardens near Rabat in Malta (see p.143), where hundreds of specimens swoop down to roost in the trees in the late afternoon. For **water birds** (herons, egrets, kingfishers, black-winged stilts, lapwings) visit the wetland reserves, maintained by local group Birdlife Malta, at Simar in St Paul's Bay and Għadira in Mellieħa Bay; both are free and open erratically at weekends. For more information on birdwatching in Malta, or to make contact with other birders, contact Birdlife Malta at 28 Marina Court, 57 Abate Rigord St, Ta' Xbiex, MSD 12 ☎347646 ⓦwww .waldonet.net.mt/birdlife.

SPORTS AND OTHER OUTDOOR ACTIVITIES

If you fancy getting active, your best plan is to head for the **Marsa Sports Club** (MSC) in Marsa (Mon–Fri 9am–9pm, Sat & Sun 9am–5pm; ☎233851), where you can rent one of the seventeen all-weather **tennis** courts from Lm3.50 per hour; or a **squash** court for Lm1.50 per 45min. However, book well ahead as evenings and weekends are usually busy. The MSC is also home to an eighteen-hole, par-68 **golf course**, the only one in Malta; you can rent clubs for Lm3 each per day, and a round costs Lm8. Temporary weekly memberships, allowing unlimited play, costs Lm50. The MSC is also the best place to watch spectator sports such as **polo**, **cricket** and **archery**; games are erratic, so check in advance to see what's on.

ROCK CLIMBING

The Maltese islands are an undiscovered haven for **rock climbers**. Cliffs girdle virtually the entire northwest and southwest coasts of Malta, Gozo and Comino, and there are also stretches of inland cliffs; together, these offer all grades of climbs, from moderate to extremely severe. Climbing is especially exciting here given that many stretches of cliffs, particularly in Gozo, are uncharted. The recorded climbs, moreover, are unbolted, a legacy honoured by the small circuit of local climbers to keep the cliffs more challenging.

To join a group of local climbers, or for further information about renting climbing gear, contact local rock-climbing fiend Andrew Warrington on ☎226100 or 09470377 (mobile).

HORSE RIDING

An enjoyable and unstrenuous means of exploring the countryside, **horse riding** is also a great way to get outdoors. A guided ride costs about Lm3.50 per hour; you can also opt to take your mount out independently for the same price. For the most scenic landscapes, head towards the ridge and cliff topography of Malta's northwest coast, where there are two **riding schools** – Hal Ferh in Golden Bay (℡573360) and Għadira in Mellieħa Bay (℡573931). In Gozo, there's just one school – Wagon Wheel Ranch, on Marsalforn Road halfway between Rabat and Marsalforn (℡556254). The table-top hills and meandering valleys that stretch on all sides of Wagon Wheel Ranch make for some scenic routes.

SPORTS AND OTHER OUTDOOR ACTIVITIES

Shopping

The Maltese islands are hardly a shopping mecca, and though local crafts are generally of a very high standard and well worth seeking out, there's not much else you can buy here that you wouldn't find elsewhere for the same price and quality. The Maltese may make a big deal about the various open-air **flea markets** scattered throughout the islands, but unless you're a bric-a-brac fanatic, it's probably best to overlook these sweaty, rickety and noisy gatherings whose stalls are piled with pirate CDs and tapes, cheap imitation gadgets, accessories, clothes and souvenirs.

Resorts and large towns have plenty of **souvenir shops** selling a generally bland assortment of memorabilia, but it's worth keeping an eye out for glassware blown in various shapes and coloured profusely, Baroque brass doorknobs and door-knockers, and replicas of Maltese archeological artefacts carved in globigerina limestone. A hunt for **antiques** – particularly furniture, household appliances, accessories and paintings – can yield some interesting objects, but you require patience enough to trawl through the tat. Staff at the Malta Tourism Authority, 280 Triq Ir-Republika in Valletta (☎220668 or 224444) will hand out a list of about fifty local antique shops and dealers on request.

Typically faceless places that hold virtually all the high-street department stores and franchises of the UK and Italy, **shopping malls** are located in the main towns, and are detailed in the box below. All open from 9am to 1pm, and 4.30 to 7.30pm from Monday to Saturday unless otherwise specified.

FOOD AND FRESH PRODUCE

The Maltese climate and the continued use of traditional farming methods mean that local **vegetables**, particularly in Gozo, have a deeper, more textured taste than what you're used to in Europe and North America. The cheapest veg are sold from the backs of farmer's vans parked along trunk roads and in the centre of every town. Each town also has its fair share of **butchers** and **bakeries** tucked in the streets branching off the high street or the town squares. **Seafood** is also hawked by fishermen from strategically parked trucks, but their presence depends on the fluctuations of daily catches; in stormy, windy or wintry weather, you'll have to resort to buying frozen fish from supermarkets or the handful of **fish markets**. The largest of these is the covered market (which also stocks meats) on Triq Il-Merkanti, Valletta (Map 2, J6; Mon–Sat 9am–2pm). In

---

SHOPPING MALLS

St Julian's, Bay Street, St George's Bay (Map 1, I4; daily 9am–7pm).

Sliema Plaza Shopping Complex, Tower Road (Map 4, K8).

Rabat, Gozo Arcadia (Map 8, G5), and the Palazz Centre (Map 9, J5); both are on Triq Ir-Repubblika.

Valletta Energy Complex and Embassy Centre, Triq Ir-Repubblika (Map 2, I6).

northwest Malta, Azzopardi Fisheries on Triq Il-Mosta, St Paul's Bay (Map 7, I5; Mon–Sat 9am–6pm), stocks the largest variety of fish in the island, including some imported varieties, but most of it is frozen. In Gozo, fishermen put up a couple of stalls in Pjazza Indipendenza (Map 9, G5; Mon–Sat 8am–noon).

Each town also has its **supermarket**, while a few large ones are strategically located. Nicholson's, on Amery Street, Sliema (Map 4, K6; Mon–Sat 9am–8pm) is the best equipped for British tastes – including Marmite – and imports virtually all its stock from Tesco's. The Price Club (Map 1, I5; Mon–Sat 9am–7pm), on the trunk road leading from Msida to Birkirkara, popularly called the Birkirkara Bypass, is the largest and cheapest supermarket in Malta, but you'll have to put up with the queues and the jostle. In Gozo, the largest supermarket, Ta' Miema, is on Triq Il-Papa Ġwanni Pawlu II toward the western outskirts of Rabat (Map 9, 3A; Mon–Sat 8am–noon and 4–7pm).

CRAFTS

Maltese **crafts** are fairly unique, and influenced heavily by Baroque themes. Pieces to look out for include mantelpiece-type models carved in globigerina limestone, particularly a *kenur* (the traditional stone hearth for stewing), *luzzus* (the local wooden boats), or the enclosed balconies you see everywhere. All of these items – and a lot more – are conveniently produced and sold in two craft villages: **Ta' Qali** (Map 1, G6), a cluster of run-down ex-RAF Nissen huts near the National Football Stadium on the road to Mdina in Malta; and Ta' Dbieġi (Map 8, C5), on Triq Franġisk Portelli in San Lawrenz, Gozo. Both open daily 10am–4pm.

Directory

Electricity The supply is 240V and plugs are three-pin.

Embassies and consulates Australian Embassy, Villa Fiorentina, Ta' Xbiex Terrace, Ta' Xbiex ☎ 338201; Canadian Consulate, 103 Triq L-Arċisqof, Valletta ☎ 233121 or 233126; UK High Commission, 7 Triq Sant' Anna, Floriana ☎ 233134 or 233135; US Embassy, 3rd Floor, Development House, Triq Sant' Anna, Floriana ☎ 235960 or 235961.

Emergencies police ☎ 191; ambulance ☎ 196; fire ☎ 199; helicopter rescue ☎ 244371; coastguard ☎ 238797.

Hospitals St Luke's, Pjazza San Luqa, Msida ☎ 241251 or 247860; Gozo General Hospital, Rabat ☎ 556851.

Internet There are several internet cafés in Malta, detailed on pp.196, 263, 264, 284 and 287 of the *Guide*. Access starts at around Lm1 per hour. Many hotels also have terminals that guests and nonguests can use for a fee, and this can be a convenient option if you don't want to travel to check your mail.

Laundry There are a handful of strategically located coin-operated launderettes in the tourist centres, particularly Sliema and Buġibba. Reliable options include: Linencare Laundry and Dry Cleaning, Dean Hamlet Complex, Upper Ross Street, St Julian's ☎ 314838 or 314840; Lion Launderette, 3 Triq It-Turisti, Buġibba ☎ 580578; JC Laundry,

Triq Paderborn, St Paul's Bay ⓣ581584. The latter two will pick up and drop off loads to addresses in St Paul's Bay and Buġibba. Many of the larger hotels and tourist complexes have laundries that are open for nonresidents; prices are comparable to regular launderettes; about Lm2.50 per load.

Pharmacies There are plenty of pharmacies in Malta and Gozo. Most open Mon–Sat 9am–7pm, but the select number that open – on a rota basis – until 10pm daily (including public holidays) are listed in the daily newspapers.

Public holidays Malta has fourteen public holidays: January 1, February 10, March 19, Good Friday, March 31, May 1, June 7, June 29, August 15, September 8, September 21, December 8, December 13, December 25.

Time Malta is one hour ahead of GMT.

Travellers with disabilities Planning rules have only had to make provision for people with disabilities in the last decade,

and facilities generally remain poor. However, many upmarket hotels have rooms equipped for people with disabilities; to get a list of these properties, or for general information and contacts, get in touch with the National Commission for Persons with Disabilities, Ċentru Hidma Soċjali, Triq Il-Kbira San Ġuzepp, Santa Venera (mid-June to Sept Mon–Fri 8.30am–1pm; Oct to mid-June Mon–Fri 8.30am–noon & 2–4.30pm ⓣ245952 or 448521 ⓦwww.knpd.org).

Weddings At the time of writing, a company was in the process of being established to handle visitors' weddings in Malta; contact the Malta Tourism Authority's head office in Valetta (see p.47) for further information. In the meantime, for civil marriages contact the Marriage Registry Division at the Public Registry, 179 Triq Il-Merkanti, Valletta ⓣ225291 or 225292.

Working You can easily get a work permit for TEFL teaching in Malta; demand for teachers is always high, and although in most cases you need to have a

TEFL certificate, non-certificate bearers are sometimes employed if schools can't fill their vacancies. It's also relatively easy to find illegal work in the building industry or in the tourist trade – doing anything from washing dishes or waitressing to acting as a guide or renting boats on a beach. However, keep in mind that the police take a pro-active, hardline stance on illegal workers, regularly clamping down on businesses suspected of employing illegal workers, and people who are caught working illegally are invariably deported.

CONTEXTS

History of the Maltese islands

Given the strategic location of the Maltese islands, their long history has often taken an importance completely out of proportion to their diminutive size. The islands had two golden ages – the protracted Neolithic era that remained in force even as the rest of the region slid into the Bronze Age, and the prosperous times under the Knights of Malta. The medieval era is among the most obscure, when the islands were appended to Sicily for several centuries.

The Maltese islands attained **independence** from Britain in 1964 – the first time they had enjoyed sovereignty – and the population is still in the process of brushing off the attitudes adopted during foreign rule. Questions of identity, the maturity of democracy, and what future the islands face in the European Union or otherwise now dominate the political and social landscape.

Prehistory

The first known human inhabitants of the Maltese islands migrated from Sicily in around 5000 BC. They came in boats, heading to the land visible on the distant horizon on clear days, 80km to the south, and carted seeds and livestock with them. They settled in caves and started clearing the scrubby forest cover of holm oaks for agriculture. Their communities flourished, and five hundred years later they started living in huts built of stone, clay and twigs; two such hamlets at Grey Skorba and Red Skorba near Mġarr, Malta, thrived from 4500–4100 BC. At Red Skorba, two huts that served for the worship of **fertility** survive – larger than the rest, they were painted with symbolic red ochre, and in one archeologists unearthed the earliest Maltese representation of the "**fat lady**", the crude statuette of a rotund, crouching female which served as fertility icons throughout the Neolithic era in the Maltese islands.

Temple culture

By the dawn of the **Żebbug Phase** (4100–3800 BC), Malta's 5000-strong population had become even more sophisticated, burying their dead in rock-cut underground tombs that evolved from crude capsule-shaped structures to clusters of interconnected sarcophagi, and then to larger lobe-shaped underground chambers of a trefoil shape, used for collective burials. Offerings such as pots, flint knives and green-stone necklaces found in the chambers suggest that burials were accompanied by elaborate rituals. But the most impressive representation of the Neolithic peoples' sophistication were the colossal **temples** they constructed around the island using giant megaliths, with symmetrical pairs of lobes culminating in an inner lobed shrine. The earliest temple so far discovered was built between 3800–3600 BC at Ta' Ħaġrat in a crude trefoil outline, and there are another 23 major temples and two underground burial shrines scattered around the islands, dating from between 3800 and 2500 BC. Building styles developed remarkably rapidly: the Ġgantija complex (3600 BC) is made up of two temples, the largest one boasting seven lobed chambers. Some archeologists believe the design of the temples is an evolution from the trefoil collective tombs; others maintain their internal wall outline is modelled on the frontal outline of the sitting "fat ladies", wherein the inner shrine serves as the head.

The temples' interiors and the artefacts within were painted with red ochre, and populated by the icons of fertility – statues of "fat ladies" that by now had become life-sized, plus stone-carved phallic symbols. The most prevalent **reliefs** throughout the temples are the spiral formations thought to symbolize the temple people's cyclical worldview, whereby all life is an ongoing cycle of birth, growth, death and rebirth.

Although there is a persistent archeological view that the Neolithic peoples were sequestered from regional influences due to the relative isolation of their island home, the presence of materials such as flint, obsidian and green stone from the Italian peninsula and the Alps, suggests some sort of trading. Another question that has baffled generations of archeologists is the Neolithic era's abrupt end at around 2500 BC. The most mainstream theory amongst Maltese academics is that, faced with chronic drought, they built the temples in a bid for salvation until, in the end, their religious obsession proved suicidal.

The Bronze Age

Bronze Age colonizers came from the north in three separate migrations between 2300 and 800 BC. During the first stage, known as the **Tarxien Cemetery Phase** (2300–1450 BC), the settlers constructed dolmens – single-roomed structures built and roofed with monoliths – all over the Maltese islands, and employed the existing Tarxien temples, built by the Neolithic peoples, to cremate their dead. Little else is known about them, however, but the discovery of some of their copper weapons suggest that they were a more warlike bunch than their predecessors.

The second group – called the **Borġ In-Nadur People** after their main settlement – arrived between 1450 and 800 BC. They built oval huts cloistered behind fortifications or atop the table-top hills which provided natural protection from enemies, and stored grain, vegetables and water in bottle-shaped pits gouged into the ground. During the **Baħrija Phase**, between 900 and 800 BC, the last Bronze Age settlers founded a community at Baħrija, and pottery made by these peoples unearthed at Borġ In-Nadur suggests a peaceful coexistence, even bartering, between the inhabitants of Baħrija and Borġ In-Nadur. Two intriguing remains – a stone bead with gold-inlay designs similar to Minoan script, and a fragment of a Mycenean cup – also suggest contact with the early civilizations of Minos and Mycenae in Greece.

Phoenician and Carthaginian control

There is no evidence to determine whether the **Phoenicians**, who arrived in 800 BC, took the Maltese islands by force from the Bronze Age peoples, or simply filtered in slowly to supplant the latter inhabitants. But as enterprising, seafaring people who originated in the Levant (modern-day Lebanon), the Phoenicians were the first power attracted to Malta – which they called *Malet*, meaning refuge – for its **strategic location** at the geographical centre of their Mediterranean trade routes. During Phoenician rule, **Mdina** (then called **Melita**) grew into the first urban settlement and the default capital.

Eventually the **Carthaginians**, the descendants of the original Phoenicians based in the Bay of Tunis, grew so successful that they ruled over the central and western

Mediterranean – that included Malta, which the Carthaginians ruled from 480 BC. The Carthaginians were even more successful in stimulating trade: they developed the principle of insurance for ships and cargo, and allowed Malta a measure of **self-autonomy**, setting up a self-governing, coin-minting Senate informed by an Assembly of the People.

During the Punic Wars between Rome and Carthage, the Maltese islands found themselves in the crossfire, and though the Carthaginians retained hold of the island after the First Punic War, the Romans took Malta during the Second Punic War in 218 BC.

Roman and Byzantine rule

The **Romans** clumped the Maltese islands under the administrative wing of the Sicilian Kingdom, a situation that relegated them to a fringe province of Sicily. They treated the islands as a foothold in trade and war, expanding the port in the Grand Harbour, establishing the fortified **Gaudos** (Gozo's citadel), but seemed indifferent towards making a cultural impact. Ruled by a Roman governor, the islands are thought to have been carved up into 25 agricultural estates that produced honey, olive oil and textiles for export. The locals were left to their own devices, and they continued to bury their dead in rock-cut tombs according to Punic tradition, and to mould pottery that was stylistically more Phoenician than Roman.

In 395 AD, when the Roman Empire split into two parts, the Maltese islands fell under the eastern wing controlled from Constantinople by Arcadius. **Byzantine** control faltered after internal squabbling and external invasions, and there is a trace of evidence that Malta may have fallen briefly to the Goths and Vandals, with Byzantines waging military assaults to recapture the islands.

Medieval Malta

Although the Byzantines foiled an Arab invasion in 869 AD, the **Aghlabid Arabs** took Malta with blazing force the following year, and retained control of the island for the next 220 years. Under the Arabs, Islam replaced Christianity, and the era saw some lasting contributions such as the establishment of today's **Maltese language**, which is derived from Arabic. Innovative irrigation techniques, such as the *sienja* – a donkey-powered system of hoisting water from wells – were quickly adopted, while cotton became Malta's main cash crop, and remained so until its viability petered out during the latter stages of the Knights' epoch. But even these advances in agriculture were dampened by the Arab's forceful and violent supplanting of Christianity with Islam, and the few Christians that kept the religion alive underground lived in constant fear of unmerciful punishment.

The locals probably resented their rulers, a discontent that may have afforded **Roger the Norman** a tacit welcome from the Maltese people when he captured the island in three days in 1090. He immediately liberated captive Christians and put the Maltese islands under the jurisdiction of the Sicilian bishop, and also encouraged the nobility of Sicilian and Norman origin to relocate to Malta, hence drawing the islands towards the cultural and political orbit of his kingdom. But it would appear that Roger the Norman failed to set up robust political structures, because Arabic culture and influence trickled in once more. In 1127, a group of Arabs were caught plotting a coup, and this time King Roger II reacted swiftly, massacring the insurgents and deporting most of the Arab population.

Roger's successor William I (aka William the Bad) was himself succeeded by William II (William the Good); on his death in 1190, the Maltese islands had their first sour taste of autocratic fiefdom when Margarito of Brindisi, a former Genoese pirate, was appointed Count of Malta by the pope. Like all the other succeeding Counts, Margarito was more interested in carving his personal empire in the islands than in improving the lot of the locals; as an undisputed provincial overlord, he ruled his subjects in an arbitrary fashion. Similarly, his successor, Henry Pistore, was interested in the islands only as a base for piracy.

Swabian rule

In 1194 Emperor Henry VI of Hohenstaufen became King of Sicily, and the Maltese islands, by extension, became a **Swabian** possession. What little has been pieced together about this period from Sicilian archives indicates that Malta was a pawn of little importance. The Maltese had little say in their own affairs, though the *Curia*, the administrative body, saw some income from royal estates and nurtured an economy based on cereal production. When Henry VI died in 1197, his son, Frederick II – revered as *Stupor Mundi* (Wonder of the World) – inherited the kingdom when he was three years old. Frederick II's lasting legacy is the falconry he established, which set the stage for the subsequent reputation of the **Maltese falcons** (see p.76).

Angevin rule

In 1266 Pope Clement IV brushed aside German influence by crowning Charles of Anjou as King of Sicily. The Angevins seem to have exerted a more direct form of rule in Sicily and Malta than their predecessors, and the overall effect was that under **Angevin rule**, Malta stepped assuredly into Europe's political sphere, including the adoption of Latin script. While allowing a measure of self-rule, the Angevins also imposed crippling taxes, and to pre-empt insurgencies they installed a garrison of 150 men and 25 seamen in Mdina and Castrum Maris (Fort St Angelo). In 1282, the Sicilians rose against their rulers, and as the Angevin fleet fleeing Sicily regrouped in the Grand Harbour, Admiral Ruggiero Lauria of Aragon grabbed the opportunity to capture Malta by ambushing them. The Angevins retreated to the Castrum Maris, and it took Manfredi Lancia seven months to flush them out and complete the Aragonese conquest.

Aragonese rule

The Maltese welcomed **Aragonese rule** with jubilant hope, but the Aragonese were not interested in improving the islanders' lot. Malta served simply as a strategic outpost which the Aragonese handed to Lancia, the Sicilian Count who helped them conquer the Angevins.

Corrupt and tyrannical, the **Counts of Malta**, as they became titled, were greedy Sicilian magnates who carved their personal empires in the islands. Malta's strategic importance became their bargaining point with the Aragonese crown: Aragon would be guaranteed a loyal Malta at its military disposal as long as it sanctioned the Counts' rule, however oppressive for the inhabitants. Understandably, the Maltese abhorred the Counts, and in 1350, the nobles – the educated class in Mdina who spoke on behalf of the people – petitioned King Louis of Aragon to banish the Counts and put the Maltese islands under his direct domain. This request was granted, but as soon as the situation cooled, Giacomo de Pellegrino of Messina re-asserted his right as Count; the Maltese rebelled against Pellegrino, and in 1372 Frederick IV squashed the revolt and expelled Pellegrino.

Power struggles between the Counts and the Maltese continued until the Aragonese crown, fearing the perilous loss of control on the ground, acted decisively in 1397 by officially removing the Counts as Malta's rulers, and promising the locals that the islands would never again be assigned to them. To strengthen self-determination and further appease the Maltese, Aragon established the **Universita** as the governing body; accountable to the Aragonese Crown, its brief covered maintenance of the fortifications and the market, as well as public hygiene and the collection of taxes. Comprised of nobles, notaries, judges, and other members of the upper classes, the *Universita* also counted former Counts among its members, though they were reined in under the *Universita's* jurisdiction. The **Catholic Church** provided a balancing power more likely to defend the populace, and in its frequent disputes with the *Universita*, the church had the final word. The effects of these developments seem to have afforded the inhabitants a larger share of profits from the production of cotton, cumin, wine and meat for export.

In 1429 the **Hafsid Saracens** of Tunisia invaded with a force of 18,000 men, and by the time they were beaten back they had kidnapped some 3000 Maltese for slavery. The rest of the fifteenth century passed with little incident, and the islands prospered from agricultural exports and **piracy**, a lucrative business that saw Maltese pirates operating as far afield as Cyprus and Rhodes.

In 1469, the marriage of Ferdinand II of Aragon and Isabella I of Castile united the crowns and territories of Aragon and Castile, and the Maltese islands formed part of this larger empire. In 1500, **Charles V** – the grandson of Ferdinand and Isabella – was enthroned Emperor, and in 1530, he bestowed the Maltese islands to the Order of St John (now the Knights of Malta), a grouping established during the Crusades to tend the wounded and provide military support. For Charles V, gifting Malta to the Knights was a means of establishing the frontline of defence against the **Ottoman Empire** that was expanding invincibly towards the central Mediterranean.

MEDIEVAL MALTA

The Knights Of Malta

When they arrived in Malta, under Grand Master Philippe Villiers de L'Isle Adam, the **Order of St John** set up base at Fort St Angelo at the tip of the Grand Harbour and left the nobles to their devices in Mdina. In tribute for the islands, Charles V of Spain asked only for one Maltese falcon a year to be gifted on All Saints Day, but L'Isle Adam viewed Malta with **scepticism**. It was unfortified, arid and unable to achieve self-sufficiency in feeding itself – grain had to be imported from Sicily. In recompense, the Knights also possessed Tripoli, which, together with Malta, allowed them to control the sea routes through the central Mediterranean. However, L'Isle Adam's hidden agenda had been to use Malta and Tripoli as springboards to recapture Rhodes, but he died four years later with his mission unaccomplished.

After their losses in Rhodes, the Knights did little in their first twenty years in Malta except regroup, assert their authority on the Maltese and carry out largely cosmetic work on strengthening the fortifications of Fort St Angelo and Birgu (later Vittoriosa). In 1551, the Barbary corsair **Dragut Rais** sneaked a surprise invasion, but when he realized he was under-equipped to penetrate Fort St Angelo or Mdina, he invaded Gozo and kidnapped the entire population for slavery. His unpredictable manoeuvres confounded the Knights, and a few days later news arrived that Dragut had captured Tripoli. The Knights realized their vulnerability and quickly erected new forts – particularly **Fort St Elmo** on Mount Sciberras (where Valletta is today) to guard the mouths of Grand Harbour and Marsamxett Harbour – and beefed up the fortifications in Senglea and Birgu.

The Great Siege

Elected Grand Master in 1557, military-minded **Jean**

Parisot de la Vallette was well aware that Ottoman Emperor Suleiman the Magnificent needed Malta as a stepping stone to attack Western Europe. As intelligence reports from Istanbul outlined the Ottoman's preparations for war, La Vallette consolidated his defences in Malta; he also asked Sicily and Spain for any forces they could spare. On May 8, 1565 the Ottoman armada, led by General Mustapha Pasha, landed in Marsaxlokk with 138 galleys and some 40,000 men. For La Vallette, with his 8500 men (6000 of whom were Maltese militia), the odds of winning what became known as the **Great Siege** looked terrible.

Pasha first attacked Fort St Elmo, which he calculated he would capture in three days, but the fort's excellent design withstood the Turks. When **Dragut Rais**, who had been assigned to lead the invasion but had got delayed in Tripoli, arrived, he mounted cannons on the three points of the triangle around Fort St Elmo and pounded it mercilessly. Shortly afterwards, Rais was supervising work on trenches around St Elmo designed to isolate it from Fort St Angelo, when he was killed by a rock that splintered nearby under cannon fire. Pasha took the reigns again, and as he blasted the fort, the Knights wanted to surrender, but La Vallette ordered them to defend to the last man, in accordance with his strategy to delay the Turks as long as possible until the expected reinforcements arrived. On June 23, Pasha's men seized Fort St Elmo, but it was an anti-climactic victory: they had lost a month and 8000 men, while the Knights had sacrificed just 1500 men.

To taunt La Vallette's nerves, Pasha beheaded the wounded and captured Knights, tied them to wooden crosses and set them afloat in the Grand Harbour. In retribution, La Vallette cannon-fired the severed heads of Turkish prisoners into the Turkish trenches across the harbour. With Fort St Elmo secured, Pasha then shifted his force into Marsamxett Harbour and set up camp in Marsa Creek. Dragut Rais's son-in-law, Hassem, arrived from Tripoli, and while Pasha approached the fortified towns of Birgu and Senglea from land, Hassem attacked from the sea. The Knights withstood these assaults, and several others over the following weeks. Pasha's resources and ammunition were diminishing perilously when, on September 7, a Spanish relief force of 8000 fresh men landed, forcing Pasha to gather his survivors and flee.

After the Great Siege

Against all prognoses, the Knights had emerged victorious, and six years later they spearheaded an attack in the **Battle of Lepanto** (near modern-day Austria), suffering great losses, but eventually winning that day too. This victory, on the heels of the Great Siege, dealt a fatal blow to the Ottoman Empire's territorial ambitions. La Vallette became Europe's celebrated hero, and in Malta, the personal effort and sacrifice during the Great Siege had united the Maltese and the Knights. La Vallette pressed ahead with the mammoth task of building **Valletta**, strengthening the Knights' fleet and improving its hospital, all despite outbreaks of plague in the 1590s and the 1620s.

The Knights' income mainly came from the European estates owned by their aristocratic, landed families, that passed a third of their annual income to the Order. Corsairing and the slave trade brought in more money, and cotton exports were booming, so the Knights could afford to cut their tax regime to occasional one-off levies to fund the new fortifications. In this atmosphere of confidence, the Knights drifted away from their reliance on Spain and the pope in a move to establish themselves as the default rulers of their new state in Malta.

Throughout the seventeenth century, the Knights' fleet reigned supreme in the central Mediterranean – the Spanish recognized the severest storms as those "which only the galleys of Malta could weather", and the Knights employed their invincibility at sea in their **corsairing**. Barbary corsairs operating from Algiers were regularly ambushed, and the Knights even attacked the vessels in the ports of Tunis and Tripoli. Corsairing peaked between 1660 and 1675, when thirty ships operated from Malta, manned by a crew of 4000. Given the Knights' assured protection, trade vessels also increasingly used the Grand Harbour for storage and refuelling. To encourage further vessels and cargo passing through the Grand Harbour, Grand Master Emmanuel Pinto de Fonseca turned the harbour into a partial **free-trade port**. Malta prospered, and Grand Master de Fonseca paid for the construction of Manoel Theatre, one of Europe's oldest theatres. As a symbol of their prestige and power, the Knights embraced Baroque, redesigning many of their buildings in the new style as well as building more churches.

Although the Knights had asked the pope to set up the **Inquisition** in Malta in the sixteenth century, and had given up one of their palazzos in Vittoriosa to the Inquisitor, they later clashed with the Inquisitor over thorny issues of jurisdiction. The Knights feared that the executive powers that both the Inquisitor and the bishop wielded would corrode their power; at the time the Maltese Catholic Church still formed part of the Sicilian diocese. The Inquisitor cited the moral corruption of the Knights' debauched lifestyle to keep his grip on the executive powers invested in him. The Knights, for their part, were alarmed by the fact that many opportunistic Maltese exploited a loophole in the legal setup by registering themselves and their property under the jurisdiction of the Inquisitor or the Bishop and, in so doing, were automatically exempted from paying taxes, from military service, and from prosecution via the Knights' courts of law. This anomaly undermined the Knights as the ruling body, and led to a bitter **power struggle**.

THE KNIGHTS OF MALTA

THE KNIGHTS AFTER MALTA

After Napoleon Bonaparte kicked the **Knights** out of Malta in 1798, Grand Master Hompesch was deposed, and the Knights sank into a constitutional quagmire, as they could not elect another Grand Master except by a decree from the pope, their patron. They took up temporary residence in **Sicily** with an eye on regaining Malta, but when British rule took root on the island, they set up base at Malta Palace in Rome in 1834. By 1879, when Pope Leo XIII restored the grandmastership, they had scrapped their military role and downgraded the criteria for membership: no longer did all Knights require proof of nobility. Without territorial and military activities, the Knights reformed themselves throughout the twentieth century into a **charitable organization** which now numbers about 30,000, one of the world's richest charities, providing voluntary humanitarian, social and development assistance around the world.

But this highly unconventional charity is an international legal anomaly, operating as a sort of **virtual state** similar to the

The Knights' princely lifestyle – which contrasted sharply with the lives of the Maltese – and their autocratic ruling style estranged many inhabitants, and the Catholic Church fanned this mood of discontent to consolidate its power. Things came to a head in 1775 when Grand Master Francis Ximenes de Texada outlawed hunting and introduced harsh economic reforms that triggered unemployment. A group of 24 priests led an **uprising**, but when the planned revolt failed to materialize elsewhere, the priests' severed heads were fixed to spikes at the gates of Valletta. Texada's successor Emmanuel de Rohan eased the economic measures and opened the doors of Knighthood to the Maltese nobility in conciliatory gestures.

Meanwhile, a wave of **secularization** washed over Europe, and some of the Knights' European estates began

Vatican. They assemble under a Constitutional Charter, and have sovereign status, with their independent Courts of Law at the heart of the legal framework of the Order. They have diplomatic relations with 81 countries, permanent delegations in the Council of Europe and the EU, and in 1994 the United Nations admitted them as **Permanent Observers**, the same status enjoyed by the Vatican.

In 1997, the Vatican model was taken up by the MLP prime minister Alfred Sant as the inspiration for a plan to hand **Fort St Angelo** to the Knights as a state within a state, a proposal that provoked accusations that Sant would be committing treachery by handing a chunk of Malta to a foreign power. After the PN entered government following the 1998 election, they opted for an agreement that gave the Knights a 99-year lease of the upper part of Fort St Angelo – not as an independent state, but as a centre of study where novice Knights would undergo their spiritual training. The Knights' headquarters is still in Rome, and their Maltese embassy is at St John's Cavalier in Valletta.

to withhold their annual contributions. Rohan rejected a proposal to secularize the order, but its disgruntled proponents continued to marshal support for their politics, leading to internal divisions. In 1792, the leaders of the **French Revolution** confiscated the Knights' property in France, worth Lm3 million, thus severing three-fifths of the Knights' revenue from their European estates.

It's often claimed by Maltese historians that the Knights' downfall was due to their moral decline and a hedonistic lifestyle which impoverished Malta, yet the Knights were more powerful than ever in their last half-century in the islands. What exposed them to outside dangers was a variety of developments, chief among them their inability to respond to trends of secularization, which led to internal cracks. When danger materialized, in the shape of

THE KNIGHTS OF MALTA

Napoleon Bonaparte, the last Grand Master in Malta, **Ferdinand Von Hompesch**, lacked the military resolve or the solidarity to face it down.

Napoleon and the French

Victorious in France, **Napoleon Bonaparte** wanted the Maltese islands so that "we shall be masters of the whole Mediterranean". With the inside help of four out of the eleven members of the Congregation of War (the body that would supposedly be co-ordinating the Maltese defence), Napoleon plotted an invasion.

On June 7, 1798, Napoleon's entourage of 500–600 ships and 29,000 soldiers converged outside the Grand Harbour. In a ruse, Napoleon asked Hompesch for water supplies, and when Hompesch stipulated that only four ships could sail into the harbour, Napoleon replied that such a restriction constituted a declaration of war and invaded. The Knights' response was uncoordinated: Bonaparte's soldiers insinuated to Maltese soldiers that the French Knights would betray them, which led to defections, and in some instances the Maltese militia even butchered the French Knights in their ranks. Hompesch approached Bonaparte for a **truce**, and Bonaparte bullied the feeble Grand Master into signing away Malta. The Knights were given three days to depart.

French rule

Napoleon publicly promised to end "the absurd and oppressive yoke of the treble jurisdiction [the Knights, the Inquisitor, the bishop] under which you were groaning". In a spate of decrees, he abolished the Inquisition, stripped the bishop's prerogatives, annulled feudal rights, freed the slaves, and courted the nobles and upper classes by putting them into office. The Maltese let out a collective sigh of relief, overlooking the fact that, to raise funds for his military expansion, Bonaparte carried off as many of the Knights' riches as he could pack onto his *L'Orient* flagship. In the seven days he spent in Malta, Bonaparte introduced a French republican style of government, and installed General Claude-Henri Vaubois as commander-in-chief.

General Vaubois continued what Napoleon began by obliterating the Knights' escutcheons, and with the stroke of a pen changed the land lease regulations, which made many farmers homeless. These developments, coupled with the fact that most of Malta's riches were being pumped into the army's coffers rather than reinvested in ways that benefited the wider populace, crippled Malta's finances. The locals seethed with resentment as they witnessed the French looting churches for riches to generate funds for their military campaigns. Three months after the French conquest, the Maltese had had enough, and when the French authorities were preparing to auction valuable and sacred objects ransacked from the Carmelite Church in Mdina, a mob rampaged through Mdina slaughtering every French soldier. By the next day the population was up in arms, beating the French back into the fortified towns of the Grand Harbour.

The Maltese **insurgents** banded together under an arbitrarily-convened national assembly. Poorly armed to fight the French into submission – who held 40,000 inhabitants, almost half the population, with them in the fortified towns – they sent delegations to Sicily and Naples for help, and pleaded with **Admiral Horatio Nelson** (later Lord), commander of the British fleet in the Mediterranean, for assistance. Within two weeks, Nelson's senior captain Sir James Saumarez arrived in Malta with ammunition for the insurgents, and the Maltese started showering the cities with cannon shells.

General Vaubois realized that his problem would be the finite resources, so he ousted thousands of "useless mouths"

NAPOLEON AND THE FRENCH

(the Maltese inhabitants) from the fortified cities. In October, Captain Alexander Ball of the British fleet arrived in Malta to police the blockade, the idea being to maroon the French inside the fortified cities and prevent outside help from breaking through until they were starved into surrender. Inside Valletta, Gulielmo Lorenzi, Father Michael Xerri and Matthew Pulis hatched a plan to over-power the French: according to the plot, Valletta insiders would subdue the sentries guarding the gate to Marsamxett Harbour and let in 200 trained Maltese troopers waiting nearby. The French, however, accidentally uncovered the plan and shot the 49 ringleaders.

A stalemate ensued and the French withered from malnutrition. In the first year of the blockade, 555 French soldiers starved to death, and many more suffered from intestinal diseases, scurvy and night-blindness. In September and October of 1799, Nelson landed a contingency of sev-eral thousand British troops. Another year passed, and inside the fortifications the French and the remaining 700 inhabitants were desperate, driven to eat domestic animals and vermin to stay alive. Eventually, on September 4, 1800, General Vaubois **surrendered**, and Captain Ball took over as the islands' caretaker on behalf of the British.

The British

Bonaparte fumed, "I would rather see the British on the heights of Montmartre than in Malta". The **British**, how-ever, failed to fully recognize the strategic value of the Maltese islands, and under the Treaty of Amiens, which made uneasy peace between France and Britain in 1802, Britain agreed to cede the islands back to the Knights. Furious at not being consulted, the Maltese, who had no wish to live under the arrogant Knights again, petitioned Britain to keep the islands under her protection. When war broke out again between Britain and France, the treaty was in any case, suspended, and Lord Nelson had enough time to convince his superiors of Malta's strategic value – in 1814, under the Treaty of Paris, the Maltese islands became a **British Crown Colony**.

Although the representatives of the Maltese appreciated the security that British rule would bring, they also wanted a say in the running of the islands, requesting self-rule, a free press and the establishment of trial by jury. But a Commission of Inquiry recommended only cosmetic changes, including abolishing the *Universita*, because it feared that drastic changes might stir up the volatile population as the French had done. Malta was to be ruled by the British government in London via a locally-installed governor, who was changed every few years. These early years established the pattern of the Maltese–British relationship, based on Malta's role as a fortress, prosperous in war but unproductive in peace; the British would allow the Maltese self-rule only as long as it was exigent to keep them loyal.

By the 1830s, however, the Maltese had gained some indirect say in the administration, filling civil service posts and advising the governor through an official **Council of Government**. The press was declared free and schools and hospitals were improved. Malta developed politically under Governor Richard More O'Farrell when, in 1849, he introduced a **constitution** that provided for a minority of Maltese to be elected onto the Council of Government. When the Suez Canal opened in 1869, the Grand Harbour became an important coaling port for the imperial steamship route between Britain and India. The Royal Navy, too, set up the **headquarters of its Mediterranean fleet** in the Grand Harbour.

The islands' limited advances were, however, undermined in the first part of the nineteenth century by a split in Maltese politics. On the one hand, the pro-Italian faction

THE BRITISH

comprised of the conservative upper classes and supported by the clergy, all spoke Italian (the language of regional currency inherited during the medieval era when Malta formed part of Sicily), and wanted to make it Malta's official language. The pro-Britain faction, which was more progressive, promoted the teaching of Maltese – the language of the working classes – alongside English. The governor favoured the reformist view, ruling that teaching in schools would be in Maltese with English being a second, compulsory subject. But the issue did not stop with the language, and there was constant quarrelling as the conservative upper classes and the church ambushed any change, including an economic plan to build an industrial base. In this climate, the British government had to override the Council of Government.

World War I and the 1921 constitution

World War I brought mixed fortunes to the Maltese islands. The naval dockyard employed 12,000 in shipbuilding and repair, and the island became known as the "nurse of the Mediterranean" – fifteen hospitals were erected, providing 25,000 beds for the wounded. Things weren't easy for most Maltese, however, as importation of major foodstuffs, particularly wheat, was restricted and greedy merchants exploited the situation to drive up prices. At the war's end, there were mass redundancies at the dockyards, and when the price of bread went up, it was the last straw for many. **Protests** in Valletta on June 7, 1919, erupted into a riot, with the angry mob attacking the homes of pro-British politicians and the *Malta Daily Chronicle*, and looting flour mills; British troops shot four people dead.

These developments led to widespread resentment of the British, who needed to move swiftly to win back the people's loyalty. They did so by introducing a new constitution in 1921 that gave Malta its first **elected Maltese govern-**

ment based on proportional representation. **Parliament** was organized into the lower house and upper house (modelled on the principle of the British House of Commons and House of Lords), with a Maltese government and prime minister for local affairs, while the British retained decision-making on defence and foreign affairs. The main two parties, who still dominate the political scene today, were the **Malta Labour Party** (MLP) and the **Nationalist Party** (PN). In 1927 the Maltese Lord Gerard Strickland became Prime Minister, and revived the plan to build an economy based on industry, but the upper house, dominated by the reactionary Church and upper classes, blocked the move. The dispute escalated into a running battle, and when the Church decreed spiritual penalties on people who voted for Strickland, the British government had to **suspend** the constitution, and over the next decade political wrangling stifled Malta's development.

World War II

When **World War II** broke out, Britain, suspecting that Mussolini might join Hitler's war effort, took stock of Malta's role. Military strategists feared that the Maltese islands would be indefensible. The Royal Navy, on the other hand, with its Mediterranean headquarters in the Grand Harbour, argued that the islands were crucial, given their strategic position, to disrupt Axis supplies to North Africa and control the sea routes in the central Mediterranean; the navy deployed submarines to this effect. But this indecisiveness meant that Malta was unprepared for battle when, on June 10, 1940, Mussolini entered the war, and the next morning Italian aircraft dropped the first bombs on Malta. Four revamped Gloster Gladiator planes engaged the Italians in the skies for the following months, and though they weren't effective in air combat, they forced the Italian planes to drop their bombs from inaccurate heights.

THE BRITISH

Over the next year, the navy was vindicated, with their submarines sinking up to sixty percent of Axis convoys. As a result, the Axis powers intensified air raids aimed at the navy fleet stationed in the Grand Harbour; simultaneously, Italian submarines targeted cargo convoys on their way to Malta, forcing the navy to use submarines rather than boats to transport vital supplies. Meanwhile, the Germans were planning an invasion, code-named **Herkules**, and although it never materialized, this prospect spurred the British government to beef up Malta's defences: 7600 troops landed in the summer of 1941, while 14,650 troops were enlisted within Malta, and hundreds of aircraft were deployed to the island. On the ground, preparations began apace, with bomb shelters constructed and anti-aircraft guns placed strategically to shower an umbrella of anti-aircraft shells over the Maltese islands.

In January 1942, the first month of the **blitz**, Malta was subjected to 262 air raids, and in the next three months only eleven nights saw no raids at all. In April, when the blitz peaked, some 6700 tonnes of bombs fell over the islands. Convoys to Malta were torpedoed, the navys ships and submarines were sunk in the harbour, and Sir William Dobbie, the governor, told his superiors that Malta could only hold out until June. The island had become the most heavily bombed place in the war, and in May the navy's submarine flotilla had to make a run to Alexandria in Egypt. To boost morale, King George VI made the unusual move of awarding the **George Cross** (the highest ever civilian bravery award bestowed by the British Crown) not to a few especially brave individuals but to the entire Maltese people. As the population slid towards starvation, it was small consolation, however.

When soldiers' rations dropped by half, the Allies pinned their hopes on one last attempt at getting the vital supplies to Malta to prevent surrender – **Operation Pedestal**.

Fourteen merchant ships and two oil tankers bound for Malta set out from Britain guarded by eight submarines, three aircraft carriers, over thirty destroyers and six cruisers; only a handful of merchant vessels and one oil tanker made it, but the supplies they carried provided enough food and ammunition for the Maltese to hit back at the Axis powers. The navy stepped up its offensive to cut Axis supplies to North Africa, and the success of this mission over the next year forced the Axis forces in the region to surrender in May 1943. Malta now moved into an offensive role as the headquarters for **Operation Husky**, the invasion of Sicily. The successful invasion led Italy to surrender, and by June 1943 the Maltese islands were virtually out of war, at a total cost of 1490 civilian deaths and half a million tons of rubble, particularly in the towns surrounding the Grand Harbour.

Postwar Malta

Though the relationship between Britain and Malta was somewhat uneasy at the start of the war, the situation had reversed by 1945. Several years of fighting a common enemy united them, and close co-operation ensued, with the British government spending some Lm30 million rebuilding bomb damage. The language question was settled when Italy joined the war.

In the first postwar **election** in 1947, the MLP shot to victory. **Dom Mintoff**, then Minister of Public Works and Reconstruction, disagreed with Prime Minister Paul Boffa over the handling of negotiations with Britain over redundancies at the dockyards, and true to his fiery character, Mintoff split the cabinet; Boffa resigned and called fresh elections. In three subsequent elections between 1949 and 1953, no party got an absolute majority, but in 1955, the MLP, led now by Mintoff, got a clear majority.

One of the MLP's first acts was to hold a **referendum** on its proposal to integrate Malta with Britain. Crown

THE BRITISH

Colony status had become an unacceptable halfway house for the Maltese, so the choice was either **integration**, which would give Malta the full socioeconomic advantages enjoyed in the British mainland, or independence so Malta's development would not be hindered by Britain's expedient military and foreign policy considerations. The PN asked their supporters to boycott the referendum, which they did: almost half the population did not vote, although the result positively affirmed integration. However, the British parliament procrastinated over integration to such an extent that Mintoff had little choice but to ask for **independence**.

The PN, under **Dr George Borg Olivier**, ousted the MLP in the 1962 elections, and continued to press for independence. Negotiations proceeded and a formula was worked out that was acceptable for both sides: the Maltese islands would become independent and the British forces would continue using Malta as a military base until 1979. On September 21, 1964 the islands duly became **independent**, but retained their membership in the Commonwealth and the British queen as its figurative head of state.

Independent Malta

With the Maltese basking in a post-independence glow, Borg Olivier and the PN managed victory in the election of 1966, and went on to petition Britain for technical and financial help to develop the Maltese economy. However, the British government, itself reeling from the war, moved to slash defence spending in Malta that would make thousands of workers redundant; Borg Olivier resisted, and Britain agreed to extend its phase-out programme to preempt any anti-British sentiment that might threaten its bases in Malta. The PN started developing an economy based on **tourism**, a drive that was also taken up by

Mintoff after he was elected prime minister in the 1971 elections.

Mintoff believed Britain should pay for its military bases in Malta, and asked the British government for an annual "rent" amounting to Lm30 million. When the British government made a counter offer of Lm5 million, Mintoff picked a protracted fight to change its mind that led at one point to an ultimatum to the British forces to depart. After painful negotiations, including shuttle diplomacy by Mintoff with Libya's controversial leader Colonel Gaddafi and Eastern Europe that were aimed at titillating British fears that Malta might sway towards the Eastern Bloc, the issue was settled at Lm14 million in rent plus Lm7 million in economic aid.

On March 31, 1974, parliament changed the constitution and the Maltese islands became a **republic**, with a Maltese President replacing the queen as the head of state. Throughout the 1970s, the MLP successfully courted manufacturing industries to set up base in Malta, and with tourism on the up-and-up, the economy was strong enough for the MLP to establish a welfare state with an extensive raft of social services, as well as increase spending on education and health. The rapid economic development also meant, however, that the change hurt some sectors of the economy and there were sticky **industrial disputes**. Mintoff's bully tactics and impatience for change hardened the hearts of his supporters and his opponents – Malta was dividing into two factions, the MLP versus the PN, a rift of personal vendettas that still persists today.

When the military agreement with Britain ended in 1979, Mintoff wanted to rid Malta of foreign occupation forever, and to this end he established a clause in the constitution declaring **neutrality**. Yet he was aware that Malta, given its size, would be unable to defend itself against foreign aggression, so he sought an agreement with a larger power that would militarily protect Malta's neutrality. He negotiated with various countries until Italy offered financial assistance and military intervention if Malta was threatened, an agreement that is still in force today.

However, Mintoff's autocratic rule edged Malta towards civil war: bombings became regular occurrences, MLP thugs carried out beatings on dissenters, and the PN carried out reprisal attacks. Mintoff pursued a policy of **nationalizing** companies and kept a tight grip on the economy. There were price and wage freezes, and strict protectionism, a situation that fostered corruption.

Mintoff's downfall

In the late 1970s, Mintoff picked a fight with the **Catholic Church** that led to his eventual downfall. There were three points of contention: the government wanted the Church to pay tax, and wanted the rights to buy the land the Church had inherited during the Knights' rule when Maltese put their property under its jurisdiction, and for the Church to offer free education in its schools (promising the government would reimburse the Church to do so). The Church resisted what it saw as a corrosion of its power, and rallied the populace against the government.

To add to the MLP's woes, the 1981 elections produced an anomalous result – the PN got a majority of votes but the MLP got a majority of seats in parliament. The PN wanted fresh elections, and when Mintoff's cabinet refused, they boycotted parliament and launched a campaign of civil disobedience, mainly consisting of incessant strikes by different sectors, which crippled the economy. Mintoff reacted heavily, threatening to expropriate shops that shut on strike days, and violence intensified. Meanwhile the **negotiations with the Church** had failed, and in September 1984 the government refused an operating permit for Church schools. The bishop opened the schools in defiance, and Karmenu Mifsud Bonnici, the government's negotiator, led Malta drydocks workers in a demonstration which ended with participants attacking the law courts, the teachers' union MUT (for toeing the Church's line) and the Curia. When a bomb was planted at the bishop's residence, teachers nationwide went on strike. Mintoff **resigned** and co-opted his puppet Bonnici as Prime Minister.

Into the 1990s

The PN, led by Eddie Fenech Adami, won the 1987 election, launching widespread **economic reforms** to create a market economy, spurring rapid growth; in 1990 they also applied for membership of the EU. Tourism reached an all-time high as the Maltese islands received one million visitors annually. Full employment was achieved, and the islands underwent an economic boom that led to greater social freedoms and opportunities, particularly the emergence of a new, educated and socially liberal middle class. In 1992, the green party **Alternattiva Demokratika** (AD) contested the election on a platform of fringe issues, particularly environmental concerns and civil rights. AD bagged almost two percent of the vote (a level of support they maintained in later elections), but the PN, elected on a larger majority, pressed on with economic and fiscal reforms. However, they lost support in the mid-1990s when the economy slowed down, and over the introduction of the unpopular Value Added Tax (VAT).

Alfred Sant, a Harvard economist, repackaged the MLP as **New Labour** and, against all predictions, won the 1996 elections. But the freezing of Malta's application to the European Union and the imposition of an austere budget led one of Sant's ablest ministers, **Lino Spiteri**, to resign in the first signal of internal divisions in New Labour. Sant wanted to streamline the inefficient civil service and the sluggish

DOM MINTOFF

Born in Cospicua in 1916, the young **Dom Mintoff** belied his working-class background to earn two degrees in Malta and, in 1939, won a Rhodes scholarship that led to an MA in engineering from Oxford University. During his stint in England he honed his **left-wing** ideology, later marrying Moyra Bentinck, daughter of a prominent British socialist. In 1944, he returned to Malta and joined the MLP, quickly rising up the party ranks. In 1949, by then deputy prime minister, Mintoff split the MLP in a power struggle that saw him snatching the reins of the party. The anthropologist Jeremy Boissevain called him "the island's first orator", and in mass meetings he excelled in theatrics by recounting anecdotes from his childhood and firing his audience with humorous set-pieces and sexual innuendoes.

He was sure-footed and fiery, at his best when he was fighting, and a legendary **workaholic** who thought nothing of calling his ministers in the dead of the night to discuss policy. His single-mindedness made him impatient, however, and under him, government became a one-man show. To his credit, he guided Malta towards an economy based on industry and tourism, while introducing a generous welfare state. He was

economy, but he projected an indifferent, managerial style of leadership, and his economic measures hit the working class hardest, a scenario that ruffled Mintoff, now a back-bencher in his eighties. Mintoff, who held the government's crucial one-man majority, hijacked parliament by voting against pieces of legislation, and as disgruntlement within New Labour intensified, Sant called a snap election in September 1998.

Malta today

The PN, still led by Eddie Fenech Adami, were returned to government in 1998. They reactivated Malta's EU member-

INDEPENDENT MALTA

also a shrewd **strategist**, who exploited the violent wing of the MLP to silence his opponents under a mantle of fear and thus force through unpopular decisions. Given this personality, his ministers and aides only told him what he wanted to hear – but behind his back, some of his ministers and senior civil servants were riddling the country with corruption.

He despised the **Catholic Church** for its influence on the populace, its wealth and hypocrisy, and for its reactionary conservatism that had interfered with political development since the Knights' epoch. But the Church resisted his attempts to corrode its power and the various Church–state battles catalyzed his eventual downfall.

Alfred Sant, leader of New Labour, sidelined Mintoff until, in 1998, now 82, he stirred from political dormancy to **revolt** against an austere budget, and his eight-hour marathon monologue was broadcast live on national TV. He told friends, "If it's in Malta's interest I will bring down the government". After a parliamentary career lasting fifty years, including four spells as prime minister, he resigned from parliament in 1998 and now spends the last of his years penning his memoirs and mentoring young socialist ideologues.

ship application, and formal negotiations started in 2000. **EU membership** now dominates the country's politics, and once again the country is split into two factions along party lines. The former MLP prime minister Karmenu Mifsud Bonnici now heads an organization called the Campaign for National Independence, a xenophobic body which is campaigning against EU membership, and the General Workers' Union, the largest union, is also rallying against membership. EU accession is scheduled for 2003 at the earliest, and the PN have promised to hold a referendum on the issue.

Although the Maltese now enjoy a standard of living and

INDEPENDENT MALTA

a level of education almost on a par with Western European countries, the sluggish economy shows no signs of revival. The budget deficit stands at a dangerous nine percent of the GNP, the burden of state pensions is unsustainable given an ageing population, the overstaffed and inefficient civil service is a drain on resources, and the protectionism of the local economy jars with the policies of a free market. Whether the country joins the EU or not, reforms of the structurally obese economy are moving ahead too slowly, which is likely to protract industrial and social instability.

Wildlife and the environment

though the parched summer countryside gives the impression of a rather barren place, Maltese wildlife is disproportionally rich given the diminutive size of the islands, and the fact that over a third of the land is gobbled up by built-up areas and roads – Malta is one of the most densely populated countries in the world – while another third is devoted to agriculture.

Land habitats

The Maltese climate is **semi-arid**, and supports a handful of major ecosystems. Before the arrival of humans, the islands were covered with thick forests of evergreen oaks; a cluster of these 900-year-old trees survive at Wardija, 3km south of Buġibba. The only sizeable tract of mature woodland is within Buskett Gardens in central Malta, which were planted by the Knights in the seventeenth century. **Aleppo pines**, **oaks**, **olives**, **sandarac gum trees**, **cypresses** and **carobs**, plus a low-lying cover of **hawthorn** and **buckthorn** (a dense, prickly creeper), cover an area roughly the same size as Comino. Some migratory birds, particularly birds of prey such as the **honey buzzard** and **marsh harrier**, roost in the trees during autumn; other notable feathered inhabitants, seen throughout the year, include **nightjars**, **turtle doves**, **song thrushes**, **scop's owls** and the distinctive **golden oriole**. A few pairs of spotted fly-catchers have nested in the woods over the last few years.

Maquis

Now reduced to belts at the foot of inland cliffs and on the bottoms and sides of deeper valleys, **maquis** ecosystems feature small, scrubby trees (mostly **olives**, **carobs** and **bay laurels**), beautiful flowers such as **lords-and-ladies**, with waxy, dark-green arrow-shaped leaves and bell-shaped beige blooms, as well as climbers such as **ivy**, **smilax** and **spiny asparagus**. Maquis is also a favoured territory for **snakes**, the most common varieties being the black snake, which can grow to a length of two metres, and the more camou-flaged spotted snake, with a variegated beige and green colouring; neither creature is venomous. During the migra-tory season, you'll see birds of prey such as **kestrels** hover-ing above maquis slopes, as well as large flocks of **house-martins**, **sandmartins** and **swallows**, which visit to feed. **Blue rock thrushes**, the fist-sized, dark blue or dark brown national bird, nest in the cliff formations above the maquis. At dusk, lesser mouse-eared **bats** fly out of caves eroded into limestone cliffs, and are a common sight.

Garigue

Rugged, rocky plateaux, typically found along elevated stretches of land where the pockets of soil that gather in rock clefts support low-lying, hardy aromatic shrubs, **garigue** plains are major ecosystems by default, in that they're not suitable for agriculture and so have been mostly left alone. Common garigue plants include

Mediterranean thyme, yellow-flowering **St John's wort**, purple-blooming **Mediterranean heath**, **white hedge nettle** and abundant amounts of **capers**. **Orchids** are among the most attractive of the plants that favour garigue habitats: look out for the **fan-lipped** variety, whose flowers, with a dangling red-purple lower lip, appear in spring. The flowers of the "**bumble bee orchid**", which bear close resemblance to a female bee, are designed to encourage pollination from one plant to another – when a male bee hovers on the flowers expecting to mate, pollen is transferred to its underbelly, to be deposited on the next flower it visits. You'd be lucky if you stumble across the rare and small Maltese **pyramidal orchid**, an endemic variety with large, blade-like leaves and, in early spring, a bushel of pale-pink flowers growing from the stem. Other spring-flowering blooms include the common **yellow-throated crocus**, a bulbous specimen with six spindly purple petals and a red stamen, while the large purple-white-and-yellow flowers of the **barbary nut iris** open only for a few hours between early afternoon and twilight.

Steppe

Steppe – sloping open land covered by short grasses, often formerly used for agriculture – is found throughout the islands, and is characterized by a wintry-green cover of grasses such as **esparto**, as well as yellow-flowering **cape sorrel** and thorny-flowered **wild artichokes**, their fan-like leaves stirring in the wind. In the spring, some steppes, particularly in Gozo, bloom into a dramatic, dried-blood coloured blaze of **clover**, the crimson flowers of the field **gladioli**. Further up the slopes, among scattered boulders dislodged from cliff faces, you might come across the rare and endemic **Maltese spider orchid**, its leaves wrapped round a single stem that, in the spring, supports a dark-purple flower with a prominent lip. A surprising but rare

LAND HABITATS

steppe plant is the **Sicilian iris**, whose 1m-long stem bears a large purple flower in spring, with drooping fingery petals. In the autumn, glistening **buttercups** splatter across the steppes, breaking up the otherwise monotonous stubby grass.

Commonly seen birds in steppe landscapes include **skylarks** and **meadow pipits**, which winter in the islands. **Fan-tailed warblers**, characteristically uttering high pitched calls as they fly, nest in clumps of grass, while migrants such as **hoopoes** and blue-feathered **rollers** are frequent visitors. Other commonly seen migratory birds are **wheatears**, with a white band on the tailfeathers, and orange-breasted **whinchats**. Stout, sparrow-like and light brown, **corn buntings** nest on steppe slopes and can be seen roosting in large numbers at Il-Wardija, southwestern Gozo.

Valleys

The undulating Maltese islands are peppered with deep valleys, most of which hold seasonal streams during the winter. Many valleys are dominated by **poplars**, while rarer valley trees include **Mediterranean willows**. Dense stands of **bamboo**, interspersed by clusters of **bulrushes**, cover the valley floors. In terms of birdlife, valleys attract plenty of **passerines** during the migration season – particularly **reed warblers**, with their greenish plumage – as well as grey and yellow **wagtails**. Other common valley birds include **moorhens**, **ringed plovers**, **stints**, **redshanks**, **greenshanks** and **sandpipers**. Though **bitterns** are relatively common, you'd be lucky if you spot one of these secretive birds hiding amongst the bamboo. **Cetti's warbler**, a small, dark grey specimen that nests in dense valleys, is also rarely seen, but you'll surely hear its explosive, melodious call.

Valleys also support the endemic **freshwater crab**, a creamish, hand-sized specimen that inhabits the streams of

Lunjzata Valley, on the outskirts of Rabat in Gozo, and Chadwick Lakes northwest of Mdina in central Malta.

Cliffs

The last of the major habitats are the vertical cliff faces that ring the south and west shores of the islands. **Cory's shearwaters**, **yellow-lugged gulls** and **blue rock thrushes** nest in cliff crevices, and plants growing here include **rock centaury**, the Maltese national plant, recognizable by its succulent leaves and, in the summer, small purplish flowers as well as its precarious favoured position at the edge of cliffs. During the autumn, you might spot the relatively rare **Eleanora's falcon** soaring above the cliff faces.

There are numerous rocky islets offshore of the main islands, which hold several subspecies. Filfla, off the south coast of Malta, supports an endemic **lizard** (*Lacerta filfolensis*), speckled black with white spots, as well as the Mediterranean's largest colony of **storm petrels** (some 8000 pairs), and smaller colonies of **Manx shearwaters**: dark, pigeon-sized seabirds.

Marine life

The waters surrounding the Maltese islands boast diverse **marine life**. The clear seas allow light to penetrate to a depth of some 40m, enabling the long, leaf-like blades of **posidonia algae**, which covers large areas of silt and sand, to photosynthesise. Posidonia meadows serve as ideal fish-spawning grounds, and their presence signals rich marine life in the vicinity – many of the fish that live in the meadows employ excellent camouflage, however, and you're only likely to spot common species such as the 30cm-long, red-coloured **flying gurnard** when they are disturbed, opening their blue pectoral fins as they dart away. A more prominent

MARINE LIFE

and colourful species is the **painted comber**, with a reddish body patterned with a white web; it's easily seen as it slips calmly through posidonia.

Rocky shores and **shallow pools** support numerous finger-sized fish, including variegated blue, green and dark grey **triggerfish**, and various species of **blennies**, particularly the triplefin **blennies**: tiny red specimens with large black eyes, which characteristically hover around rocks, and the equally motionless dark brown **Connemara sucker-fish**. The inquisitive common **octopus** is still abundant near rocky shorelines, despite being extensively targeted by spear-fishermen; spiny, dark brown **sea urchins**, which embed themselves into rock clefts, are present in even higher numbers. Around the size of a man's hand, common red **starfish** are found near the shoreline; these are distinguishable from their relative, the giant red starfish, by their behaviour – while common reds cling to rocks in shallow water, their arms splayed out straight, giant reds, which favour slightly deeper waters and are double the size, characteristically fold their tentacles over one another. You'll see large shoals of flat, silvery **saddled bream** and **two-banded bream** (recognizable by the two dark stripes on the head and tail) near the shorelines, as well as red **mullet** and the thick-lipped grey variety, and cloud-like schools of small fish such as **sardines**. Among the most colourful fish inhabitants of Maltese waters, **Turkish wrasse** boast a green body with bluish fins, and speckled brown and red heads.

Amongst the static underwater inhabitants are gnarled pomegranate-red **sea potatoes**, simple organisms that grow from the rocks and feed by filtering tiny particles from the water; they hardly twitch in the current. The Mediterranean has no true coral reefs, and the coral-like organisms that cling to rocks (known as **false coral**, and properly as cnidarians) come in many different shapes and

MARINE LIFE

sizes. In shallow waters, **golden cup** clusters in large numbers on shaded surfaces or the mouths of underwater caves, its fingers flapping in the current. Inhabiting the same shady spots are the most colourful cnidarians, the **zoanthids**: huge golden sheets elevated from the rocky surfaces to which they are attached via a stem.

Deeper waters

At depths of ten metres and more, you'll spot **parrotfish** (bright red with contrasting silvery heads), and orange **cardinal fish**. Two types of **scorpion fish** skulk along the bottom amid rocks by day and foraging for food at night: both have protruding foreheads, large black eyes and prominent spindly dorsal fins, but the black scorpion fish (actually dark brown) is less conspicuous than its relative, the red scorpion fish. Both have venomous spines, so don't get too close if diving. Deeper waters also harbour **groupers** – up to 1m long, with a rotund, bulging green-brown body. These were once commonly seen skulking around rocks, but overfishing has led them to retreat to ever greater depths. Perhaps the most charming undersea residents are **sea horses**, with delicate, 15cm long translucent bodies; look for them hovering among the rocks. Maltese waters also harbour seven species of **hermit crab**, which make their homes inside discarded triton or giant tun shells; the largest variety grows up to 12cm long. They're usually found on the seabed scavenging for morsels of food – you can see their brown antennae and pinhead eyes protruding from the shell. Secretive **moray eels**, up to 1m long, venture out of rocky crevices only at night; their beautiful gold-patterned skin makes it easy to tell them apart from dull-grey, 3m-long **conger eels**, which have a menacing look.

Even further from the shore, open waters are patrolled by small, loose groups of **barracudas** feeding on small fish;

around 2m long, they have pointed silver bodies and heads tapering into a snout-like face. **Rays** also glide effortlessly through the depths (look out for 3m eagle rays), while **dolphins** are fairly common; if you're lucky, you'll see the bottlenose variety, with its distinctive snout. Perhaps the most exciting inhabitants of Maltese waters are **loggerhead turtles**; these once nested at Gozo's Ramla Bay, but are very rare these days; many are killed when they mistake floating plastic bags for their main foodstuff, jellyfish.

Threats to the environment

The Maltese islands hold the dubious distinction of having one of the poorest environmental protection records of any developed country. Thanks to the efforts of local **hunters**, the barn owl, peregrine falcon and even formerly common species such as the jackdaw no longer inhabit the islands, and the overall list of locally extinct species is rising annually. Malta's indifferent attitude towards conservation is demonstrated by the fact that while the islands are inhabited by 153 animal and bird species recognized by international treaties as having ecological importance (and hence are legally protected by those treaties), Maltese legislation protects only 68 of these species.

The islands have just a handful of **protected areas**, which in total account for less than one percent of the overall land area. The islet of Filfla, for its colony of storm petrels; St Paul's Islands in the mouth of St Paul's Bay for their undisturbed garigue plains; and Fungus Rock in Gozo for its endemic fungus. Two wetlands in northern Malta, maintained by environmental group Birdlife Malta, are also protected reserves. Simar Nature Reserve in Xemxija, which is densely covered by reedbeds, is inhabited by the rare little bittern, and is a nesting spot for great reed warblers, while Għadira Nature Reserve in Mellieħa

Bay is an important rest-and-refuel stop for waterbirds such as herons and egrets and ducks. None of the waters surrounding Malta have official protection, and as there's no closed fishing season, fish stocks have been severely decimated. Even Dwejra, widely considered as offering the best scuba diving in the Mediterranean, is open ground for fishermen.

Bird hunters and trappers

Though the Maltese islands have long served as a crucial outpost for birds migrating across the Mediterranean, the activities of some 16,000 **hunters and trappers** have had a devastating effect. Hunters overrun the countryside, as well as shooting from secondary roads, breaking into nature reserves with impunity, and taking to the seas in dinghies to blast exhausted birds flying low and slow. To make it all the more galling, of the three million-odd birds shot in Malta every year, 68 percent are protected species, including 96,000 birds of prey, 32,000 herons and egrets, 11,500 owls, 55,000 cuckoos, 48,000 hoopoes and 2000 kingfishers among others. Trappers' nets account for another three million finches. With what some would class as compulsive obsession, Maltese hunters compete to shoot the largest and rarest specimens – game birds are considered worthless, while vultures and eagles the ultimate prizes. A glass cabinet brimming with stuffed **"trophies"** takes pride of place in many living rooms, and some collections make natural history museums seem pitiful.

Unsurprisingly, the hunters' activities have not gone unchallenged. In 1987, when the PN were elected to government, Birdlife Malta launched a protracted campaign to **lobby** the government to restrict the hunters' excesses. EU countries, too, pressurized Valletta into updating its hunting laws (Malta is the only European country to allow hunting and trapping in the spring breeding season), and both

THREATS TO THE ENVIRONMENT

initiatives were widely supported by the Maltese public. By 1993, the government was driven to act, bringing in new **regulations** that were stricter than ever before, though still short of Europe's level of restrictions – despite being banned all over Europe, trapping was allowed to continue, as was hunting in spring, the main breeding period for many species. The police then embarked on a campaign to enforce the new laws, rounding up hundreds of hunters in a matter of months and busting taxidermists, one of whom was found with some 2000 deep-frozen birds, ninety percent of which were protected species. Hunters were up in arms at the new approach, and **protested** by spraying pro-hunting graffiti on street signs and historical monuments, damaging roadside trees, attacking birders in the countryside and pouring oil into wetlands, while an ambush of the Environment Parliamentary Secretary ended in a punch-up. Their intimidation worked, and in 1996, with the upcoming election very much in mind, the government relaxed the new restrictions in a bid to appease the hunters and their votes – crucial in a country where elections are won by a few thousand votes.

The opposition MLP party then courted the hunters' vote with promises to further diminish 1993 regulations, and they honoured their promises when elected to power in 1997. Today, birds are offered even less protection than before the 1993 legislation – the hunters continue to massacre Malta's birdlife while the authorities look the other way.

Architecture

Maltese architecture has been dominated by Baroque since the seventeenth century. The Maltese took the characteristics of Baroque – wide spaces, high ceilings and a frothy ornateness of motif – to their hearts in a flowering of extra-lavish Grand or High Baroque that continues to this day: the various parish churches, by means of their excessively elaborate Baroque architecture, dominate the towns, and even today ordinary houses boast large rooms, exuberant staircases skirted by stone or mahogany balustrades, protruding balconies and three-metre-plus ceilings. Although Baroque is still in vogue, recent decades have seen architects experimenting with modern styles influenced by contemporary European design, while also incorporating older vernacular styles such as the loggias of medieval farmhouses.

Much of this distinctive architecture is due to the soft **globigerina limestone** from which most of the Maltese islands' buildings are constructed. This is the only vernacular stone suitable for construction – the local clay cracks during temperature fluctuations, while Malta's upper coralline limestone is too hard to work – and it weathers elegantly to the colour of natural sandstone; in addition, its plasticity allows it to be sculpted into very fine detail.

Prehistory

With no other stone available, **Neolithic** peoples of the fourth millennium BC built their temples out of the native hard upper coralline limestone; it was cut in blocks of megaliths, which were trundled towards the site on round stones and erected into place by hoisting them over ramps of rubble. The earlier temples, such as at **Ġgantija** in Gozo, were built entirely in this way. With their series of lobed chambers, the temples were either designed on the outline of the sitting "fat ladies" (see p.329) or evolved from the interconnecting chambers of the collective rock-cut tombs. Their curvaceous designs are thought to express fluidity, continuity and the conduit of human and divine energies – in a sense, a spatial representation of the spiral motifs that frequently recur. At one point, the Neolithic peoples discovered the softer, easier-to-manage globigerina limestone, building later temples, such as at **Tarxien** and **Mnajdra**, almost entirely from this stone.

These temples are the oldest built structures on earth, and Malta's Neolithic peoples are generally accepted as the earliest-known **architectural civilization**. Architecture became a study, and the stone model of the temples exhibited at Valletta's National Museum of Archeology illustrates the studied considerations of temple design – the corner megaliths placed strategically to support the entire structure, the stepped roof, and the corbelling rising towards the dome in what is the earliest, crude development of the principle of the **arch**.

The medieval era

The next principal stage, **medieval architecture** (from 870 AD) is marked by the introduction of Arabic influence. Medieval people converted caves into churches and hewed simple rock-cut chapels such as the **catacombs** of St Agatha and St Paul in Rabat (Malta). Whole communities throughout the Middle Ages – up to the arrival of the Knights – lived in caves; **Għar Il-Kbir** in Dingli, the largest cave settlement, housed 27 families made up of 117 individuals, each family's allotment defined by rubble walls. In the countryside, peasants lived in the **girna**, an oval hut built of rubble. In later centuries, *girnas*, which retain a cool and constant air temperature, were used to store vegetables; some still survive intact.

Country farmhouses show a combination of Sicilian and Arabic influences – cube-shaped houses built around a courtyard, the walls plastered out of rubble and mud, with rainwater spouts sticking out from their roofs. They faced south for maximum sun exposure, and their loggias were backed by a corridor, which trapped an insulating buffer of air so that the temperature in the rooms which branched off it remained constant. Many had a set of pigeon nestboxes hollowed out of the walls of a purpose-designed square turret rising from one corner of the building. Some sported the Arab-style *muxrabija*, a fine-meshed wooden window-screen or projecting box from which the occupants could watch comings and goings outside their house without being seen. Built **chapels**, too, were cube-shaped, with one nave and a slightly pitched roof; the best-preserved examples include the **Annunciation of the Virgin** in Hal Millieri, **San Bazilju** in Mqabba, and **Santa Marija ta' Bir Miftuħ**.

In Mdina and Birgu (Vittoriosa), the only two towns of medieval Malta, more sophisticated **palazzi** resembled country houses but had decorative trimmings of simple geometric patterns. Dated loosely to the fourteenth and fifteenth centuries, some survive in Mdina, including the palazzi **Santa Sofia**, **Gatto Murina**, **Inguanez** and **Falzon**, dubbed "Siculo-Norman" due to their Norman influences, particularly in their twin-arched windows.

THE MEDIEVAL ERA

369

Enter the Knights

When the Knights moved to Valletta in 1571 they gave the job of designing their buildings to the Maltese architect **Ġirolmu Cassar**, who proceeded to marry different styles in his designs for Valletta's **Grandmaster's Palace**, **St John's Co-Cathedral** and the seven original *auberges*. Born in Birgu in 1520, Cassar first came to the attention of the Knights when he worked on the repair of the fortifications following damage in the Great Siege of 1565. Later, he assisted Francesco Laparelli in designing the new city; when Laparelli departed, Cassar was a natural replacement. His designs had to reflect the austerity of the Knights as a military and religious order, but he also employed vernacular styles in the flat and undecorated facades, particularly using panels as articulation, and introduced elements of the Renaissance and Mannerist styles picked up from his internship in Rome.

In the early seventeenth century, the new style of **Baroque**, which took hold in Italy and France, spread through the Roman Catholic countries of Europe. The Knights' resident architect **Francesco Buonamici** introduced Baroque to Malta in 1635, when he designed the Jesuit Church. Thereafter a Baroque makeover swept through Valletta. The Knights erected new churches, rebuilt the *auberges* and public buildings, and dressed the gates piercing the city fortifications with Baroque plumes. The interior of St John's Co-Cathedral was crowned with eruptions of flame-like forms. The obsession culminated in 1741 with the rebuilding of the **Auberge de Castille**, the most monumental Baroque building in Malta – imposing, square, and boasting a wide staircase that draws the eye to its main door, topped by triumphal motifs carved in stone. Baroque symbolized prestige, power and wealth, with its curvaceous forms, the colossal size of the buildings, the coats of arms, broad interior courtyards, and so on: noble families took the cue and started icing their facades with Baroque motifs, building in grand style to flaunt their wealth and status.

Meanwhile the Catholic Church was competing with the Knights to create Baroque landmarks: in the late seventeenth century, a new drive began to build grander churches, topped by fat domes and belfries to stand proud over the townhouses. The most outstanding examples were designed by **Lorenzo Gafa** (1639–1703), one of the most influential architects in the development of Maltese Baroque. Gafa was born in Vittoriosa to a family of skilled stone carvers and sculptors, and his older brother Melchiore achieved international fame for his sculpture, and spent much of his working life in Rome. Lorenzo undertook no formal architectural training, but was lucky to serve as an assistant to Buonamici. In his work, he opted for simpler, less ornate exteriors than his contemporaries, and excelled in their composition. He designed the **Gozo Cathedral** and **St Lawrence Church** in Vittoriosa to stand on a dais, reached by steep, broad external staircases – an effective device to amplify their visual presence. He designed Mdina's **St Paul's Cathedral** with a square facade, lending the church an image of grandeur and drama. The belfries rise only marginally over its pediment, but together with the dome, they are deeply sculptured like braids.

Military architecture

In less than three centuries, the Knights erected 40km of **fortifications** on Malta, pierced by 54 gates. The Grand Harbour was almost encircled with fortifications, and the entire low-lying east coast was protected by a chain of coastal towers, forts, redoubts, batteries and entrenchments.

Once Valletta was complete, the Knights sent for the Italian military engineer **Pietro Paolo Floriani** to look

THE FOUGASSE

Amid the array of military structures on Malta, the **fougasse** (a rock-cut mortar) is most obscure in origin, and found in just a handful of other countries; it was probably invented by the Italian engineer Marandon in 1740, though some evidence suggests an earlier date. It comprises a cone gouged into a boulder or rocky surface, wide enough for a man to crouch into and about four metres deep. Overlooking the flanks of landing bays, these *fougasses* – of which the Knights built around sixty – were designed to be packed with rocks and gunpowder, so that, when fired, they would shower stones over enemy boats. In February 1802, the British **Brigadier-General Lawson** tested one, loading it with 64kg of gunpowder and ten tonnes of rocks. "The explosion," he wrote, "resembled the tremendous discharge of a volcano." The best example of a *fougasse* that exists today can be seen on the eastern flank of **Ramla Bay**, carved into a rocky boulder facing the bay at an angle of 45°; ironically, it was never fired, and in 1798 Napoleon's troops landed in Ramla Bay unhindered.

into strengthening the defences around the Grand Harbour. At this point the Knights' policy in the event of an attack was to corral the entire population behind the fortifications. Floriani arrived in 1635 and he proposed an outer ring of bastions to encircle the towns around the Grand Harbour. His **Floriana Lines** sealed the Valletta peninsula and the emerging suburb of Floriana, and the same concept was borrowed for the Three Cities: the **Margharita Lines** to protect Cospicua, and beyond, an outer ring of bastions to envelope all three cities, the **Cottonera Lines**.

As Malta's population increased and settled further north, on a coast pockmarked with bays where an enemy could disembark, the Knights had to review their defences. In 1715 a more strategic policy emerged, based on the "active defence of the islands". About thirty **coastal towers** had already been built in the seventeenth century, intended to signal news of an attack to Valletta and act as assembly points for reinforcements in the event of an attack. Now, additional waves of larger, stronger towers were built (such as the **Red Tower** in Mellieħa), and Grand Master Adrien de Wignacourt initiated the drive to beef up the coastal defences. The coastal **batteries**, designed by Phillippe de Vendome, are semicircular, perched over the sea, with cannons poking through a saw-toothed parapet and a barracks housed in the basement underneath the parapet. Twenty of these batteries still stand, although in a half-ruined state. Twenty similar, but smaller, **coastal redoubts** survive (the most intact is the recently restored **St Mary's Battery** on Comino), and between the two emplacements, the Knights built **coastal lines**, walls of bastions and entrenchments that skirted the entire east coast.

Architecture under the British

Following their takeover in 1800, the **British** made their architectural mark slowly: for their 164 years of rule, there are probably less than a dozen surviving examples of British architecture in Malta (excluding military buildings and small clusters of private homes).

At the beginning of the nineteenth century, the **Neoclassical** style was in vogue in Britain; it marked a reaction against the excess of Baroque and Rococo, and a return to the styles of ancient Greece and Rome, borrowing and reusing the harmonious ensemble of columns framing a facade topped by a pediment. The Neoclassical imprint can be seen in Malta's early British buildings, notably the **Anglican Cathedral** in Valletta, as well as in secular buildings, many of which sport colonnaded porticos

– Villa Portelli in Kalkara, Capua Palace in Sliema, Dragonara Palace in St Julian's, and so on. Malta's dominant Neoclassical building is the **Mosta Dome**, whose cornerstone was laid in 1833; it is one of the largest buildings in Malta, a monstrous circular church with a colonnaded facade and bell towers that are lost amidst the overbearing columns and dome. In the 1860s the principal proponent of **Gothic Revival** in Malta, Emmanuele Luigi Galizia, designed the **Addolarata Cemetery** and later the **Carmelite Church** in Balluta Bay. (Galizia also designed three **Moorish** houses on Rudolph Street, Sliema, the only examples of their kind in Malta.)

Throughout the nineteenth century, the British constructed **forts** and **batteries**, especially north and south of the Grand Harbour, and around Marsaxlokk. Meanwhile, advances in military technology rendered the Knights' coastal defences obsolete; in 1832 one Colonel Morshead put forward a plan to demolish 15 coastal towers and 25 redoubts – fortunately for posterity, his recommendations were shelved. However, the British did expand on the Knights' concept of defensive walls of fortification, constructing the extensive **Victoria Lines** that straddle Malta east to west. Taking advantage of the Great Fault, a geological rift that dissects Malta on two levels, the idea was to reinforce this escarpment, 239m at its highest, along the line of the rift that runs from Fomm Ir-Rih in the west to Baħar Iċ-Ċagħaq in the east – in effect dividing Malta in two. "A few detached forts on this line," wrote Brigadier-General John Adye, the proponent of the Victoria Lines, "would cut off all that westerly portion of the island where there are good bays and facilities for landing." The Victoria Lines were built in the 1870s, a low-lying bastion that threads its way for 15km along the edge of the Great Fault. To back the Victoria Lines with firepower three **forts** were built, at Bingemma, Mosta and Madliena.

Modern and contemporary architecture

At the beginning of the twentieth century, architects began to experiment with more styles: the **Romanesque** Ta' Pinu Basilica, the **Gothic Revival** Għajnsielem Church, the **Art Nouveau** Balluta Buildings. All the while, however, Baroque remained the dominant style, matching the Maltese taste for the grand gesture. After World War II, many people built for themselves grand Baroque houses, with prominent enclosed or balustraded balconies and exuberant interiors. The most recent two churches built in the Maltese islands – Our Lady of Mount Carmel Church in Valletta and the Xewkija Church on Gozo, both completed in the 1980s – are grander than ever, reasserting Baroque dominance. Even *luzzus* (wooden fishing-boats) and ordinary buses and lorries are these days painted with the lavish colours and curlicued designs of Baroque.

The last two decades have witnessed the introduction to Malta of more innovative, hybrid styles, influenced by an increased appreciation of the islands' architectural heritage and current trends in Europe. Farmhouses, whose design harks back to medieval times, are now being restored to become highly-prized country villas. The latest large-scale project, **Portomaso** in St Julian's, incorporates loggias as a recurrent motif in the design, juxtaposing the balconies and wide spaces of Baroque with a modern glass tower (also Malta's highest building).

Richard England, Malta's most famous living architect, has spent a lifetime perfecting a distinctive style of circular architecture, seen to best effect in his churches, most notably Manikata's parish church, and in his excellent restoration of **St James's Cavalier** in Valletta. He has also recently designed an extension to the **University of Malta** in Msida, where he created a cluster of stout tower-like structures, some squarish, some round, most with slanting roofs and various geometrically shaped windows. The overall effect makes the eye range over this cluster of "ivory towers", which simultaneously express the university's intellectual distinction and its esoteric isolation. Along with the internationally renowned Italian architect Renzo Piano, England is also the co-designer of the **Valletta Master Plan**, where his flair is given free rein. The design proposes transferring the bus terminus underground to make the surrounding fortifications stand out more gloriously, and redesigning the ground-level plaza in a triangle shape, mimicking the proportions of a bastion. Freedom Square nearby will also be completely rebuilt, and England chose this location to showcase his circular architecture, its fluidity acting as a conduit of urban energies – a conceit which harks back to the motivations underpinning the Maltese innovation, in the Neolithic era, of the concept of architecture.

Books

There's a huge amount of Malta-related written material, much of it pertaining to the islands long and rich history. Publishers of each book are given, where available, in the UK and the US. Titles published by Maltese companies, many of which are available only in the islands, are denoted by the abbreviation MA. The best place to find these titles is Sapienza's, Triq Ir-Repubblika, Valletta (Mon–Sat 9am–7pm; ☎233621), the largest and best bookshop in the islands.

History and politics

Warren G. Berg, *Historical Dictionary of Malta* (Scarecrow Press, UK & US). Excellent but expensive thumbnail reference book including entries on personalities, salient epochs and historical monuments.

Christina Biaggi, *Habitations of the Great Goddess* (Knowledge, Ideas and Trends, US). Taking over from the late archeologist Marija Gimbutas, Biaggi writes about the Goddess and matriarchal culture of Malta's Neolithic peoples in greater detail, citing more archeological remains, and analysing the data via cultural symbolism.

Brian Blouet, *The Story of Malta* (Faber & Faber, UK; Progress Press, MA). A readable, condensed chronicle from prehistory to the present.

Ernle D. Bradford, *The Great Siege: Malta 1565* (Wordsworth Editions, US). Translated from Francesco Balbi di Correggio's eyewitness journal account of the Great Siege, this gripping memoir reads like a suspense thriller.

Ernle D. Bradford, *Siege: Malta 1940–1943* (Progress Press, MA). A factual story of Malta in World War II; anecdotes and re-created scenes add colour to the extensively researched facts.

Peter Elliott, *The Cross and the Ensign: A Naval History of Malta 1798–1979* (Grafton, UK). Recounts the activities of the British Royal Navy, from the early sea adventures during the French Blockade to the glory years when Malta was the headquarters of its Mediterranean fleet. The prose is fleshed out with plenty of detail and drama.

Leonard Mahoney, *A History of Maltese Architecture* (Self-published, MA). Detailed account of the development of Maltese architecture from the prehistoric era to World War II, with most of the book dedicated to the development of Baroque during the Knights' epoch.

Edgar Mizzi, *Malta in the Making 1962–1987* (Beck's Graphics, MA). Former attorney general, and right-hand man to prime ministers Borg Olivier and Mintoff from 1962 to 1987, Mizzi recounts the inside story of the turbulent post-Independence years; the style is archaic, but it's riveting stuff.

Henry J.A. Sire, *The Knights of Malta* (Yale University Press, US). The most scholarly, authoritative book on the Knights from their foundation to their present status, including an in-depth analysis of the order's achievements and history in Malta that dispels some widespread myths concerning the Knights' decline in the eighteenth century.

Fiction

Anthony Burgess, *Earthly Powers* (Penguin, UK; Carroll & Graf, US). Based in Lija, Malta, where the author lived for several years as a tax exile, this is Burgess at his best. The octogenarian protagonist is much given to reverie and bitterness against priest-ridden Malta: a veiled grudge Burgess nursed against the country, and which eventually drove him away.

Linda C. Eneix, *People of the Temples* (OTS Foundation, US). A fictionalized account, inspired by the Neolithic Goddess and New Age worship in Maltese temples, which tells the story of how Malta's Utopian Neolithic society came to an end.

Nicholas Monsarrat, *The Kapillan of Malta* (Cassell Military, UK). Set during World War II, this historical novel, by a British expat who lived in Gozo, recounts the suffering and the glory, as well as the claustrophobia of the air raid shelters from the point of view of a village priest.

A.J. Quinell, *Man on Fire* (Orion, UK). A suspense novel set in Gozo, where the author – a sometime resident who writes under a pen-name – is well-known for his late-night drinking bouts in the island's bars.

Nicholas Rinaldi, *The Jukebox Queen of Malta* (Black Swan, UK; Simon & Schuster, US).

Another historical novel set in World War II, which forms a bleak and senseless background to an intense love story between an American soldier and a Maltese woman.

Guidebooks

Anthony Bonanno, *Malta: An Archeological Paradise* (OTS Foundation, US). Illustrated introduction to Malta's archeological temples and remains.

D.A. Brawn, *Malta Walking Guide* and *Gozo Walking Guide* (both Discovery Walking Guides, UK). Reliable guide to scenic country walks all over the islands, which includes sketches of routes. Detail on the flora and fauna encountered on the routes is scanty, though.

Mario Buhagiar, *The Iconography of the Maltese Islands* (Progress Press, MA). A detailed guide illustrating works of art in churches, as well as insignias, such as coats of arms, that are prevalent throughout the islands.

Anne and Helen Caruana Galizia, *The Food and Cookery of Malta* (Prospect Books, MA).

Dozens of forgotten recipes unearthed and explained in detail, this book provides the definitive lowdown on Maltese cuisine.

Quentin Hughes, *Malta: A Guide to the Fortifications* (Progress Press, MA). Extensive guide that details the design and construction of all of Malta's military architecture from the Knights to the British.

Edwin Lanfranco and Alfred Baldacchino, *Wildlife of the Maltese Islands* (Environment Protection Department, Ministry for Environment, MA). Definitive guide to the wildlife of the islands, with detailed descriptions of species accompanied by colour prints.

Guido G. Lanfranco, *The Fish Around Malta* (Progress Press, MA). Descriptions and photos of marine life found in local waters.

Lawson and Leslie Wood, *The Dive Sites of Malta, Gozo and Comino* (New Holland, UK). A comprehensive guide to virtually all the dive and snorkelling sites, including short descriptions that rate accessibility, depth and visibility.

Society and culture

Jeremy Boissevain, *Saints and Fireworks: Religion and Politics in Rural Malta* (Progress Press, MA). Written by a Dutch anthropologist who's spent a lifetime studying Maltese culture. This is a profound anthropological analysis of parochial and tribal politics, including the relationship between religion and politics, as manifested in town festas.

Ronald Sultana and Godfrey Baldacchino, *Maltese Society – A Sociological Enquiry* (Mireva Publications, MA). This collection of essays, putting forth a sociological analysis of subjects as diverse as village feasts, ex-Prime Minister Dom Mintoff, drug and alcohol use and political allegiances in Malta, form a perceptive overview of the sociological fabric of a small society.

Language

Malti, known in English as "Maltese", has its roots in the Arabic of western North Africa, but has gathered many words and influences from Italian, English, French, German and Spanish. It sounds a lot like Turkish and – like Turkish – it is a Semitic language written with Latin letters. Maltese script evolved only at the beginning of the twentieth century: Italian was Malta's default language up to 1934, when it was officially replaced by Maltese and English.

In many ways, this has placed the language under threat of being swamped. Officially, Maltese and English have equal status, and documents have to be in both languages in order to be legally binding. Culturally, though, Maltese is much less important, and the extensive vocabulary of Maltese linguists is largely lost on the general populace. Grammar and spelling are widely corrupted, and large sections of the population speak either English or a hybridized form of Maltese-English in everyday life.

Everything from menus to roadsigns to official proclamations are in English and, regrettably, you won't impress anyone by trying to speak Maltese – which, in any case, is very difficult to pronounce and fraught with peculiarities and exceptions. You'll only need the basics, to help you get your tongue around place-names.

MALTESE PRONUNCIATION

ċ as **ch** in chur**ch**

e is short, as in b**e**t

g is hard, as in **g**oat

ġ is soft, as in **j**oke

h is silent (except at the end of a word, when it's pronounced like ħ)

ħ is strong and definite, as in **h**ail

i is long, as in b**ee**

j as in **y**es

għ is silent in most instances

q is a glottal stop – the sound at the beginning and in the middle of "uh-oh"

x is an English "sh", as in **sh**ear

ż is soft, as in **z**ebra

z as in ba**ts**

The Maltese **alphabet** has 29 letters – five vowels (as in English) and 24 consonants (some of which are unfamiliar): a, b, ċ, d, e, f, g, ġ, h, ħ, i, j, k, l, m, n, għ, o, p, q, r, s, t, u, v, w, x, ż, z. Pronunciation of most of the letters differs from English, in that emphasis is placed on a drawn-out twang. The box, above, details instances of markedly unusual pronunciation.

Glossary

AD Abbreviation of Alternattiva Demokratika, the green political party.

Auberge An inn of residence for a group of Knights forming a particular *Langue*, grouped under the region they came from.

Baħar Sea.

Bajja Bay.

Bastion A triangular outcrop, jutting from a line of fortifications to produce a zigzag outline, that provided a larger range of fire coverage and reinforced structural resistance to destruction.

Bieb Generic term for any door or doorway, as well as the gate to fortified cities.

Cavalier Tower within fortifications that acts as a raised gun platform and rearguard position.

Corsair Sea-based pirate licensed by the state and international law to carry out piracy against a defined enemy.

Curtain The main trace of fortifications linking two bastions.

Daghjsa Boat.

Demi-bastion A smaller, less-defined bastion with one flank instead of two.

Fat ladies The generic term attached to any of the well-endowed stone figures and statues from the Neolithic era.

Festa Generally refers to the three-day feasts of fireworks and brass bands held in every parish every year during the summer to commemorate the parish saint; the same term also refers to public holidays.

Fliegu A sea channel but refers particularly to the channel separating Gozo from Malta, the Gozo Channel.

Forn Bakery.

Fortizza Fort.

Fougasse A large hole gouged into solid rock on the side of a bay, which was packed with gunpowder and rocks to fire on boats attempting to land.

Garigue An adopted French word that defines the rugged stretches of rocky landscape, where aromatic and hardy bushes and flowering plants grow in pockets of soil.

Għar Cave.

Għassa tal-Pulizija Police station.

Għolja Hill.

Ġirna Small stone hut found in the countryside, originally used as a dwelling in medieval Malta and later for storing vegetables and agricultural implements.

Globigerina limestone Local limestone used in many Maltese buildings.

Ġnien Garden.

Grand Master the absolute ruler of the Knights, functioning as the king in a monarchy and informed by the Council as a cabinet of sorts.

Gvern Government.

Gżira Island.

Hobża Bread or rolls.

Ħut Fish.

Il-Belt "The city", usually applied to Valletta.

Irdum Cliff.

Ispiżerija Pharmacy.

Karrozza Car.

Kastell Castle.

Kenur Stone cooking hearth.

Knisja Church.

Kunsill lokali Local council.

Langue A branch of Knights hailing from a particular region, such as the Langue of England, Langue of Bavaria, and so on.

Luzzu Colourful, vernacular wooden fishing boats.

Maquis French word that refers to the clusters of trees and large bushes that thrive in the shadow of inland cliffs.

Misrah The old Maltese word for a square or clearing.

Mużew Museum.

Parroċċa Parish.

Passiġġiatta Walk, but particularly a summer evening stroll near the sea.

Pjazza Square, usually a large church square.

Posta Post office.

Pulizija Police.

Ravelin Triangular defensive outbuilding in front of fortifications.

RTO Abbreviation of Reserved To Owner, this is used by hunters to mark their territory.

Sies A cliff.

Sqaq Alley.

Tabib General doctor.

Tal-Linja Bus.

Tempju Neolithic temple.

Torri Tower.

Triq Street or road.

Vapur Ship.

Wied Valley.

INDEX

X

Y

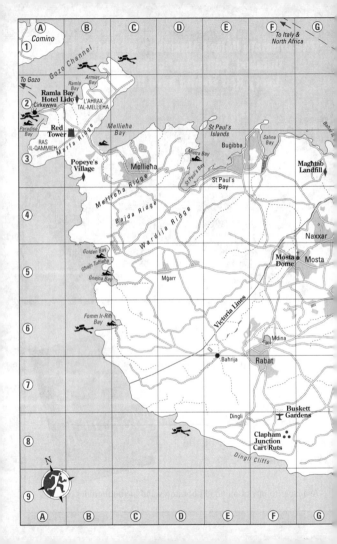

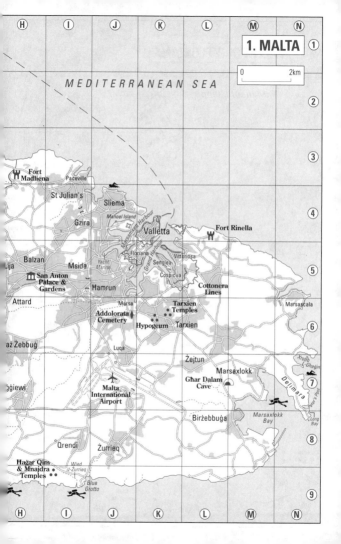

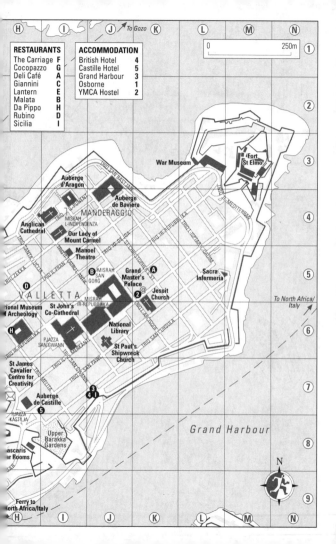

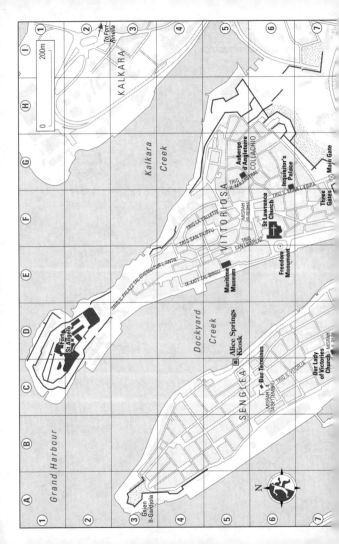

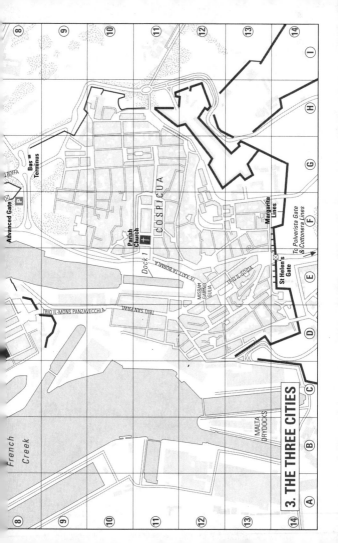

3. THE THREE CITIES

French Creek

MALTA
DRYDOCKS

COSPICUA

Parish
Church

Dock 1

Advanced Gate

Bus
Terminus

J BOFFA

TRIQ IL-MONS PANZAVECCHIA

TRIQ SAN PAWL

TRIQ XATT IL-BORMLA

MUSEUM
GAFFINO
GULIA

TRIQ IL-GDIDA

St Helen's
Gate

Margarita
Lines

To Polverista Gate
& Cottonera Lines

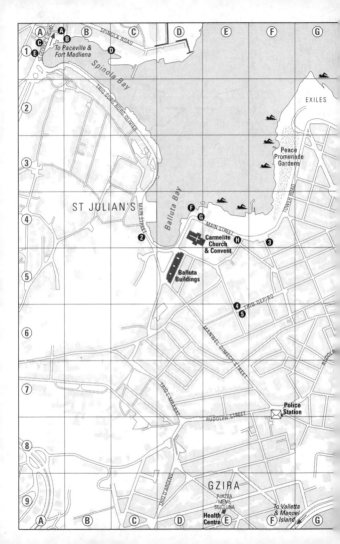

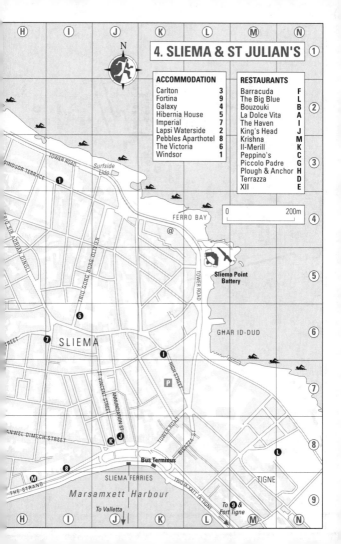

4. SLIEMA & ST JULIAN'S

ACCOMMODATION

Carlton	3
Fortina	9
Galaxy	4
Hibernia House	5
Imperial	7
Lapsi Waterside	2
Pebbles Aparthotel	8
The Victoria	6
Windsor	1

RESTAURANTS

Barracuda	F
The Big Blue	L
Bouzouki	B
La Dolce Vita	A
The Haven	I
King's Head	J
Krishna	M
Il-Merill	K
Peppino's	C
Piccolo Padre	G
Plough & Anchor	H
Terrazza	D
XII	E

0   200m

TOWER ROAD

WINDSOR TERRACE

Surfside Lido

TRIQ GORG BORG OLIVIER

TRIQ SIR ADRIAN DINGLI

FERRO BAY

@

TOWER ROAD

Sliema Point Battery

GHAR ID-DUD

SLIEMA

HIGH STREET

P

ST VINCENT STREET

AMMUNITION ST

ANWEL DIMECH STREET

TOWER ROAD

BISAZZA

Bus Terminus

SLIEMA FERRIES

TRIQ IX-XATT IX-TIGNE

TIGNE

THE STRAND

Marsamxett Harbour

To Valletta

To ⑨ & Fort Tigne

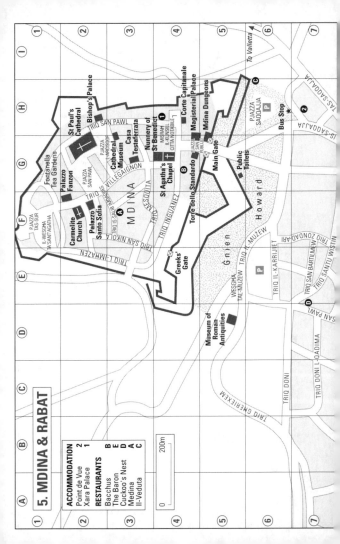

5. MDINA & RABAT

ACCOMMODATION
Point de Vue 2
Xara Palace 1

RESTAURANTS
Bacchus B
The Baron E
Cuckoo's Nest D
Medina A
Il-Veduta C

0 200m

St Paul's Cathedral
Bishop's Palace
Fontanella Tea Gardens
Palazzo Falzon
Carmelite Church
Palazzo Santo Sofia
Casa Testaferrata
Cathedral Museum
Nunnery of St Benedict
St Agatha's Chapel
Corte Capitanale
Magisterial Palace
Mdina Dungeons
Main Gate
Torre dello Standardo
Public Toilets
Greeks' Gate
Museum of Roman Antiquities

MDINA
TRIQ SAN PAWL
PIAZZA T-ARCISQOF
PIAZZA SAN PAWL
TRIQ VILLEGAIGNON
TRIQ INGUANEZ
TRIQ MESQUITA
TRIQ SAN NIKOLA
TRIQ IL-MHAZEN
MESRAH IL-KUNSILL
CITTA NOTABILE
PIAZZA SAN PUBLIJU

Gnien Howard
Gnien

WESGHA TAL-MUZEW
TRIQ IL-MUZEW
TRIQ IL-KARRIJIET
TRIQ SANTU WISTIN
TRIQ SAN BARTILMEW
TRIQ ZONDADARI
TRIQ DONI L-QADIMA
TRIQ DONI
TRIQ GHERIEXEM
SAN PAWL

PIAZZA SAQQAJJA
Bus Stop
To Valletta
IS-SAQQAJJA
TAS-SAQQAJJA

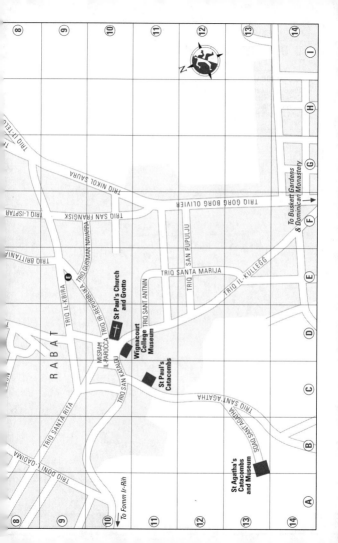

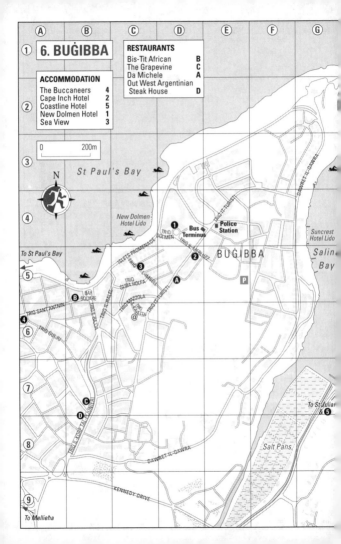

6. BUĠIBBA

ACCOMMODATION

The Buccaneers	4
Cape Inch Hotel	2
Coastline Hotel	5
New Dolmen Hotel	1
Sea View	3

RESTAURANTS

Bis-Tit African	B
The Grapevine	C
Da Michele	A
Out West Argentinian Steak House	D

0 200m

N

St Paul's Bay

New Dolmen Hotel Lido

To St Paul's Bay

Suncrest Hotel Lido

Salin Bay

TRIQ DOLMEN

Bus Terminus ①

TRIQ IL-KAĦLUZZ

Police Station ■

BUĠIBBA

TRIQ IT-TURIST

② The Grapevine

③ ISLETS PROMENADE

TRIQ IL-KANSEL

④ ②

TRIQ GUBA HOLFA

P

BAY SQUARE Ⓑ

TRIQ SANT'ANTNIN

TRIQ IL-MALEK

TRIQ IT-TRUNĊIERA

TRIQ MAZZOLA

TRIQ BALLUT

@

TRIQ BUĠIBBA

TRIQ IL-KORP TA' DUMNI

Ⓒ

Ⓓ

To St Julian's & ⑤

Salt Pans

DAWRET IL-QAWRA

KENNEDY DRIVE

To Mellieħa

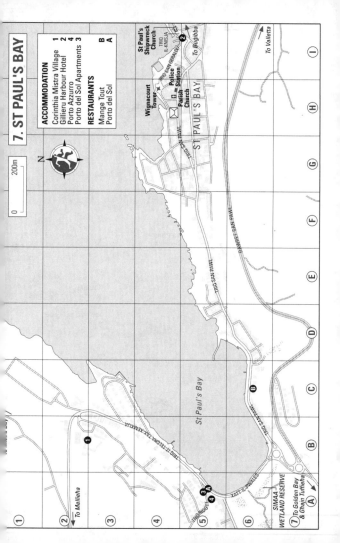

7. ST PAUL'S BAY

0   200m

N

ACCOMMODATION

Corinthia Mistra Village	1
Gillieru Harbour Hotel	2
Porto Azzurro	4
Porto del Sol Apartments	3

RESTAURANTS

Mange Tout	B
Porto del Sol	A

St Paul's Shipwreck Church

TRIQ IL-KNISJA

Police Station

Wignacourt Tower

Parish Church

ST PAUL'S BAY

TRIQ IS-SALINI

TRIQ SAN PAWL

 It-TELGHA TAL-KORÇ

St Paul's Bay

TRIQ IS-SALINI

DAWRET SAN PAWL

XATT IL-PWALES

TRIQ IL-PWALES

SIMAA WETLAND RESERVE

To Mellieħa

To Buġibba

To Valletta

To Golden Bay & Għajn Tuffieħa

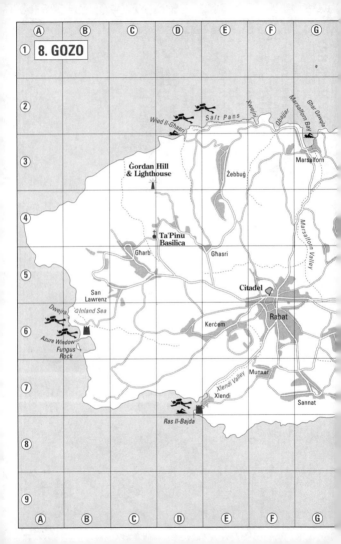

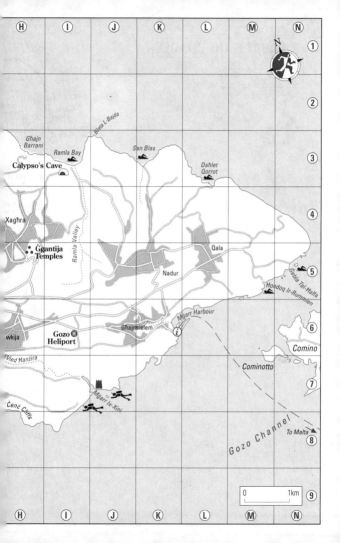

9. RABAT & THE CITADEL

0   100m

N

To Dwejra

TRIQ SANT ORSLA

TRIQ L-IMGHALLEM

CITADEL

Natural
Science Museum

Id-Demibastjun
ta San Martin

TRIQ LAWRENZ SAN MARGON

Medieva
ruin
TRIQ IZ

Folklore
Museum

Old
Prisons

PJAZZA
KATIDRAL

Citadel
(Mdina Gate)

Museum of
Archeology

Il-Bastjun
ta San Miki

PJAZZA SAVINA

TRIQ L-ASSUNTA

TRIQ SANTA MARIJA

TRIQ SAN GORG

TRIQ S. CASSAR

TRIQ BEFARO

TRIQ IT-TIGRIJA TAL-BEL

Banca
Giunatale

i

PJAZZA
INDIPENDENZA

R   A

PJAZZA
SAN GORG

OLD
QUARTER

TRIQ IL-LIBRERIJA

St George
Basilica

TRIQ IL-KARITA

Il-Panzi

PJAZZA
SAN WISTIN

TRIQ
L-ISKOLA

TRIQ VAJRINGA